DATE DUE

TO BRECHT AND BEYOND

HARVESTER/BARNES & NOBLE STUDIES IN CONTEMPORARY LITERATURE AND CULTURE

General Editor Patrick Parrinder, Reader in English, University of Reading

This is a new series of original, full-length studies of modern literature and its cultural context. Although a variety of historical, theoretical and critical orientations will be encouraged, each title will aim to illuminate the common themes and conditions of twentieth century writing, rather than to explicate the work of an individual author. Taking 'literature and culture' to indicate the whole of organized verbal expression, the series will include studies of modern drama, film and the communications media, as well as offering new and stimulating approaches in the fields of English and comparative literature.

TO BRECHT AND BEYOND

Soundings in Modern Dramaturgy

DARKO SUVIN

Professor of English and Comparative Literature
McGill University

THE HARVESTER PRESS · SUSSEX

BARNES & NOBLE BOOKS · NEW JERSEY

First published in Great Britain in 1984 by
THE HARVESTER PRESS LIMITED
Publisher: John Spiers
16 Ship Street, Brighton, Sussex

and in the USA by
BARNES & NOBLE BOOKS
81 Adams Drive, Totowa, New Jersey 07512

© Darko Suvin, 1984

British Library Cataloguing in Publication Data
Suvin, Darko
  To Brecht and beyond
  1. Drama – History and criticism
  I. Title
  809.2   PN1721

  ISBN 0-85527-975-3

Library of Congress Cataloging in Publication Data
Suvin, Darko, 1930–
  To Brecht and beyond.
  1. Brecht, Bertolt, 1898–1956—Aesthetics. 2. Brecht
Bertolt, 1898–1956—Influence. 3. Drama—20th Century—
History and criticism. I. Title.
PT2603. R397Z88924   1984   832'.912   84-252
ISBN 0-389-20463-3

Photoset in 11 pt. Bembo by Thomson Press (India) Ltd.,
New Delhi
and printed in Great Britain by
Butler & Tanner Ltd., Frome, Somerset

ripae ulterioris amore
(Virgil, *Aeneid*, 6)

Contents

Apologue and Dedication

I like to think of Brecht, Lukács and Benjamin carrying on a debate in the Elysian Fields. Looking aslant and askance at us, they know all we do, but they know it better. The wizened Lukács sits on his fluffy cloud of ethical aesthetics, somewhat uncomfortably glancing now and then at the sketched-in open door. Benjamin, still pale from neglect, fingers nervously his fading aura, while looking with a mixture of sorrow and delight at yellowed photographs of nineteenth-century Paris. Brecht returns from visits to his favourite houri to write new variants of a Lehrstück on the three Tui gods descending into our bitter–sweet follies. They eat a lot of cheese, read a lot of newspapers, catch all our satellite beams, and do not stop debating.

Outside, in front of the empty door-posts, with grave courtesy and patience sits Kafka, listening intently. Thomas Mann wanders by, feigning indifference. Bloch is occasionally consulted on difficult salvational points. When Rimbaud passes, the Masters feign nonchalance.

I hope this book might give the three Masters a ten-minute subject for debate, and that Brecht might be moved to put into his latest rewrite a two-minute appearance of a minor Tui character mouthing my views – much better formulated yet ironically estranged, of course.

The book is affectionately dedicated to the Old Masters;

– to Nena, whose span of cohabiting with its notions it almost covers:

– and to Patrick, the Customs Officer curious and patient at the Pass.

Preface

The following nine essays were all written between 1967 and 1977 for publication in different periodicals and, in the case of chapters 2, 5 and 7, in a pamphlet and two books of essays. Thus, though they are variations on and evolutions of the same theme – modern dramaturgy as explainable by the history that constitutes it and into which it returns – their formats (length, technical apparatus, etc.) vary. Little could be done to correct this. I trust, none the less, that their cohesion will be apparent. I shall point out here some roots and aspects of that coherence, as well as (in the following Introduction) some second thoughts in hindsight.

The first factor of cohesion should arise out of the essays' genesis and ideological context. From my student days in 1951, I was a theatre critic for dailies and weeklies in Yugoslavia, with frequent travel to and study in Italy, England, Paris and West Germany, as well as, somewhat later, to other places, from Prague, East Berlin and Warsaw to New York. Freelance reviewing and translation were in fact what I did until my appointment as assistant lecturer in Theatre Arts and Comparative Literature at the University of Zagreb in 1959, at which point the criticism shifted to longer pieces in monthlies and scholarly publications. At the same time, I was a member of two self-managing student theatres in Zagreb, as their dramaturge and Yugoslav representative in the International Student Theatre Union, and I was intimately involved with the organising of the annual student theatre festival in Zagreb.

In 1967, sharp differences in opinion with a nationalist group at the Zagreb Faculty of Philosophy forced me to leave that university and take an appointment in North America, where I also taught primarily modern drama. Thus, I have been deeply marked – second in importance only to my boyhood marking by the World War and the Yugoslav revolution – both by my experiences in the struggle for socialist culture and theatre in Yugoslavia and by my participation in the student theatre movement. These student theatres from most of Europe, with the exception of the USSR, met yearly at four festivals: Parma, Erlangen, Zagreb and Istanbul (the latter replaced by Nancy in the 1960s), where many of the most prominent theatre and media-shapers of my generation – young directors, dramaturges, organisers, etc. – came together.

In retrospect it is clear that their movement was an important forerunner of the continent-wide student revolt in Europe in 1968. The central attitudes arising out of these formative experiences of the essays' genesis – the sense that the world is radically wrong and must be changed, and thus the acute sense of interaction between dramaturgy and existential or salvational politics, the sense of historical and inter-European heritage, the refusal to separate text and stage, the willingness de prendre son bien où on le trouve, be it Aeschylus, Lenin, Brecht, Marivaux, Kropotkin, Stuart Mill, Meyerhold, or the Mysteries, the joyous internationalism of the intellectual eros, the deep sense of scale analogies between world and stage (i.e. of stage as world model) – all these, I assume and hope, provide the main coherence for the following essays.

In analytical terms, this coherence is visible as the use – continued from Part 1 – of some encompassing strategies and terminologies. The dramaturgy at hand is explored through its cosmology (the implied view of universe and of people's place in and relationships to it) and anthropology (the implied view of stage agents or dramatis personae and their mutual relationships). Both are seen as being exclusively and fully explainable by the historical constellation which permeated that particular dramaturgy. Not that I have any ideological commitment to History. Often, I feel like exclaiming with Joyce that history is a nightmare from which I would dearly like to awaken. Simply, the crucial dates for my generation are 1945, 1968 and a third in between: for me, 1948 – the year of the Cominform break with Yugoslavia; for most others, 1956. Therefore, such a generation of intellectuals, hacking with pain and effort its way through the jungle of cities, in running-battles both with capitalism and Stalinism, realised in its most intimate structure of feelings that it had been moulded by historical forces colliding in its flesh. With cool passion, we understood what generations of slower times and places might have disregarded: that history was, like it or not, our destiny. This, then, is at least as much a factual as a value-judgement. Quarrels about values can arise only after the fact is faced.

Montreal, January 1983

Introduction

The chapters in this book were first published as follows: Chapter 1 in Zagadnienia Rodzajów Literackih – Problems of Literary Genres, 1966. Chapter 2 was adapted from a 1972 lecture as 'Dramaturgy and Communication' in the Working Papers Series of McGill University Graduate Communications Program (Montreal, 1982). Both have now been partly rewritten, and subsume also the essay 'Modes of Political Drama', published in The Massachusetts Review(1972). Chapter 3 was first published in The Drama Review (1969), and slightly enlarged in Travail théâtral (1971). Chapter 4 was published in The Drama Review (1967), and reprinted both in Erika Munk (ed.), Brecht (New York, 1972) and in Lee Baxandall (ed.), Radical Perspectives in the Arts (Harmondsworth/Baltimore, 1972). Chapter 5 was published in Siegfried Mews and Herbert Knust (eds), Essays on Brecht (Chapel Hill, North Carolina, 1974; 1979). Chapter 6 was publslished in Clio (Wisconsin) (1974), and reprinted in Norman Rudich, (ed.), Weapons of Criticism (Palo Alto, 1976). Chapter 7 was published in Henrik Birnbaum and Thomas Eekman (eds), Fiction and Drama in Eastern and Southeastern Europe (Columbus, Ohio, 1980). Chapter 8 was published in The Tulane Drama Review (1967) and partly reprinted in Ruby Cohn (ed.), Case Book on 'Waiting For Godot' (New York, 1968). Chapter 9 was published in The Drama Review (1970), and the subsequent exchange with Lee Baxandall (reproduced here as an Appendix to the chapter) in the same journal later that year. All, except Chapter 2 have also been published in Yugoslavia, Chapter 1 being the reworking of some previous articles brought together in my book Dva vida dramaturgije (Two Aspects of Dramaturgy – Zagreb, 1965).

1. It will be apparent that the coherence of this book, and some changes it might evidence in relation to the original texts, call for comment. This will be found in the Afterwords to Parts 1 and 2. In

*this general introduction, I would like to glance briefly at the outer
limits of the book, at the level of analysis and type of approach
which seem most useful to me today and which I would have used
had I begun this enterprise in the mid-1970s rather than a decade
earlier. I would retain, of course, the same ideological horizons. But
the analysis would be stricter and more formalised, while the
approach would insist on a more intimate permeation of dramaturgic
elements with the authors' and the social addressees' historical
premises and attitudes. Though labels do not much matter and
doctrinaire schools even less, I would call such an approach*
dramaturgic semiotics, *a discipline that would be at the crossroads
of the semiotics of spectacle and the semiotics of narration. It would
use a number of Structuralist and post-Structuralist insights about
the technical advantages of formalisation, but in principle, it would
be opposed to the horizons of Parisian and US technocracy. The
most useful names from this corner would perhaps be Propp,
Shklovsky, some Lévi-Strauss and some Barthes. It would, further,
situate itself within a prolongation of the great Marxian tradition of
cultural critique, but it would do so by avoiding the pioneering
insufficiencies that run from Lukács and Adorno to, say, Thomson
and Ubersfeld in favour of a synthesis adumbrated by Bakhtin,
Brecht and Benjamin, and today perhaps approached most closely
by Luis Prieto and Umberto Eco in general semiotics, Bernard Dort
in performance analysis, and Yury Lotman, Raymond Williams and
Fredric Jameson in narrative analysis. To this should be added some
basic probings into a putative dramaturgic semiotics, briefly touched
upon by Eco and Lotman, and developed by Keir Elam (*The
Semiotics of Theatre and Drama *(London, 1980)) and Marco
De Marinis (*Semiotica del teatro *(Milano, 1982)). The position
of such a dramaturgic semiotics might best be clarified by a
rudimentary discussion of what dramaturgy is and how it relates to
the system of performative or 'spectacle' genres. I shall then conclude
with a few paragraphs on Individualism and allegory.*

*   'Dramaturgy' originally meant playwriting, but its root meaning
of 'working on a play' easily slides into, first, 'the principles or
guidelines of composing a play', and second — as pioneered by
Lessing — a critique, analysis and theory of such basic principles
extended from the play both to its performance (which is to be judged
in the light of those constructive guidelines) and to the whole
technical and ideological context of theatrical performance. If one
were to enter into a theory of* spectacle, *defined as* activities by

consciousness-endowed agents ostended to an audience – *as I gingerly do in chapter 9 – then spectacle is to be divided into two main sub-groups. First, the 'plotted' or diegetic group, embracing drama theatre, opera and other 'musical plays', ballet and other diegetic dance performances, mime, and similar genres, all of which narrate a story. Second, the non-plotted or adiegetic group, embracing pageants, circus, fair shows, street jugglers, Happenings, and similar genres which do not tell a story but are none the less delimited by an attitudinal (thematic, 'topical') field. Of course, there are also intermediate genres, such as music-hall, cabaret, vaudeville or burlesque, oscillating between the first two groups. Dramaturgy is usually applied only to the first or 'theatrical' group, to verbal-cum-gestural drama proper, as well as to plays which use partly and exclusively other sign-systems.*

However, I think this limitation is not necessarily correct. Dramaturgy could, then, be initially defined as the theory and analysis of paradigmatic and syntagmatic composition of plays as well as of non-diegetic spectacle. *At any rate, even diegetic spectacle alone would today comprise not only theatre but also, very importantly, the plotted or story-telling segments which comprise almost all movies, much television and a part of radio. (I discuss this further in the Afterword to Part 2.) Such new technical media – which may soon include computer and laser-based video/ audiotapes, holograms, etc. – are differentiated from 'theatre drama' by a crucial factor: in the latter the human performers are immediately and directly present to the audience, with whom they communicate in a feeback relationship that determines the framework of theatre dramaturgy. I would argue that the performance/audience relationship in the case of the new media based on technical multiplication is derived from the basic or 'zero' theatrical relationship, so that the necessary elements of theatre performance constitute the basic parameters of dramaturgy for all possible media.*

The basis of theatrical performance, and the subject-matter of most dramaturgic scholarship, could be defined as composed of five interlocking elements: (1) a non-empirical organisation of space/time; *(2)* borne by performers; *(3)* who represent by means of a sensible action; *(4)* significant human relationships; *(5)* to a human group. *Each of these elements should be discussed at length, but I shall note here only that the performers' 'holy circle', the stage, is neither a totally magical nor a totally empirical place or locus. A fully magical locus, in the tribal rituals,*

*cannot allow any division between performers and spectators. The
ritual group as a whole is bathed in a special – magical or
religious – space/time. Theatre and drama are born from but also by
being delimited against rituals. Attempts to abolish the difference
between spectatorial and performative space and time must logically
(as the most intelligent theoretician of such attempts, Richard
Schechner, has realised) also abolish theatre as we have known it in
all post-tribal societies. (I do not wish to enter here into a
value-judgement on such attempts; I think they are sometimes very
interesting, sometimes very dangerous, and finally unfeasible in class
society.) On the other hand, neither are empirical or physical space
and time identical to the space and time on the stage: the spectator
sees an* imaginative or dramaturgic *space and time, much more
flexible than the x square metres of the stage or x hours of
performing. The space/time of the stage is simultaneously a
concrete, sensually (visually and auditively) present reality, and yet
out of reach of the spectators' empirical (tactile, manipulative)
intervention. It is a (more or less) different,* alternative *world,
where different relationships between the dramaturgic agents become
possible. With respect to the spectators' empirical reality, the
dramaturgical reality is an epistemological experiment or model: a
space/time which is simultaneously a hypothetical and a concrete one
is precisely an experimental or model space/time.*

*From the very large number of modelling possibilities, one or (at
exceptional periods of strife) a few become* dominant *in a given
socio-historical constellation or age. Thus, the subject-matter of
dramaturgic history is not simply a history of dramaturgic creators
(writers, performers, directors, etc.), nor simply a history of isolated
plays (even including their main performing possibilities), nor even
simply a history of dramaturgy as a part of the general history of a
homogeneous 'culture' or 'art' – though all of these may be valid
partial approaches, if not absolutised. The subject-matter of a
relatively autonomous history of dramaturgic production, whose
elements arise in socio-historical reality and whose consequences flow
back into it, would be the dialectical feedback between the different
historical* groups of plays *(whose principle of composition and
dominant model may be called a dramaturgy) and the different* social
addressees *for whom they were written and whose values, interests
and norms they presupposed.*

*The basic question of dramaturgic analysis is then: What is the
relationship of such a residually numinous or aesthetic locus, of its*

space, agents and events, to the audience's englobing existential space, activities and underlying system of human relations? According to the ways this question is answered for different epochs, overall historical types of dramaturgy (in abbreviated usage: 'historical dramaturgies') can be distinguished. I speak in this book of medieval or Gothic, Renaissance, and Individualist dramaturgies, and I think there is a post-Individualist dramaturgy striving to be born. Of course, for any particular dramaturgic generation (e.g. the Elizabethans) or smaller units (e.g. Brecht's Lehrstücke), *additional codes or conventions based on class, ethnic and other ideological particularities have to be taken into account. But it seems to me that in all cases the aesthetic, dramaturgic locus is built up by a selection from elements or relationships available in a given culture. Though the dramaturgic locus may therefore be more intensive and more significant than what the audience thinks of as its empirical locus, it is more restrictive. The stage can therefore again be called a microcosm in relation to the existential macrocosm. As in a model, no single element – action, agent, aspect of space and time – has to be identical with an element from existential reality (though it* may *be). However, the basic unit of dramaturgic analysis is, I believe, never a single element but always a* relation *between two elements. And the basic relationships of the dramaturgical model do in some way reproduce, correspond to or simulate basic relationships from the audience's existential reality, sometimes adding carefully foregrounded changes in such relationships. This reproduction is futile, that is to say, aesthetically insignificant, unless it strives to make the human relationships in question somehow clearer than in the audience's existential reality. It does so by means of conventional yet changeable signifying systems in which, for example, empirically non-existent elements, such as gods, speaking animals or science-fictional aliens, can signify and indeed clarify central existing relationships between people.*

For historically clear but still very strange reasons, what is discussed at length in this book as the Individualist dramaturgy (beginning, say, in some Shakespeare and culminating in the nineteenth century) uses an illusionistic *model. Its basic convention is that it in some mystically unexplained way directly reproduces, mirrors, or 'gives us' the empirical societal world which is its exclusive subject-matter (bourgeois drama cannot deal with man's relationships to the universe, with non-Individualist forces such as gods, et sim.). This is a departure from most (or all?) previous dramaturgic models throughout history which were basically* analogical, *that is to say, whose basic convention is that it produces an analogue to the empirical macrocosm permitting 'only' the understanding of the basic forces at work in it. All dramaturgic models or microcosms have to condense and displace existential time, space and activities into a* dramaturgic story *or fable (the ensemble of events, as Aristotle says) with its own dramaturgic space, time and agents. However, in the illusionistic model, the performance or representational time, space and agents are supposed to be identical to the represented or performed time, space and people; in the analogical model they do not have to be identical. The illusionistic verisimilitude makes for the consumer's passivity: her or his impossibility of intervening into what looks like an exact replica of the empirical world stands for his or her impossibility of intervening into that empirical world, for which the surrogate of empathising into the protagonist(s) is offered. On the contrary, a truthful recognition that the dramaturgic space/time and agents are experimental conventions resorted to for pleasurable investigation allows the audience to avoid pure consumerism through its activity of translating the findings of the stage into possibilities of empirically alternative practice.*

Perhaps this is the place to put in some preliminary clarifications about my attitude in this book toward Individualism. As any Marxist, I do not believe that judgements of facts and judgements of value can finally *be sundered. Even the initial choices of subjects for discussion, the terminology used as cognitive instrument, and so on, are strongly bound up with the writer's values. On the other hand, I recognise that any dramaturgy, indeed any 'structure of feeling' and world-view, necessarily selects while setting up its models. It is salutary and instructive to compare relationships shown on the stage with those historically attested to through other writings at the same time and place. Such a comparison has shown for example that in the dramaturgy of Molière (surely a 'popular' playwright), the common people or lower classes (in other words, the overwhelming majority of the French population) appear only as* personnages ridicules. *The contemporary dramaturgy of Racine is even more thematically selective: not only is the people in it mentioned at best in very general and vague terms, but no economic topic is admitted. Indeed, Racinean tragedy shuts out the whole of everyday existence except upper-class power struggles, the correlative psychology of passions, and (later) some religious motifs. Now I would resolutely refuse to blame Molière or Racine for this, and furthermore maintain that their very or (as the case may be) somewhat narrow thematic and characterological range can transmit insights significant not only for their society, or for the social classes shown in their dramaturgies, but also directly or parabolically applicable to (at least) any class society. It is not necessary to choose between these two playwrights and the certainly wider range of Shakespeare or Brecht, and it would be downright unintelligent (unmaterialistic) to choose Shakespeare* over *Racine or Brecht* over *Molière. None the less, what is absent from a dramaturgic microcosm delimits and determines it far more intimately than thematics alone might suggest. To put forward only one argument: it is no accident that the 'limited' giants named wrote (in their significant plays) either tragedies or very bitter comedies; certain ways of envisaging life were denied them, as they were not to the 'embracing' giants. I believe there is a correlation between the limitation in thematic domain and agential range and the limitation of possible stances and visions (implicit, for example, in Lucien Goldmann's argument on Racine).*

Thus, were I writing a history of dramaturgy I would dwell at length on the historical necessity and even value of the rise of Individualism and its dramaturgy — the 'round' characters as agents, the laicised space and time empirically accountable for, and so on. In this book, I am concerned mainly to look backward at Individualism from its artificially delayed collapse, and to find the inherent elements making for its decay. Like Baudelaire's charogne, *it is today an unburied corpse that menaces us with a universal epidemic. If we ever overcome this threat, we shall be able to speak in less angry ways about the Individualist structure of feeling: 'Anger, even against injustice/Makes the voice hoarse . . .' (Brecht). Trying to prefigure such a balanced judgement on a huge subject, about which we need much more investigation, I would note the following:*

The rise of Individualism — just as the rise of its economical and social analogues and bearers, the market and the bourgeoisie — has brought great advantages as well as great limitations. The advantages were principally apparent during the ascending historical phase, in Europe, say, up to Balzac, George Eliot and Tolstoy. To take only the agents as an example, in that phase the 'character' was the agential formulation of the freedom to break through the consensual constraints of hierarchically frozen social types and dogmatic normative systems (connected with despotic monarchism and a stagnant subsistence economy) toward larger horizons of life. The multiplication of traits and their conflictuality, the illusion of agential 'roundness' and 'three-dimensionality', connoted that human agents and actions were not explained, foreseen or fixed once and for all. Their richness allowed these freshly conceived agents to slip through the insufficient, clumsy and restrictive net of old 'universal' agents (i.e. the types). The new dramaturgic space/ times were analogous to this new structure of agents: where the types were timeless and set against a fixed background, so that they pretended to eternal and ubiquitous validity, a character can and does evolve in linear time and within the environment. But all such aspects turn into their contraries with the contraction and exhaustion of Individualism in our century. On the one hand, the price of its particular kind of freedom begins to weigh more heavily than its achievements as the bourgeoisie shifts from personal competition to fictitious corporative 'individualities' and state institutions. On the other hand, this shift as well as the failure (so far) of radical alternatives to bourgeois rule threatens all freedom, in the true sense of enlarging possibilities of life, bringing about new monopolistic and stereotype-producing Leviathans – states, corporations, armies, culture industry, etc.

Finally, my book converges toward what I take to be the central problem of any theory of literature and culture that focuses on their significant relations with historical and societal dynamics: toward allegory, *in the widest sense of intimate relationship between a fictional text and a cognitive teaching or belief. Such a belief about human and cosmic nature may be placidly accepted in stable ages, or it may be furiously worried over in unstable ages such as ours, but it can certainly not be reduced to a technical problem for medieval or Antiquity or sinological philologists. One of the worst ideological sins of Individualism is to have expunged all such englobing value-problems from the cultural horizon: we need to put allegory back on the top of our cultural agenda. If this is not done, it will be there anyway, but in debased forms. Allegory is, I believe, the privileged way of getting at the relationship between aesthetics and salvation (a subject I develop in my Afterword to Part 2 à propos Brecht, Beckett, etc.). Therefore, it is a bone that a number of us have been gnawing at inconclusively for quite some time.*

2. *As can be seen, and as I point out in other places in this book, perhaps the main red thread running through it is dramaturgy (as part of what for want of a better word is called aesthetics) in a* *feedback loop with history. History means – these essays are increasingly aware of it, though today I think not enough – a ruthless collision of people and institutions in* power structures *as a rule inimical to humanisation. Its sense is in the long march to what in theological language would be called a salvation through but against the Terrene City. Thence the theme of alienation (desensualisation, reification), first taken up in Part 1, and running through all the chapters. And yet this is, I hope, very far from Andorno-type gloom and doom, from what Lukács somewhat unfairly sneered at as Grand Hotel Abyss or Despair. If life is alienated, alienation is shot through with life: a strange symbiosis is implied here, an optimism whose precondition is pessimism (as in Brecht). The symbiosis is, philosophically speaking, unnatural: but that is the nature of our times (of class society in general). This is what culture is (up to now). The basic constituents and aspects of dramaturgy – time, space and* dramatis personae, *or anthropology and cosmology – are all shot through, and indeed formed by, such contradictory, analytically interesting but axiologically unnatural categories swayed by the alienation of humanity.*

Is theological language legitimate for atheists? Possibly it might be better, in a different world, to do without it. But first, this is impossible. In the European tradition of systematic thinking (philosophy), without which we, in Europe at least, cannot manage, coherent investigation of basic questions of people's destiny has been – for reasons of political power and ruthless suppression of alternatives – largely done within theology. Even when the argumentation was laicised, its basic bricks often remained theologemes: e.g. the Nation State; or the People; or indeed History. But conversely – second and more important – why leave this vocabulary to theology only? Why let salvation be treated merely as a heavenly and not an earthly matter? Why must the Saviour be god and not a political force? Out there and not in here? Why not have – with folk tales and William Morris – an earthly paradise? Lucretius and Epicurus were, after all, before Augustine and Aquinas. Let us socialise the means of intellectual production too, rescuing them from sectarian property. (Historically seen, monotheism is a sect limited in time and space – the tribes, the Chinese, classical Antiquity, or the classless society do not need it.) In fact, I would maintain all the major literary/theatre/cultural critics of this century have used theologemes: literally, as Eliot or Frye; or in a more useful refunctioning, as Lukács, Bakhtin, Benjamin, Bloch, or Brecht –

critics decisively marked by their encounter with Marxism.

   And so I have arrived at the central position of Brecht in this book – and further, in cultural as well as dramaturgic criticism today. I shall discuss that in the Afterword to Part 2. Here, I want to clear up two other questions of analytical technique or terminology used in this book. First, how useful are the terms of cosmology and anthropology? And second, what about the occasional use of topology (or, more modestly, graphs from analytical geometry, opposed – isotopic – columns, and a few other non-linear discursive devices)? Both are of Renaissance and Rationalist provenance, from Descartes to Kant, say. As to the latter, when these papers were first published, in English or Serbo-Croat, I was taken severely to task for (very occasionally) deserting verbal explication by some Left-'humanist' critics who, I imagine, believed they were defending the Poetry of Art against the Prose of Science. Now, I shall readily acknowledge that in my youth I committed six years of natural science studies, and have therefore neither superstitious respect toward science nor a reluctance to use some of its witty tools. As Tomashevsky wrote in his study on verse, 'Science cannot tolerate a prohibition on using any method . . . . The number, the formula, the graph are symbols of thought just as the word is . . . . Numbers do not decide anything, they do not interpret, they are simply a way of realising and describing facts.' Such a pre-, semi- or quasi-Structuralist use (excogitated before I encountered the pleasant novels or sonatas of Lévi-Strauss) seems to me allowable where economical; and I wish I had used it more. But I do not wish it to signify agreement with the latter-day Structuralist terrorism which holds (against the more intelligent Formalists such as Tomashevsky) that graphs simply by being there do decide a matter – which is not true even in mathematics, much less in culture. My conclusion is that verbalistic humanism could be, and often was, as terroristic as Structuralist technocracy when it filled the identical position of ruling ideology. Such hysterical reactions are incomprehensible even within its own tradition: don't humanists like painting? or architecture? or music and its clearly mathematical architecture? When applied to theatre and dramaturgy it becomes especially obvious that they are, as I argue in Part 1, simply a piece of standard bourgeois ideology, reifying the sensual world of three dimensions, poetry, colours, sounds, etc., into the two-dimensionality of verbal prose – the medium of the nineteenth-century market. That this became compatible with left-wing politics is one of the unhappy aporias of European socialism. Yet materialist dialectics is the only way I know that can, when used intelligently, transcend both romantic humanism and rigid technocracy – if it first absorbs both.

Somewhat similar reflections, with a somewhat stronger self-critique, could be addressed to the terms of cosmology and anthropology. The names of these two scientific disciplines developing after, say, Cusanus and Bruno or Lyell and Frazer respectively, are used metaphorically in cultural studies to signify the particular views of environmental and personal relationships, both always suffused by values, in a given corpus of texts (in the widest sense: plays, paintings, etc.). But the scientific term vehiculating the metaphor, the suffix -'ology', indicates an approach that wishes to emulate in precision – though, since it is used within a metaphor, not necessarily in method – a natural science. So far, so good: I would still defend the union of observation and rigour, of factography and flexibility implied in such a hybrid of science and art. The categories of cosmology and anthropology can in fact mediate between the empirical world of the audience and the fictional world, and help to situate the fictive microcosm inside a collective societal macrocosm. None the less, we need instruments which can better reveal the intimate interpenetration of 'the fictive' and 'the real' (what we think of as real is a convention akin to fiction, etc.). Whatever terms we use, even if we just call it idiolect vs. sociolect, they should avoid both mechanical reductionism and idealist formalism. I would today rather use terms which are equidistant from these extremes, more philosophical and simultaneously more technical, such as dramaturgic space and agents, or topoanalysis and agential analysis. But this would be of a piece with a fairly wideranging rearrangement of perspective, for which this is not the place.

3. *Some other problems raised by the essays that follow and their juxtaposition are discussed in the two Afterwords. Here I want to point out the pivotal position in this book of chapter 3, on the Theatre Law of the Paris Commune. This chapter takes up the overviews of Part 1 and introduces accounts of exemplary modern dramaturgies. This is not at all accidental. First, the reference toward the end of its first section to an intelligent theory and practice of politics merging with a critical anthropology (and cosmology) – i.e. with a critical view of people's relationships to each other and their common societal universe – provides the general context and horizon of the whole book, which strives to understand dramaturgy*

*as a privileged – cognitive and pleasurable, one because of the
other – series of glimpses into such relations and their freezing by
different societal power relationships. The institution of theatre is,
then, born as a tension between two poles. The original tribal magic
impulse and traffic between the largely identical performers and
audience of a collective story has been shaped into theatre by its
counterpart, the emergent State. The State (its jurisdiction, its
police) always subtends the ideological justifications and contesta-
tions of theatre, and of its constructive principle and axis,
dramaturgy, as a huge, today usually occulted but necessarily
inferrable iceberg or indeed continental ice-shelf. In the truly
exemplary and radical case of the Paris Commune, these two
interlocked institutions, State and theatre (organisation and dramaturgy), are both revealed and demystified.*

*The title 'organisational mediation' can therefore branch in two
directions. Synchronically, it indicates the crucial role of the
perennial interface between community – both as audience and as
state power – and theatre. This is technically and legally difficult to
study except in overviews such as those of Part 1, but I have
discreetly attempted to particularise it in chapters 5, 6, and 9.
Diachronically, it indicates the epoch-making failure of the
revolutionary mediation between Individualist and (let us call it)
Communalist theatre in the last hundred years, which is one of the
few basic parameters for any history of dramaturgy. As British
readers may have glimpsed in the case of the Ardens vs. the Royal
Shakespeare Theatre – though the careers of practically all other
playwrights, most clearly of Brecht, could be taken as examples
too – the matter of who manages the theatres and thus who decides
what is staged, how, and for whom, is inseparable from the
(usually) failed passage from Individualist to post-Individualist
dramaturgy.*

*A second reference in the Paris Commune chapter to a neces-
sary debate on 'Theatre now!' which is not to be put off until society
as a whole has been rid of its murderous antagonisms – though I believe only then would a decision become possible – contains the greatest
part of the* raison d'être *of the whole book. The conclusions of this
chapter are twofold. First, that organisational liberation is a necessity
of life, and that, for this necessity to be met, it is indispensable to prepare
for it by 'mental experiments' based on lessons of the past and on a
coherent and significant methodology. Second, that a critic who is, as
I am, for ideological and organisational reasons on the whole*

prevented from direct cooperation in daily, collective theatre life, can decently contribute to the cause of the liberating theatre – identical to the cause of understanding the possibilities and built-in limits of significant dramaturgy – only by methodologically clear judgements on the preconditions, coherence and implications of given historical practices. These judgements will, for reasons of economy, have to focus on exemplary practices – be they positive or negative, be they the dramaturgy of a single (sufficiently representative) play, play-wright, spectacle genre, or indeed – as in this essay – a major turning-point in theatre organisation delimiting much of the dramaturgy to come. The Paris Commune is such a delimitation by its very suppression: a convex mould explains its concave mouldings. The rest of Part 2 proceeds to probe such exempla: *the standpoint of Brecht's dramaturgic opus, deepened and qualified by examinations of three plays – one each from his Weimar, exile and GDR phases; Beckett's first and most representative play; and the curious, evanescent, but very indicative genre of Happenings. I would hope all of this also suggests how a horizon of 'Dramaturgy now!' is both scantier and yet wider than 'Theatre now!': more abstract and yet applicable also to other spectacle genres beyond drama, and indeed to film and television.*

Lawfully, the pivotal methodological position of the Paris Commune chapter is also a pivotal historical *position. I wish I had found world enough and time to substantiate it by more probes into the great tradition of liberating (practical and mental) experiments toward a self-governing, popular or plebeian theatre. Never interrupted, but mostly driven underground throughout history, this tradition surfaced at favourable times of resurgence of lower classes and relaxation of repression. In European civilisation (and the situation is basically similar in Asia) it runs from the medieval guilds and* joculatores, *through the popular compromises with aristocratic and monarchic patronage in the* Commedia dell'arte *or the theatres of Shakespeare and Molière, to the issue raised anew by Diderot and Rousseau, brought to a head by the practice of the 1789 Revolution, and transmitted thence to the ideas of the young Wagner, to Romain Rolland and Firmin Gémier (and the whole current of* théâtre populaire *down to Copeau and Vilar), to Nietzsche's reappraisal of Hellenic tragedy, and to the galaxy of early Soviet effervescence in and around theatre, only too scantily indicated by the brilliant solar systems of Bogdanov, Kerzhentsev, Meyerhold, Lunacharsky, Mayakovsky, Eisenstein, Vakhtangov,*

Okhlopkov, amongst others. The early Soviet experiments have prefigured further debates in our century on the guerrilla and agitprop theatre, on the street and participative, the 'poor' or 'empty space', the pleasurable and the didactic, and so many other variants of theatre and dramaturgies. The only area not covered by the early Leninist prefigurations seems the still budding discussion of the 'house dissemination' media of radio and television, though even there the Russian Futurists or Brecht and Benjamin were significant precursors (see Chapter 5).

Finally, Chapter 3 is pivotal because of the new light it throws on the book's argument, begun in Part 1, about the downward trajectory, the splendour and misery, of Individualist dramaturgy. As mentioned, this debate was fed by centenary and millenary strivings toward self-managing de-alienation in theatre as well as in society at large. This enabled it to become the clearest attempt yet – or, at any rate, between the medieval-cum-Renaissance attempts (perhaps even the tribal or Hellenic spectacles) and the Soviet attempts – at finding an organisational form within which the currents of Individualist reification could be counteracted and reversed. However, the attempt was suppressed by fire and sword: not by argument and reasoning, but by the ultima ratio regum, *the violent hacking of people's bodies and spilling of human blood. The greatest continuator and re-focusser of the liberating tradition of the Paris Commune, Brecht, wrote plays both on it and – with characteristic obliqueness – on the Soviet experiment. In* The Mother, *he focused on its presuppositions and necessity; in* The Caucasian Chalk Circle, *he collocated it within the encompassing perspective of historical figuralism; and finally in the* Coriolanus *adaptation, he speculated on its future prospects. One could also argue that a number of his other major plays are warning anti-types arising out of the Leninist experiment: for example, the universe of* Mother Courage and Her Children *has as its awful premise and non-dit the experiment's failure in the domain of international peace. Three of these four plays are analysed in this book. Yet Brecht was a political dramatist, but not a politician, and he focused on the torturing of flesh in the victims and saints of the slaughterhouse age which ensued from the suppression of the Paris Commune and the partial (as he saw it) failure of the early Soviet impulse. I preferred to analyse his* Saint Joan *rather than the more famous but largely derivative* Galileo *in order to show this basic Brechtian motive and motif.*

However, Brecht is, after all, a sociological or statistical exception in modern theatre: as in one of his own plays, the exception proves the rule. Most plays disbelieve in the possibility of radically new horizons. Their dramaturgy either pretends to ignore the deeper societal and dramaturgical aporias of Individualism, whose unravelling has been and is being forcibly suppressed (West End, Broadway, the boulevards). Or, in significant cases, they grow despondent and nihilist. The worlds of Beckett and of the Happenings are in a way the obverse of Brecht's – though the interactions are much more complex than that. But they are no less determined by structures of feeling arising out of a continuing rule of the bourgeoisie and of a totally discredited Individualism, usually bound up with illusionist theatre. In that sense, the subjects of my last two chapters are negative grandsons of the Paris Commune: nay-saying themselves (as I discuss), but also the offsprings of the non-Commune (of its suppression). Negative does as negative is: in that sense, Adorno's defence of negativism as immeasurably superior to status quo positivism is quite right. That is why I argue that a sympathetic understanding of, though not identification with, those horizons of modern art best represented in dramaturgy by Beckett (and elsewhere by Schönberg, Kafka, etc.), as well as by the Happenings, is indispensable for any believable twentieth-century radicalism. The history of socialism has proved this to the hilt: this understanding is the cultural equivalent of the difference between a socialism dominated by bureaucracy (Stalinist or 'social-democratic') and one dominated by plebeian democracy. Which, I suppose, is one of the main debates within this book.

PART 1

1

On Individualist Dramaturgy

0. Hypothesis: Individualism and Illusionism

Each and every performance or (re)presentation is *a sight and show of a fictive universe* (with a non-empirical space/time), i.e. the prospect and inspection *of believable and meaningful human relationships, presented in a sensible and sensually direct way, to a spectatorial community which has not seen them yet and is therefore struck by them* (see Appendix, Some Semantics as Frozen History). The onlookers' community has not seen such relations either because they might be familiar but their inspection was beclouded by too great proximity and/or complexity and/or mystifying class interests, in other words, because they might have been known as disjointed details but were never 'seen' in their meaningful entirety (*bekannt* but not *erkannt* (Hegel)). Or, on the other pole, theatre might show the prospecting community 'the jab of other worlds on this' (Rossiter), an unfamiliar but possibly alternative universe or set of human relationships. Often, what is beheld is a blend of the familiar and unfamiliar, both so far uncognised or 'untheorised'. The central purpose of theatre is to articulate, deepen and clarify the vision of its collective spectator(s).

It should be stressed that *relationships between people* are a central – *the* central – aspect of all fiction. They are processes shared and indeed necessarily transferred back and forth between fiction and empirical apprehension of life in a way that the much more rigid categories of space, time and *dramatis personae* cannot be. For example, even if the stage figures are gods, talking animals, Martians, Robinson Crusoes, or even animated objects, they necessarily and unavoidably convey human relationships and attitudes only: and therefore as necessarily imply a human culture and

19

community as their context and moulder. Thus, both in regard to the beholders and to the beheld, all theatre, all plays (and indeed all artefacts as well as all other human products) are, in the wide and fundamental sense of the terms, civic (from *civitas*) or political (from *polis*) – concerned with the health or sickness of the body politic. This means, of course, that within the spectrum or spread of meanings ranging from 'politics as everyday pragmatic, party bickering' and 'politics as fundamental questions of the community's sickness or health, life and death' we have chosen the latter pole as the only relevant one. The first meaning finds man alienated by, and what is worse alienated *into* the Leviathans of states, corporate companies, parties and bureaucracies of all kinds and stripes. The second meaning assumes man is biologically and sociologically a communal animal – a *zoon politikon* as Aristotle remarked. In this latter sense, politics means 'the affairs of the *polis*, of the community', and concerns itself ultimately with the community's salvation in historical time and space. Aristotle's teacher, Plato, called his dialogue treatise on an ideal form of social or community organisation the *Politeia;* the best English translation of that is not the Republic or the State, but the Cromwellian and Miltonian translation of the 'Commonwealth'.

If all theatre and drama are political, and since they emerge together with class society (tribal societies use instead powerful but undifferentiated rituals), they will, in fashioning their ordered *theoria* (originally, that which is beheld or contemplated), be faced with a spread of salvational choices situated between the existing order and their own order of vision, between seeing the alienated actualities and seeing the ideal human potentialities. Very rarely, the usually grim societal *status quo* and the intrinsically utopian, artistic vision of existence as creative pleasure will, if not coincide, then at least be understandable as concentric circles. As a rule, the necessary harmony in human relationships will be incompatible with the relations and institutions contemporary to the artist.

Within this incompatibility it is useful to distinguish playwrights – or better, modes of composing plays or *dramaturgies*, usually associated with prominent names for brevity's sake – whose fundamental form is correlative to a belief that a liveable balance between utopian existence and societal organisation *can*, or to a belief that it *cannot*, be struck. In the first case, such a balance can be worked toward by means of (explicitly or implicitly) 'workable' or practically usable suggestions of a better polity, a different system of human relationships, as in Aeschylus, Shakespeare's comedies or Brecht. In the second case, theatre and dramaturgy can only bear witness to the qualities of some unavoidably defeated *dramatis personae* as in Sophocles, Shakespeare's tragedies or Ibsen. But this is not a matter of the pragmatic outcome, a happy or unhappy ending, which is a dramatist's appraisal of what is believable at a particular historical period for a particular type of spectator. It is, rather, a matter of stressing either (in the Aeschylus to Brecht group) a given intrinsically dynamic constellation of forces to be understood by the spectator in view of his own orientation, whatever might have happened to the play's hero(ine); or of stressing (in the Sophocles to Ibsen group) the intrinsically unalterable, static condition of Man in the universe. In both types of dramaturgies, the supreme norm of the societal group functions as Fate or Destiny, the arbiter of the play, but in the first case Destiny is composed of human interactions, and in the second of transcendental revelation.

In modern times, say from the French and American Revolutions on, the central categories determining the structure of feeling or viewing of any historical epoch have become laicised. These central categories which link the work of art (the specific *theoria*) with the common societal reality (*praxis*) from which it arises as a signifying model and into which it returns by signifying to determined audiences how the world is fashioned, are: (1) the human relationships which provide the *subject-matter* (theme or domain) for artistic situations; and (2) the approach to them from a determined *point of view* (the world-view or *Weltanschauung*), i.e. a valorisation of such human relationships. It is a specific feature of bourgeois art that (1) it cherishes the *illusion* that its artistic world picture in some mystically unexplained way directly reproduces or 'gives us' the objective outer world, its subject-matter; and (2) it conceives, views and feels the world from the standpoint of *the individual*, as the final brick or unit of the envisioned universe. Thus, it hinges on the two axioms of *illusionism* and *Individualism*. Developments during the decadence of Individualism in the last hundred years seem to indicate that it is the more fundamental axiom of the two, and I therefore focus mainly on it.

1. The Individualist and Renaissance View of the World: Dehumanisation and Environment

Individualism became a decisive element of the bourgeois world-view when the bourgeoisie was contracting out of the Renaissance popular mainstream and turning against it. I shall therefore contrast it with the vision of the Renaissance, the epoch when the bourgeois structure of feeling was not yet fully developed, since the bourgeoisie was still the articulate vanguard of a broader popular movement. The great achievements of the then truly 'middle' classes were therefore anything but limited in a bourgeois way, representing as they did the *civis* rather than the *bourgeois,* and can both genetically and typologically serve as a legitimate foil and test.

The Renaissance ethics were absolute, universally applicable, and of universal relevance. By their light, a human being was analogous to the macrocosmos, diminished in scale but qualitatively of the same importance. Because of this, the Titanic figures of Renaissance drama, a Tamburlaine, Faustus, Prospero, Antony, Macbeth, Lear, Timon, *can* be equivalent to cosmic forces, harmonising or conflicting with them. Their tragedy does not lie in quantity – in Macbeth's being finally less cunning than the witches, or Tamburlaine's being less powerful than Death – but in a wrongly oriented quality, in their having transgressed against the cosmic order. But even in its doom, a Renaissance personality involved the universe – during Duncan's and Caesar's murder the elemental frame is shaken; Lear struggles with the hurricane as an equal. *Qualitative values are inherent in the personality*, not in an ideological view of the world. The views of Prospero and Antonio, or Faustus and Mephistophilis, differ only in quantitative awareness of a common, clearly defined, and absolutely relevant qualitative anthropology and cosmology: and the views of Claudius the murderer,

and Hamlet the rightful avenger, differ only in the consistency of applying such shared awareness.

The relationships within the Renaissance view of the
universe were trans- or supra-individualistic: not only was
the single person englobed in an all-embracing unity, but this
unity had as its irreducible bearer an articulated collectivity
rather than the atomic individual. This holds true also for the
later middle ages, i.e. for the universal Gothic drama of the
Mystery cycles, although the collectivity involved – well
symbolised by the Ptolemeian concentric shells and the
vertical Great Chain of Being with their rigid patriarchal
power layers – was considerably dehumanised. Deprived of
either the human or the divine 'organic unity' (as the
Romantics will put it) or collective completeness, Individualist drama and theatre could envisage the universe only as an
antinomic reality split into *the individual* and *its environment*.
This kind of 'reality' was simultaneously the subject-matter
of Individualism and its world-view. The ideal-typical
horizon of this radically new structure of feeling was a
thoroughgoing reorientation from use-value to exchange-
value, flowing out of the very essence of money economy,
and resulting in the desensualising of human relationships
through abstraction and their depersonalising through
reification; as the Renaissance writer Sacchetti commented:
he who does not know himself, how shall he know things
outside himself? Conversely, for the individual it is the things
outside people which are important: more particularly those
attributes which can be translated into the numerical language of measures and money, the one language pertinent to
only quantitatively measurable units. The international
merchant Marco Polo is, in all his descriptions of Cathay's
wonders, primarily interested in their wealth and size, in
their 'millionness'; Dante, the supreme articulator of qualitative relations structured within a medieval framework, but
already bearing significant features of Renaissance humanisation, found 'all the gold under the Moon' less important than
one person(ality), even one tired, wealth-beguiled soul in
Hell (*Inferno* VII).

The pervasive dehumanisation has profound effects. As
Marx expressed it, the direct consequence of Man's alienation
from the product of his work, is 'the alienation of man from

man, the alienation of man from his generic activity
signifying that one man is alienated from another as well as
that each of them is alienated from human being' (*Economic
and Philosophical Manuscripts of 1844*). Thus, the bourgeois
person is not analogous to the cosmos, but a fragment
opposed to an *a priori* alien cosmos, to his *environment*. More
and more, the individual exists only as a sum of relationships
to things outside him, the 'external reality'. Other people too
are included among the external things: in the Individualist
world Man is primarily an object, a moving and speaking
thing, to Man. It is because of this that he can behave towards
another person as if that person were a usable thing, slightly
more complicated to use. The Renaissance prince, Hamlet,
was still outraged at such Guildensternian behaviour:

Why, look you now, how unworthy a thing you make of me: you
would play upon me; you would seem to know my stops; you
would pluck out the heart of my mystery; you would sound me
from my lowest note to the top of my compass; and there is much
music, excellent voice, in this little organ, yet cannot you make it
speak. S'blood, do you think I am easier to be play'd on than a
pipe?

(*Hamlet*, III. iii)

The ideal of *plenty* – of a full compass, a qualitatively
articulated but literally harmonious plenitude or universe
(here the universe of sounds) – is, in Renaissance view, *the*
means of attaining beauty and excellence. It implies an
enjoyment of life in which intellect and senses, the brain and
the sensorium, are not opposed but integrated. This was, no
doubt, an ideal horizon, practically accessible only to a small
affluent minority at court or in the city, between Palermo and
London, while the bourgeois horizons drew their power
from and triumphed because of the lure – and, in limited but
real ways, the actual possibility – of participation in its ideals
by a significantly greater number of people. But while this
number was absolutely much greater, it was relatively still
very small in comparison to the popular masses of peasants
and townsfolk. And the qualitative price for the quantitative
enrichment of a larger societal class was the substitution for
the ideal of harmonious plenty of the ideal of arithmetic
plenty (more and bigger equals better). In such a quantified

view of the world individuals are reduced, even in the realm of music, to counting according to an arithmetic scale, to making the abundance of things an end unto itself. Hamlet's Renaissance critique rightly identifies this philosophy (which became dominant after Bacon and Descartes) as making things out of or *reifying* all relationships – those between people in society as well as those between Man and the universe.

Man's being a thing to Man is the final expression of a situation where everything outside the individual is inanimate as far as he is concerned, where unquantifiable personal qualities are increasingly irrelevant. Each individual is in the final analysis alone, a Robinson Crusoe on his own cosmic desert island of objects. The Renaissance dream of a person being fulfilled as a member of its harmonious ensemble of autonomous personalities yields place to individuals dominant 'at the expense' of other, subordinated and exploited individuals. In such a climate the individual's relationships with other individuals become increasingly unbearable bonds. The very notion of 'bond' is transmuted from that of a naturally just relation to that of fetters to be burst by the enterprising individual. In *King Lear*, the great tragedy of the downfall of medieval qualitative hierarchy, such individuals are presented as the villains Goneril and Regan – the wily merchandisers of love exchanged for land and power – opposed from the beginning to Cordelia and Kent, who love according to their 'bond'. For Shakespeare, when 'natural' quality is shaken, the chaos of nothingness has come again ('nature' and 'nothing' being two terms that reverberate through the whole play).

Thus at the very outset of the newer European theatre the single personality was – paradoxically – most heroically affirmed in the not yet fully Individualist drama of Marlowe and Shakespeare (and, in a feverishly concentrated way, in that of Corneille and even Racine). The paradox is explainable by the fact that playwrights (and other artists) do not adopt basic epistemic and aesthetic axioms, such as Individualism, on any given New Year's Day. On the contrary, such presuppositions and frames gain sway only in slow, scores of years long, complex, sometimes less than coherent but sometimes (as here) very fruitful interactions with earlier presuppositions and axiomatic systems. However, once the fruitful tension of the Renaissance had collapsed, together with its socio-historical bearers – various forms of the compromise between absolute monarchy and the middle class as representative of the people or as *cives* – Individualist art began to permeated by increasingly acute manifestations of *accedia*, melancholy, *Weltschmerz*, boredom, spleen, *mal du siècle*, anxiety, nausea. That is why the protest against the universe grows so hysterical as already in some aspects of Robinson Crusoe – sensitively noted in Buñuel's film treatment – or as in European Romanticism after de Sade, Rousseau and Byron (e.g. Schiller's *Die Räuber* [*Robbers*] or Dumas père's *Antony*). The Individualist cosmos is in the final analysis composed of *one character (subject) and his real (objective) environment*: all-pervading, and therefore all-important.

However, the Individualist cosmos exists not only in space, but also in time. The abstracting of human relationships into bonds between men of property, owners of commodities, flowing out of the Individualist greed for quantitative magnitudes, leads to universal antagonistic competition. Man is not only a thing to Man but, in a mystical way, also a wolf, a competing Other or inhuman being. He is alive and a subject only in so far as he is competing: the war of each greedy individual against each is a normal Hobbesian state of the Individualist world. And the persistence of this warfare is made possible by the boundlessness of promised spoils, by *the factual and notional appearance of capital*. Land property in a given area has natural boundaries, financial property theoretically has none. The financial areas acquired in time are potentially vaster than even the Roman Empire: Cortez's and Pizarro's America was more of a financial than a spatial discovery. *Time*, the measure of acquiring things, becomes the equivalent of finances: its quantity begins to be measured in the fourteenth century (the first town clocks), in the same period when literature begins to mourn its swift flow. The reified Individualist space and time environment is therefore to be comprehended only as a sum total of quantities, in the numerical language of measures and money. Money is, in its turn, the measure of all saleable goods or commodities, including most prominently human energy in clock-time: 'Time is money.' Shakespeare's times were still qualitative and multiple, galloping with some and ambling with others: there is 'no clock in the forest' of *As You Like It*. Now the metaphor of time as a river and devourer, the theme of 'seizing the day', is emerging. Among the most significant examples from a host of such testimonies is *Troilus and Cressida*, the drama of time which, bringing in its flow the war, destroys generic love relationships:

> Time hath, my lord, a wallet at his back
> Wherein he puts alms for oblivion,
> A great sized monster of ingratitudes
> (*Troilus and Cressida*, III. iii)

Individualist relationships finally exist only as a capricious, thankless flux, determined by the positions of figures in a competitive and inimical environment, constantly changing in an unsafe Time.

2. Background, Dramaturgical Space and Time

All this means that the *dramatis personae* are determined at least as much by their relationships towards a dramaturgically transposed 'real environment' as by their mutual relations. More precisely, these mutual relationships are themselves to a considerable extent determined by a narrative transposition of the environment.

The spatial and temporal (i.e. societal) environment of the epoch is transposed into Individualist drama as *the background*, which represents and signifies the dominant social norms of the environment (e.g. the Code Civil with its marriage and inheritance paragraphs in European nineteenth-century drama). Up to the present day, the background – usually of societal power – has remained the defining formal device of Individualist dramaturgy. It determines the outcome of the dramatic conflict with the figures in the foreground, at first by being explicitly incarnated in a spokesman such as von Walter in Schiller's *Kabbale und Liebe* [*Intrigue and Love*], Master Anton in Hebbel's *Maria Magdalene*, Armand's father

in *La Dame aux camélias* [*Camille*], Dr Stockmann's brother in
Ibsen's *An Enemy of the People*, or the Court in Shaw's *St
Joan*. But this explicit incarnation has, especially in more
recent times, been supplemented and sometimes supplanted
by impersonal forces around the main figures, as in the
Maeterlinckian and Chekhovian 'mood'; or within them, as
in Pirandello's split personalities; or both around and within,
as in Beckett's pervasive games with Fate. Different secondary groupings around such a main axis of tension – e.g. the
love-partner and the virtuous father alongside the main
character in bourgeois tragedy from Lillo and Diderot to
Lessing and Schiller, or the doubling of the main figure in
Beckett – constitute characteristic features of smaller units in
the history of Individualist drama. However, through all
metamorphoses the existence of a dominant dramatic background endures. This apparently neutral, formal category in
fact defines the historical limitation, the ideological and
finally political nature, of practically all Individualist drama
between the eighteenth century and the latest Broadway,
West End and boulevard hits. It is built into the very
foundation of this dramaturgy.

It is this background which defines the relationships of the
intrinsically isolated *dramatis personae*, and looms over them,
in a quite different way from that in Aeschylus or
Shakespeare. Lady Macbeth from the Mtsensk region – or
from Kenya – is quite easily imaginable, and Hamlet's being
a prince is not his determining trait. Nora as a duchess, a
working-class woman or a Mexican is imaginable only in so
far as individualist and capitalist relationships (including
respectability, the *Code Civil*, promissory notes, a financial
fraud revealed by post-dating, and subordination of women)
have become the dominating background of, say, a Proustian
aristocracy, a Laurentian working class or contemporary
Mexico. I would assert that there was no unbridgeable gulf
between Clytemnestra and a charwoman of any present-day
Mediterranean port: between Hedda Gabler and a working-
class woman of her period's Oslo I can see no dramaturgically pertinent bridge. The background, the transposed
environment, determines, by manifesting itself in space and
time, the scenic figures of Individualist drama.

The Individualist *dramaturgical space* is thus subservient to what the most significant aesthetics of the whole bourgeois epoch, Hegel's, called drama's closed entirety. Space and the things that constitute it are antinomic: on the one hand their significance constantly rises, up to the archeological pedantry of Stanislavsky, so that the *dramatis personae* are dominated by them and not infrequently become mobile furniture (*meubles*). On the other hand space – visible or suggested – cannot actively participate in creating the basic quality of a dramaturgical situation as it did, say, in Shakespeare. To the contrary, the spatial background must be simultaneously all-pervasive and yet so unquestioned that it is 'abstracted out of the spectator's consciousness. Only thus can an [Individualist] absolute or dramatic situation come about. The more frequently the scene is changed, the more difficult this is. Also, the spatial disjunction – like the temporal one – presupposes an epic I. (Stereotype: "Now we leave the conspirators in the forest to visit the unwitting king in his palace.")' (Szondi). This is why Hegel censures Shakespeare – though with some excuses – for his too frequent changes of place, more proper to epic than drama.

As against this, almost each 'scene' in Renaissance dramaturgy – as its name testifies – involves a particular space correlative to its particular time; in fact, that space-cum-time often constitutes the basic premise of its story segment. The ideal-typical space of Individualist dramaturgy is a room or some analogue of it; its horizons are bounded by wallpaper and organised around the foreground of a very few colliding characters. The typical space of Renaissance dramaturgy is a scene in the open, or some analogue of it open toward nature – for example, toward the time of day and season – and toward a larger human collective. Indeed, the sociological basis of such 'open' dramaturgy is the nostalgia for, or prefiguration of, such a larger, super-individual collective. The *dramatis personae* of Renaissance dramaturgy represent all social classes; nobody – and no place – is insufficiently 'dignified' for tragic, or too sublime for comic events. Its space-forming objects are never conventionally given or sensational, such as the sofa, fan or chandelier of the 'well-made play'; on the contrary, whether visible or imaginatively suggested, they contribute to the basic quality of the story – for example, the imaginary knife in *Macbeth*, the red carpet in *Agamemnon* or the imaginary cliff and courtroom in *King Lear*.

The illusionistic identity of Individualist dramaturgical space with empirical space means that its *dramaturgical time* is a perpetual present. As Arnold Hauser rightly remarks:

> Only a society that had lost its faith in both the necessity and the divine ordinance of social distinctions as well as in their connection with personal virtue and merit, a society which experiences the daily growing power of money and sees men becoming merely what external conditions make them, but which, nevertheless, affirms social dynamism, since it either owes its own ascendancy to or expects it from this dynamism, only that kind of society could reduce the drama to the categories of empirical space and time. (Modified from Stanley Godman's translation, in Hauser, III. 90.)

The perpetual presentness of Individualist dramaturgical time means that it develops as an exclusive succession: any dramaturgical situation is to be explained by the development of the play as a whole, it does not, even at the moment of its presentation, exist without regard and reference to preceding and succeeding situations. The time of Individualist dramaturgy is also antinomic: communicated as an endless present, on the other hand it is predetermined by earlier dramatic moments and continually straining in a teleological movement toward the culmination, untying and end; the past and the future are the destiny of the present. The meaning of a situation is not autonomous, it will be exhausted by later effects or it is the presentation of effects from earlier causes. Instead of particular meanings of the moment, the spectator is primarily referred to the general causal nexus of dramaturgic destination in the totality of the play. Particular events do not give rise to particular temporal qualities, they only add a new quantum (*quantum satis*) within the linear time stream. The temporal succession is a neutral and transparent river flowing with a more or less equal speed, without significant dams or vortices (as in Newton).

By contrast, in the medieval or Renaissance dramaturgy – whose open forms drama began striving toward again about the end of the nineteenth century – the situational unit of speech, gesture, time and space has a significant autonomy. No doubt, it participates in the final effect of the play, but it does so in its own inimitable way, so that it is not obliged to have a direct and immediate relation to a preceding or succeeding situation. Thus, the playwright does not have to violate the verisimilitude and dream up coincidences by help of which the *dramatis personae* communicate with earlier or later situations. The time of 'open' dramaturgy is not necessarily linear, it can be cyclical, explosive, slowed down, spiral, etc. (cf. Gurvitch). Dramaturgic situations and agents are primarily significant because of their qualities, and not because of their position in a given causal, linear flow. The borderlines and planes of contact between situations are not smoothed out, but cubistically sharp and rough. Their differentiation communicates to the alert spectator the qualitative particularities inherent in them. This is one of the ways which enables him to rise above the eternal present of the stage and the figures within the plot. The inviolable *sensual presentness* of drama is thus rescued from the *ideological presentness* of Individualist 'closed' dramaturgy, allowing for a manipulation of the temporal succession.

Historically, Renaissance drama organised time round an integrated and representative personality who in a heroic struggle reduced it to the space of his actions. In Individualist drama time becomes super-ordinated to and the master of events. The absolutist statics of French Classicism (which tried to ignore the background by artificially fixing it) were an exceptional attempt at ignoring time: but the price of such isolationism proved to be excessive. During the Enlightenment the rising bourgeoisie is persuaded that time and environment work for it. But the collapse of such naive optimism in Europe after the French Revolution, and in America after the closing of the western frontier, makes of time a *peau de chagrin*, mystically connected with the protagonist who is unable to evade it. In Schiller's *Wallenstein*, time is the waiting for a propitious conjunction which does not arrive, in Hugo's *Hernani* for the horn-blast of reckoning which unavoidably does arrive. Non-banal bourgeois drama will never extricate itself from this subservience of the act to a bitter Fate which the protagonist is unable to evade in time. Be it Balzac's comi-tragic Mercadet waiting for the bell that announces his creditors (*Le Faiseur*), or Strindberg's tragi-comic Jean waiting for the bell that

announces his master (*Miss Julie*), time remains fatal for the
individual in its grip.

Of course, hardly any drama that we know, consubstantial
as it is to class society, attains in the final analysis such
de-alienated horizons as would allow it to draw the sting
from death; tribal rituals seem to have faced this task much
better. However, when we say that Macbeth and Cassandra
meet the supreme 'untimely' penalty of death, that he or she
is prematurely killed, we are speaking of a qualitatively
different kind of event. Cassandra and Macbeth realise at a
certain point that they must die, and they go consciously to
their death as bearers of certain human values established by
and around their personalities during the entire play, and
decisively stressed by the poetic dramatism of the episodes
preceding their deaths – the prophecy, or the 'sound and
fury' speech. Jean, on the contrary, not only risks no tragic
downfall (death) nor does he in fact understand what his
situation entails, he unresistingly renounces human values
and Miss Julie because he bears his master's bell within
himself, because he has been waiting for it all the time. He is
not a fighter who affirms an absolute ethic in succumbing,
but the slave of the background and its continuous presence
in time. Charged with the entire potential of his dread, the
bell changes thus from a thing to a hypnotic antagonist with a
vitality of its own: time lasts as anxiety. The winged chariot
of time is bereft of its Hellenic or Renaissance driver, it drags
its victims through the dust like a triumphant conqueror.

Finally, it is no wonder that the illusionistic scenery can be
dispensed with: the background grows so pervasive that it
permeates the *dramatis personae*. Time, from being the most
precious and the only irrevocable commodity, has become
the cheapest. Its flow has been entirely emptied (a catharsis
that would have shocked Aristotle), it is hollow within, like
the *dramatis personae*. In Beckett's world, time is only quite
residually felt as the pain of valuable chances missed, of lost
Julies or non-arriving Godots. In that peculiar, entropic
universe only a dim memory of quality flickers; what we are
left with is progressively diminishing quantity, an almost
totally evacuated duration, a simultaneously revocable and
irrevocable (because cyclical) waiting, in the first act as well
as in the second and to the end of time, Amen. For the

medieval burgher guildsmen, authors and actors of Gothic drama, time was absolute and cyclical, frozen by God's gaze (the natural economy). The contemporary disaffected and marginal intellectuals have come full circle, and we seem to be back in an everted middle age, with atheist Mystery plays. Time, as well as space, is absolute again, but now absolutely *present within* the *dramatis personae*, made diffuse by an Individualist absence of world-view – or by a presence of a wholly nihilistic world-view, embodied, logically, in up-rooted tramps. The time of middle-class anti-drama, setting (but also wry realisation) of the final lay alienation, is related to the time of religious drama as blasphemy is to prayer.

3. Historicity, Character, Fate, Ideology

The manifestation of the background in time and through the *dramatis personae* thus becomes the central structural element of Individualist drama. It flows necessarily out of an individual time and space, out of irrevocable (because unique) events, unrelated to collectively overarching ethics. Irrevocable events bound to definite circumstances (the background) and 'just such' individual behaviour (the characters) result in *historicity*. It is a 'positive' or positivistic historicity, implying not only an exclusively individual existence of each particular event, character, and thing, but also, in its final horizon, their subordination to the principle of historical individuation. This antinomic historicity is an essential characteristic of bourgeois being and drama – which is in this sense always historical, whether the characters wear doublets, a smoking-jacket or overalls. History, public of private, is the super-ordinated arbiter of Individualist drama, as Fortune was for the Renaissance or divinely personified collective Fate for the Greeks. In the *Oresteia* Athene is not only a *dramatis persona* but also the personification of the *polis* of Athens, from whose point of view the dramatist regards and organises his artistic structure; it can be said that the *Oresteia* is seen through the eyes of Athene, the goddess and the commune. In *The Tempest* (admittedly an ambiguous example) Prospero, no longer a god but still a magus – a man with a certain amount of super-individual power – stands above the plot and determines it. Even if he is not absolutely sovereign (see the revolt of Caliban), he is allied to Fortune which leads Antonio's ship to him. He does not solve human problems primarily by means of a religious power from above, but by means of a magical wisdom operating through people and their senses – the love of Ferdinand and Miranda, the music of the enchanted island as a sensual, anti-Guildensternian principle of harmony – that is, at least in part through their generic humanity. Ibsen's *Rosmersholm*, on the other hand, is dominated by an inimical History as revelation of the background, and all the efforts of the characters can only unveil it and hasten its approach until the finale of death. History stops only with the annihilation of its subjects, the stage figures dominated by it. As for bourgeois comedy, which by its very aim and nature had to attempt breaking out of the immobility induced by this freezing historicism, it concentrated on a frantic superficial intrigue of a mechanical kind. In a way differing from but com-plementary to 'serious' drama, this superficiality too did away with 'round' characters, since its trajectory from, say, Beaumarchais through Scribe to Feydeau increasingly led comedy to farcical types as the only possible *dramatis personae*.

In bourgeois drama the reified character thus finds him or herself acting in front of an historically definite background, an illusionistically 'real' scene of events. Although Shakespeare's tragedies have often been read as happening in a more or less definite time and place (a legendary Scotland and England, Denmark, Venice and Cyprus, etc.), the drama of Lear as, say, a viceroy of Cyprus would not necessarily have to be different – except for dramaturgical difficulties in motivating the division of his domain etc. In Elizabethan drama, place and time are much more abstract conventions, determined by tradition, and the relationships of stage figures are arranged according to the Renaissance views of universal analogy. (Similarly, Racine's Greeks and Romans wear – physically and ethically – Louis XIV wigs: the tradition arises in this case from court codes, not from popular legends.) Shakespeare's 'background' (properly speaking not a back-ground) can remain abstract because the play is dominated by personalities who, each in her or his own way, refract an ethical whole, the cosmos. Racine's can remain a sketchy backdrop to a specific viewing of the fixed and closed ethics of an unhappy absolutist class. Ibsen's or Schiller's background is historically univocal, and any material change in it would immediately destroy the drama – meaning neither the geography nor the calendar, but the original, unrepeatable relationships between illusionistic people in it. (See the example of Clytemnestra *vs.* Nora above, p. 28).

The main stylistic consequence of the existence of such a History, of the temporal and spatial background in Individualist drama, is a quantitative enrichment in the detailed aspects of the *dramatis persona* as a sum of relationships with the background and of the moulding of that *persona* through events. Spatial and temporal dimensions are no longer economically outlined and strictly necessary as in Greek or Renaissance drama: more aspects of the figure are filled in to produce 'round' characters 'in depth', irreducible to a type, to an allegorical or mythical personification. Looked at from different angles, these characters draw illusionistically near to persons from life, just as the stage happenings are 'realistically' limited by everyday empirical verisimilitude up to the scenery and the costumes in which they happen. The 'slice of life' is implied in bourgeois drama from its very beginning; so is its obverse, the escape from History into Symbol: Naturalism and Symbolism are the two faces of the Individualist Janus.

Indeed, *character* – the special Individualist case (enrichment as well as reduction) of the *dramatis persona* or scenic figure – is the central device of bourgeois dramaturgy. Bending Aristotle (who had observed that personality can be manifested only by its readiness to act and react to other agents) to the purposes of Individualism, Hegel's *Aesthetics* defined as the principle of dramatic events and actions 'the self-conscious and active individual' from whose inner will and character arise the events. These events 'become significant dramatically only by their relation to the subjective aims and passions. Equally, however, the individual does not limit himself to an enclosed independence, but ... his individual aims lead him into opposition and conflict with other individuals.' Therefore, dramatic poetry *'represents an action sufficient unto itself as real by means of a direct presentation.'* As Hegel here points out quite clearly, the illusion of an immediate and exclusive presence of dramatic figures brings about necessarily and directly the closure of the dramatic microcosm. In fact, drama is enclosed, artificially fenced in to exclude external irrelevancies which might pollute it. It is aesthetically defined by '*the necessity of a stronger closure of the whole work*' than in 'epical' and 'lyrical' works of art (all emphases in this paragraph are mine). This type of drama does not know or acknowledge anything outside itself as an immediate presence; in Hegel's words, it is the most perfect totality, which is why it lives truly only in its scenic performance.

Such a dramatic totality is correlative to an Individualist spectator severed from and reconnected to the stage by a proscenium. Individualist dramaturgy is differentiated from all others by the device of the proscenium, 'the fourth wall' of the scenic cube allowing only a spatially and psychologically very specific type of communication between characters and spectators, between individuals as agents and individuals as audience. Individualist drama is built to be experienced by the spectator who is, on the one hand, completely passive, silent and immobile, by convention absent, and, on the other hand but simultaneously, unaccountably active, magically involved in the stage play by *empathising*, feeling with or into the words and gestures of the *dramatis personae*. Basically, the relationship between spectator and Individualist drama is one of complete formal separation and complete psychological identification: the spectator cannot, in principle, step in between the flow of scenes or look 'sidewise' at the stage figures, he cannot judge them outside the 'dramatic totality'. He can look askance at this magical stage totality only after the curtain has fallen and the hypnotic effects have gone out together with the footlights.

In the naive beginnings of Individualist dramaturgy, accompanied by least self-deceit, Diderot had directly asked for *dramatis personae* to be formed no longer according to Classicist upper-class abstraction, but according to their social status (*condition*) of judge, merchant, father of middle-class family, and similar. Not long after that, the Romantics recognised that societal status motivates scenic figures, and erected their dramaturgy on the rebellion against it – simultaneously envying Shakespeare who did not have to recognise this. However, as the historical background becomes increasingly aggressive and the characters increasingly blurred, the feasibility of human relations, of establishing a personality, develops into a basic problem. In the Renaissance it was the scenic figure's qualitative orientation that mattered. Now the very need for action, the feasibility of a character's existence through action, is in question. Hamlet does not know what to do, but he has been created to act; Wallenstein knows that he should want to do something, but he has been created not to act: there is a chasm between their vacillations. Hebbel expressed the hysteria of Individualist drama by declaring that it does not matter at all whether the 'protagonist' meets his doom because of his good or bad actions – in other words, the important thing is to do anything at all. This drama is centrally concerned with the naked subsistence of individual integrity, with the tragedy of the individual's duration and existence as such.

The dramatic tension grows exasperated as tragedy is identified as the 'natural' correlative of individuation: 'Thus understood, the tragic is not primarily a dramaturgical but a metaphysical notion,' explains Staiger, the latest in a series of Idealist bourgeois theoreticians stretching from Kant, Hegel and Schopenhauer through whole libraries of Teutonic elucubrations on 'the tragic' (Vischer, Volkelt, Zimmerman, Dietz, etc.). The metaphysical recourse to Fate tends to a more or less explicit religiousness. Even for the Rationalists, Society was a kind of terrestrial divinity. Such a parvenu deity having been abandoned after the French Revolution, the search for a successor to Osiris, Dionysos and Christ went merrily on. The Pantheon of such candidates is rather variegated: Fate can be Public Opinion (in Hebbel's *Maria Magdalene*), the Use of Capital (*Mrs Warren's Profession*) or Heredity in Spyrochetae (*The Ghosts*), or quite openly the *personnage sublime* of Death (early Maeterlinck) and, in a more scientific guise, the entropy of the universe (Beckett).

This implies two complementary aspects. First, the final sanction of Individualist dramaturgy wears a lay semblance: its believability or verisimilitude is laicised. Whatever variant name comes up in the whirligig of ideologies, within the quickly changing composition of the Pantheon, Fate is

always brought on by the very flow of time and shaped by
History, the swift predator of human relationships. It is
perhaps a nemesis (a retribution for the ambitious existence
of individuality) but it is not divine Nemesis (a god or
goddess descending from above or a blight upon the whole
country). It is instead the Policeman who appears toward the
end of *Tartuffe* and looms behind all plays from then on.
Shakespeare's *Othello* uses a transition between super-
individual and Individualist sanction: the Venetian senate
sends a new governor to apprehend Othello, but the
inner-oriented Renaissance hero prefers to listen to the ethical
absolute within his conscience, to be his own judge. A comic
or at least a happy end variant of the arbiter at the end of
Individualist plays is the Royal Messenger, a replacement of
the Greek *deus ex machina* or the Gothic voice of God
bringing pardon and salvation at the last moment. The
double ending of *Tartuffe*, with the Royal Messenger
following hard on the heels of the Policeman in order to save
the play as comedy, represents Molière's prototypic realisation of the two possibilities.

Scondly, civil law and order thus simultaneously *is* (in
empirical reality or *de facto*) and *is not* (in axiological necessity
or *de iure*) a transcendental Fate: its 'necessity' grows
statistical rather than inescapable. Equally, the characters
become strangely equivocal – both mystically irrational and
geometrical fabrications, 'a mere contrapuntal necessity'
(Hofmannsthal). All generic human contacts outside a
doctrinaire blueprint of conflicts have become superfluous.
The disintegration of a significant story set in during the
eighteenth century; the significant *dramatis persona* disinte-
grates next. The fundamental device of Individualist drama,
the sacrosanct final atom of the bourgeois world-view, turns
out to be unsuited for the role of the basic unit with which to
build a universe. From the Romantic schizophrenia on – e.g.
Fiesco's, or both Schiller's and Hugo's Don Carlos's – the
dramaturgical character himself is increasingly disintegrating
into the nether structural elements of ideas (i.e. its Individualist special case, ideology) and language.

The author's fabrication of happenings around the reified
characters opens thus the problem of communication and
symbolics, of the suitability of the whole dramatic medium.

The lack of universal ethics means, moreover, that the characters stand in the field of drama like to Newtonian atoms, discrete particles whose linking constitutes the problem. In the abstracted world of Individualism they can be linked, 'the problem can be solved', only by an *explicit ideology* formulated by the author. Together with character, ideology thus becomes the fundamental element of Individualist drama. That is why Individualist drama has to have ideological programming, and furthermore each time a new one, corresponding to a new variant of distributing and linking the characters with regard to each other and to the background, as well as to the new variant of ideology dominant at the moment. Individualist drama knows in fact no other tradition but the ideology of the bourgeoisie, it breaks with the existing stage tradition; the consequences have already been sketched in this chapter. In this dramaturgy, traditional themes are completely restructured: Grillparzer's Medea is subject to historical background in a way which makes her essentially different from Euripides' avenger.

4. The Doctrinaire Degradation of Individualist Drama

As the first class that shapes its myths into a rationalist semblance, that advances under a pseudo-scientific banner, the bourgeoisie is also the first to have elaborated its demands in a theoretically explicit and, so to speak, pre-programmed manner. Never before have class antagonisms been formulated as conceptual principles manifest on the surface of the play. From the standpoint of a philosophy of history, *King Lear* is a drama of the conflict between the patriarchal and the Individualist – or the feudal and the merchandising – value-systems and horizons, and of their mutual annihilation in the overarching horizon of chaos. Even the ideologists (one could almost say *raisonneurs*) of the three horizons, Kent, Edmund and the Fool, are already present. Or, the *Oresteia* is from the same standpoint a conflict between the ethics of the matriarchal clan (Clytemnestra and the Erinnyes) and of the patriarchal clan aristocracy (Agamemnon and Apollo), a collision resolved in the Aeschylean synthesis of a democratic *polis* (Orestes justified by Athene – which is why the trilogy is called the *Oresteia*, though if one followed the Individualist logic of dominant *dramatis persona* it could have very well been called the *Clytemnestreia*). But Individualist drama was (as Hauser strikingly formulated it) the first historical example of a dramaturgy that made out of class conflict its very theme:

The theatre had always propagated the ideology of the classes which financed it, but class differences had never before gone beyond the latent content of its performances and become manifest and explicit, Nobody had ever before said: you Athenian aristocrats, the principles of your clan morals are contrary to the fundaments of our democratic state; your heroes are not only killers of their brothers and mothers but have also committed high treason. Or: you English barons, your frenzies threaten the peace of our industrious cities; your throne pretenders and rebels are no more than imposing criminals. Or again: you Paris shopkeepers, usurers and lawyers, know that if we French noblemen disappear, with us will disappear a world too good to enter into compromise with you. Now, however, it is quite explicitly said: we, honest citizens, cannot and will not live in the world ruled by you parasites, and if we fail, our children will carry the day and live. (Modified from Godman's translation in Hauser, III: 84–5)

In place of an ethics implicitly permeating all relationships, a unified whole both in life and on the stage, from the eighteenth century onwards – as has been suggested – a conscious polemical ideology appears, according to whose demands the playwrights establishes the conflict of dramaturgical characters. Hence a much greater mortality among plays and increasingly frequent wailings about the ephemeral character of theatre. The Elizabethan or *Commedia dell'arte* theatre was, of course, still more ephemeral – what would we not give for a film or at least a coherent critique about the actor Shakespeare? – but it considered itself a functional part of an integrated popular organism and so had, before the arrival of Humanistic professional élites, neither time nor cause to think of future glory. All Individualist drama dies with the age which provided its author with the moral demand and the problem-matter, thus bringing about the individual ideological variant of a given set of plays as a solution of this problem in applied aesthetics. The work of dramatic art, the specific definition of which is that it lives in action, is no longer realised in a generic time: it is under standable that, as soon as the modalities of such non-realisation recede into the past, nothing is left of such a work.

It can thus be seen that, at its best, bourgeois stability was strikingly different from feudal or slave-owning stability (not to speak of tribal or despotic societal formations). The underlying reason for this is the bourgeoisie's consubstantial-ity with money economy, capitalism and unceasing econo-mic development. The history of the bourgeois political hegemony is therefore a permanently conflictual one; and its cultural hegemony is much more complex than the fairly neat separation of classes (or 'estates') before capitalism and of their cultures. If we put 1792 as the date of the final victory of the bourgeoisie, we have to note that even before that year the victors had to promulgate a law against trade unions. From the English Reform Bill perhaps: but what about the Luddites, the Chartists or, earlier still, the Diggers alongside Cromwell? Germany's unification in 1871 was preceded by whole movements within European and German socialism. France finally became a republic when only the republic could stifle the plebeian movement of the Commune: many other bourgeois states, on the periphery of its world-system were caught up in new revolutionary movements even before having been fully constituted. Five centuries passed between Charlemagne and Gian della Bella, the Florentine radical leader, and roughly as many from the first *sotties* to Ben Jonson: Robespierre and Babeuf were bumping into each other on the streets of Paris. From anti-aristocratic polemics, the bourgeoisie had to redeploy with hardly any breathing space into polemics with its own revolutionary ideas of yesterday, with the popular and proletarian mainstream out of which it had arisen. From its beginnings, the bourgeoisie exists in the guise of a patricidal and incestuous Oedipus (Freud's clientele was bourgeois). This change can be noted in Schiller (in the midst of writing *Don Carlos*); the same holds true for Beaumarchais (between the second and third part of the 'Figaro' trilogy), and many others.

Now it is only during the rare periods of a political stability which lasts for several generations that the ideolo-

gical premises and institutional frameworks of the community present themselves to the audience's mind as something
fixed, sacred and possibly eternal. Drama then concentrates
either on celebrating the justice of that community, or on
following minor ripples in representative interpersonal relationships within its given framework. The best example in
our civilisation is the great European medieval drama and
theatre. However, no ideologies and institutions are really
fixed, eternal and sacred. New horizons, new tools and
means of communication (finally, new institutions) arise, and
drama follows (or leads) in the presentation of the unavoid-
able, destructive, and vivifying conflict of the old and the
new. If this conflict can be properly acknowledged and
transformed, the times of stress become also the golden ages
of theatre and drama, which thrive on oppositions and
contradictions. But the unstably durable rule of the
bourgeoisie produced neither Mysteries nor tragedies. Who
except historians of theatre and literature remembers today
the hits of the epoch when Individualism was reigning
supreme in western Europe and North America? Indeed,
where are the Scribes, the Dumases, the Sardous, the Pineros
of yesteryear? Even further, who among theatre-goers
today – except for German schoolchildren – looks at *Wallenstein*, and who does not look at *Macbeth*? The nineteenth-
century dramatists who are still alive today were either
isolated oppositional figures who, by romantic mockery or
revolt, saw beyond the seemingly solid surface of consensus – the Mussets and Büchners – or they were voices from
the periphery of Europe, where Individualism had not
managed to assert itself fully before it began to be radically
put into question: Ibsen and Strindberg from Scandinavia,
Gogol, Tolstoy and Chekhov from Russia, Verga from
Sicily, Shaw and Synge from Ireland. (This is also why the
twentieth century is producing, like Athens twenty-five
centuries ago, the Gothic middle ages, and the Renaissance,
the latest golden age of theatre and drama.)
    The historically unprecedented fact – to my knowledge
unparalleled as the rule governing a whole class epoch – that
each variant of bourgeois drama is preceded by a doctrinaire
ideological programme (from Diderot's and Lessing's writings to Shaw's prefaces and the modern manifestos) also

clearly testifies that this drama no longer grows out of a communal ethics and theatre. It is therefore either untenable on stage (closet drama, 'literature' or 'paper' in modern theatre jargon) or at least much less in touch with the exigencies of the stage. If, on the other hand, the writer comes from within theatre practice he uses his knowledge solely as a reservoir to increase his 'bagful of tricks' (Shaw), and not in order to verify his ethics: for better packaging, not for a better product. Significant playwrights, such as Merimée, Musset, Büchner, etc. (it is hardly necessary to go on up to – Mayakovsky, O'Neill and Genet perhaps?), either remain without a congenial wide public, or must woo such a public for dozens of years without much chance of a success not bought by compromising, by accepting the very bourgeois world against which they protested as poets (see, for example, the contraction of dramaturgic space, time and language between *Peer Gynt* and *An Enemy of the People,* or *The Bald Primadonna* and *Rhinoceros*). The whole epoch, from roughly the French to the Russian Revolution (starting, of course, with Lillo and finishing with – Beckett and Albee?) has not approached to the mass theatre of economically poorer periods, from ritual drama to Pulcinella. The bourgeois epoch is the first after the Huns in which the disappearance of dramatic theatre is a seriously discussed possibility. The Humanists already pleaded for a learned élite, but they, at least theoretically, hoped the learning would spread. Only at the apex of Individualism, in bourgeois drama, the very notion of a non-minority theatre will be lost (cf. Strindberg's writings in favour of a minority theatre). Long before television, the Goncourt brothers assumed that the circus, the Orpheum, the *revue,* would supplant drama. At a time when drama declines to an escapist entertainment, theatre as a popular festivity, lifting its public to a joyous awareness which cuts down class barriers, is virtually non-existent.

This also explains why drama is no longer the most comprehensive literary form, the supreme poetical cognition which it was in Hellenic or Renaissance times: it abdicated from a central place in fiction or narrative. As a rule the playwright does not dominate Individualist literature. What would Lessing, Hugo, Yeats, Chekhov, Krleža or Pirandello be without their lyrics or prose? On the contrary, Aeschylus or Molière, without any doubt significant poetic thinkers, could put all their insights into dramatic form, on a public stage. Racine's, Lope de Vega's or even Shakespeare's lyrics are secondary to their plays. Clearly dramatic temperaments, like Keats or Dostoyevsky, did not become dramatists. Certain exceptions may be found in Germany or Scandinavian literature, yet even there the compromises mentioned were serious. Schiller is today (except for *The Robbers?*) dead to the stage wherever he is not used for ideological flag-waving. Kleist and Büchner were left for the next century to discover, and even Goethe's major work has permanently kept the stage only in Gounod's sorry travesty. Of course, this in no way represents a valid judgement on the unique values of *Faust,* but it gives an eloquent *testimonium paupertatis* to Individualist theatre which found no way of accepting it. Moreover, *Faust* has remained within the Individualist dramaturgy, an isolated 'epic' or 'open-form' attempt. Shakespeare's plays are the most significant of dozens of similarly structured ones before and after him, including notably Marlowe's *Dr Faustus.* Molière is the centre of an unbroken line from Gothic or even earlier *sotties* to present-day boulevard comedy. Similar considerations hold good for Aeschylus or Aristophanes. On the contrary, around *Faust* there is nothing in Individualist dramaturgy: in it *Faust* exists more as a foreign body indicating the need for a Faustian kind of drama than as a sourcehead.

In other terms, what is the place of O'Neill's, Odets's and Miller's dramas in the literature of Norris, Dreiser, Lewis, Scott Fitzgerald, Dos Passos, Hemingway, Wolfe and Mailer? Or of Wilde, Shaw and Synge at the time of Hopkins, Hardy, James, Owen, Eliot and Joyce? Some chronologically permissible parallels in France are yet more eloquent: Scribe–Stendhal, Augier–Balzac, Dumas fils–Baudelaire, Sardou–Flaubert, Becque–Zola, Maeterlinck–Valéry, Giraudoux–Eluard ...; unequal and blasphemous matches, lost *par forfait!* Individualism, so fertile in the lyrics of the aggrieved individual and in the prose epics of his increasingly complex relationships with the environment, runs to all appearances contrary to the basic principles of significant dramatic form.

5. The Loss of the Story and of Personality

The fundamental dramaturgical event of Individualism is the recession or devolution of the plot, *the loss of a significant story*. Lear would be tragic in any case; for Karl Moor the trick of a falsified letter is necessary. Shakespeare's figure is motivated out of its own fullness, and Schiller's out of the author's fabrication. The Renaissance story flows inevitably out of the initial situation which contains the whole of it *in nuce;* the story in Individualist drama flows from an author's fanciful delineation of characters, dependent on his more or less idiosyncratic feeling for historical background. Accidental and arbitrary, such a story concerns the individual in the auditorium only if and when he identifies himself with the otherwise alien stage figure. Identification or ineffectiveness, indifference or enchantment: such are the alternatives of Individualist dramatic effect. The possibilities of an active co-operation of the public, of a critical mutual induction of new appreciation and understanding from both sides of the footlights, dwindle to nothing. The story turns into a 'well-made' escalation of sensations, where the strongest sensation must logically be reserved for the end. An analysis of the story – as well as of the ethics and the implied bourgeois view of history – points strongly to the criminal case or detection story being the primal nucleus of Individualist drama, its alpha and omega *(The London Merchant, Die Räuber, Rosmersholm,* Verga's *Cavalleria rusticana [Village Gallantry],* Wedekind's *Erdgeist [Earth Spirit], Sei personaggi in cerca dell' autore [Six Characters in Search of an Author],* Miller's *The Crucible,* right up to Agatha Christie). The final arbiter of bourgeois 'tragedy', the Policeman, is thus a Nemesis wholly pertinent to a universe whose laws are identical with the *Code Civil* (and the same applies to the final arbiter of its comedy, some version of a Royal Messenger).

Macbeth and Cassandra, as mentioned earlier, had to die from the moment their figure was what is was in a determined universe; their tragicalness is an *a posteriori* one. Ibsen can almost make us suspend our disbelief in the necessity of Rosmer's and Rebekka's death by his well-engineered fabrication, if we want to agree with his theoretical premises. But there is no real reason for doing

that. There is nothing to stop our stepping outside such
premises and envisaging a further fighting life for the
inhabitants of Rosmersholm in the teeth of their social
environment: nothing, that is, except the lugubrious atmosphere of the 'white horses', i.e. except an ideological
fabrication of the author's. Significantly, Ibsen's characters,
standing here for those of bourgeois drama in general, reach
fulfilment only in their downfall, dramaturgically speaking
in *death*. Shakespeare and Aeschylus acknowledge the inevi-
tability but deny the value of death; Ibsen and Maeterlinck
affirm the sublimity of escaping into it. Individualist drama
has a strong streak of the necrophilic: behind the best of its
tragedies a *grand-guignol* melodrama peeps out. Behind
O'Neill's *Mourning Becomes Electra,* behind the *Six Characters
in Search of an Author,* one can glimpse the skeleton of *The
London Merchant* or Dumas père's *La Tour de Nesle.* Only in
the moment of death does the Individualist sequence of
events shape itself into an 'organic' whole, thus in effect
denying both the play as such and its whole universe. In the
play, before death, the individual Rebekka or Don Carlos
could only long for a significant order (love, justice).
Nirvana is the most enlightened ideal of Individualism.

Aristotle (and Brecht too) would have categorised the
subordination of story to character as a grave structural error
which involves losing sight of the purpose, the *raison d'être* of
drama. But this subordination followed logically from the
failure of the bourgeois structure of feeling to outgrow the
abstract conceptual stage and constitute a system which
would work as if it contained no value-judgements but
self-evident, inescapable truths (i.e. to attain a presupposed
rather than a posited cosmology). The all-important characters of Individualist drama are not ethically determined
passions of the Renaissance kind, sensual as well as cerebral,
so to speak reflexes like the Elizabethan revenge or the
Spanish *pundonor;* they can only be ideology bearers,
sentimental rather than naive, determined more by the beliefs
they hold than by their personalities or generic qualities.
More precisely perhaps, their human qualities are all focused
in and exhausted by their ideological reasons. Those *dramatis
personae* who in the bourgeois culture are not supposed to be
fully reasonable – women, children, the lower classes, idiots,

etc – are therefore an important exception. Not to mention the splendid Holy Fools and women of Dostoyevsky, Tolstoy or Chekhov, one could take the example of Büchner's Woyzeck (lower class plus Holy Fool), Shaw's Joan (woman plus Holy Fool) or finally the husband's belief (*A Doll's House*) in law and order opposed to Nora's mixture of disbelief and sheer illogical or 'generically human' assumption that life is better than death.

Moreover, the dramaturgical character is itself broached from within. Growing increasingly complex and on the surface increasingly verisimilar, it is in the same process losing its ethical consistency and significance. The accent shifts from its humanity to its clothes at the time of Carlyle's paradox in *Sartor Resartus* that clothes do in fact constitute a man. Since ethics are no longer a common framework but an ideological problem for each individual, dramas change from action to rhetorical debates and declaimings. Hamlet's or Macbeth's monologues are preludes to a shift from action into musings on intellectual problems, but their rhythm – although doubtless in the tradition of Humanist rhetorics – is still strongly haptic, muscular. Compared to them, Posa is a Kantian barrister, and Hernani a high school class valedictorian. On the horizon already looms the specious *raisonneur,* more ideological function than character.

The breakdown of the story was already an expression of the Individualist theatre's dead-end, of its moving towards a relativistic structure of feeling, where the heroism of the 'hero', of the protagonist, is sanctioned only by the author's say-so. The playwright strains to make up a story, taking refuge under the fetish of originality, contemporary with the notion of copyright. On the other hand, however, this breakdown was an expression of more complicated ways of transposing the relationships from life. The characters get more complex and blurred, because the ordering and hierarchy of their thematic lines is also such. Secondary figures have become characters just as the protagonist. Thus, the main antagonists have in this general levelling of values come closer to each other than ever before. The standpoint of the formal antagonist (Schiller's King Philip, Hugo's Ruy Gomez) is relatively right: the bourgeois class-consciousness is beginning to respect the forces (the rulers) it once fought

against. Poetry communicates with knowledge, in favourable cases (Aeschylus, Shakespeare; in our days, Brecht) with
the People; rhetoric communicates with Power, with the
Court or the Prince. Individualist drama relies increasingly
on Idealist rhetoric, not on the poetry inherent in the
juxtaposition of story events. What is usually called 'poetry'
in such drama is an exclusively verbal, incantatory, elocu-
tional (i.e. ideologically evocative) effect (Rostand,
Giraudoux, Fry), not the integral *mousiké* of the Greeks nor
the poetry of understanding human relationships – Lear's
'Pray you undo this button' (V. iii) – of the Renaissance.

   The antagonists thus become relatives, brothers, and
finally the same *dramatis personae* (Pirandello, etc.). The
pinnacle of reification and dehumanising is reached in that
phase of bourgeois 'serious drama' where each *dramatis
persona* is his or her own antagonist and somebody else's
protagonist. 'Hell is other people' (Sartre): there is no heaven
in sight, nor a humanised world to which the notion of
heaven and hell would be unnecessary.

   In general, the historico-ideological motivation of the
story can become an intimate possession of the individual
only through abstraction. He/she acts increasingly against
his or her will (from Hernani, Grillparzer's Medea, and
Ibsen's Oswald, through Maeterlinck's marionettes, to
Pirandello and Beckett), and ethically partakes less and less in
his or her actions, just existing more and more as a sensitive
complexity. The basic problem of bourgeois dramatic
aesthetics, the 'hybris', is therefore not aesthetically soluble
but is an ethical and political problem, an Idealist 'hypostasis
of sociology' (Lukács). A Shakespearean dramaturgical
conflict is motivated from within the *dramatis personae* and
takes place between the protagonist and the antagonist. An
Individualist dramaturgical conflict is increasingly motivated
from within the historical background and takes place,
lacking a clear antagonist, inside the psyche of one or more
main characters. In such a context the story is fragmented
into ideologically connected reactions of individuals to the
course of History, into rhetorical beatings of characters
against the frightening barriers of the background. Yet, it is
only from the standpoint of such arbitrary, increasingly
complex and sensitive, characters that some unity and

orientation can be arrived at for a time in Individualist drama, since it lacks an all-embracing understanding of the world necessary for a harmony of action and characterisation. For a time; because character too fragments from within, and the only question remaining is: will personality survive and re-form in a new dispensation, or will the *bourgeois* destroy all the gains of the *civis?* Socialism with a human face, or a collective barbarism?

6. A Provisional Conclusion

When ethical standards cease to be clear, ethics change from an all-embracing into an initial category, into a problematic motivational focus of the plot; what was once a secure basis is now a provisional solution. The connections between the *dramatis personae* and the events are no longer strictly necessary; conflicts grow abstract in such a doctrinaire form of drama. The net of dramaturgical necessities is no more immanent to the scenic figures, it becomes fatefully transcendental. The necessity is only formal – irrational or contrapuntal – and the characters are constituted as functions of such a formal, non-generic and non-intimate necessity. The main character may be farsighted, but he is dramaturgically inactive or only mechanically active: seeing is separated from understanding, and understanding from practical cognition and mastery, leaving all necessity to Fate. The reified figures, turning to each other only that side which expresses a fatal necessity (Lukács), become Fate or agents of Fate for each other. Their conflicts are therefore merely nodal points of an ornamental pattern of fatal relationships. Also, Shakespeare took national or world history for his subject; in Individualist drama at each individual moment, for each individual, his fate becomes a world-historical one. History grows into the individual's flesh like a Nessus's shirt.

A *Cid* or *Antony and Cleopatra* – plays whose subject-matter was taken from historiographers – also treated human relationships from other periods as relationships of their own epoch. However, unlike *Hernani, Wallenstein* or Scribe's *Un Verre d'eau* [A Glass of Water], they did not pretend to be historically accurate reconstructions. The notion of history in the sense of a succession of moments with individual and irrevocable specificities was unknown to them: they just used majestic legendary types whose validity was to their minds eternal. Corneille's Augustus was Louis XIV whereas Ben Jonson's was James I, because Augustus was the perennial model of an ideal ruler. The ancient king Lear was to Shakespear as real and as legendary as the still more ancient Caesar or the mythical evil-doer Richard Gloucester. And what is the Macbeth of the Chronicles – reality or legend?

As opposed to this, each bourgeois drama is historical by its angle of vision and understanding, by its inescapable ingrown notions of the individuality and uniqueness of time and place. 'Verweile doch, Du bist so schön': Faust's supreme sin, which destroys him as a sovereign and entire personality, is the adoption of such an Individualist point of view, which does not find its values in the dynamics of events but in the statics of the perfect moment. A dramaturgy bereft of all-embracing ethics, and consequently also of an intimate permeation between sovereign personalities as *dramatis personae,* will necessarily substitute characters and ideology for representative figures and cognitive thought, and break the structure of the story down to the nethermost level of language as hermetic game.

Thus, the Individualist reality and structure of feeling for reality are breaking up the dramatic theatre as a form and as an institution. Although it put up a furious defence, condemning itself to increasingly smaller rations of significance and lower life-forms, the moment of its final annihilation was put off only by Atlantean efforts of poets and rebels, heroically opposed to an Ibsenian 'solid majority'. But even this could not be done without making increasingly drastic compromises with bourgeois reality and ideology. It is paradoxical, as well as tragical in the most technical sense of the word, that it was the Individualist poets, intimately rebelling against the consequences of Individualism, who became the historical executioners of the drama, carrying out a necessity which they did not bring about but which they, as the most sensitive instruments of the time, felt most clearly. History was also their tragic Fate: the more authentic a poet, the deeper he felt a need for order, for elastic yet all-embracing ethics, and the more stubbornly he had to try and recreate such an order formally, through aesthetics. A vain attempt: for aesthetics are free only when ethics are firm. And vainest for those who needed it most, for the potentially most creative writers: Sisyphus should be imagined as increasingly unhappy. From Faust's arresting the most beautiful moment, to Sisyphus's repeating the most difficult moment – how faithful a trajectory of the Individualist poet, of the Individualist drama!

APPENDIX: Some Semantics as Frozen History

Any work of art or ensemble of such works can be envisaged as constituting an articulated universe of discourse (or, more generally, of ostended signs) that is at the same time something beheld – an autonomous, intransitive thing to behold – and a model reproducing some significant properties of the universe presupposed as common to the artist and his addressees. The model (diminutive or small-scale representation of *modus,* the manner in which a thing is fashioned) is therefore also a 'world-view' or organon for contemplating and understanding the extra-textual world. In the original Hellenic sense of the word, any unified artistic ensemble is literally a *theoria* (that which is beheld or contemplated). *Theoria* derives from the root *theo-* or *thao-,* akin in its richness to the Latin *spec(t)-: thea* = spectacle, *th(e)aomai* = to gaze at wonderingly, *thauma* = wonder, just as *specere* = to look, its frequentative *spectare* = to gaze at attentively, to see, and *spectaculum* = show, that which can be seen publicly or communally. The subject of such attentive, wondering seeing is a *theoros* or *spectator,* and the object is the *theoria* or the *spectaculum,* even in English still both a thing seen and something out of the ordinary (spectacular). Such a seeing is therefore not simply a registration on the retina, it is not an act of mindless staring ('Glotzt nicht so romantisch' [Do not stare so romantically] was the slogan the young Brecht put up in the theatre at one of his earliest performances), but a 'sight' in the sense of 'doesn't he/she look a sight!' In other words, this is not only a 'normal' look or sight but a sighting, an insight, a foresight (*prospectus*), a looking forward to or expectation, a looking closely into or inspection, a looking at again and again (a re-specting or regarding). The spectacular spectacle can also be a *spectrum* = appearance or image, and the place or space where things can be seen or inspected a *speculum* = mirror (e.g. a 'mirror for princes' or a 'mirror for magistrates' as the Elizabethans had it, or simply a mirror for every spectator, for the time as a historical monad, as Shakespeare's Hamlet defined the staged spectacle of actors). *Specula* were watch-towers from which one spied out or observed (*speculari*) things coming from afar: in seventeenth-century English, theory and speculation, theoretic and speculative, were practically synonyms, just beginning to be opposed to practice or *praxis*. What does such a *theoria* or *speculatio,* what does a wondering theoretician, an attentive spectator, one given to speculation, see as spectacle? She/he sees a *species* = appearance or thing seen (and by extension, kind of thing inspected, as well as beauty), in any case something with its own 'special' or 'specific' characteristics of 'special-ties'. 'Mirror', of course, comes from late popular Latin *mirare* = look at, itself from *mirari* = wonder, the exact synonym of *theaomai* and the source of 'admiring'. Finally, for anybody interested in communication, this whole net-work of terms and concepts originating in *theo-* and its Latin (and Germanic) equivalents culminates in the earliest form of communal communication, the *theatron:* originally the place of all this wondering gazing at or spectacle, akin to both the root for *theos* (Latin *divus* or *deus* = god, the incarnation of the wonderful appearance) and for *tithemi* (to set, place or see, whence *thema* = a circumscribed place, location, region or, by extension, subject-matter).

Of course, all of this does not simply imply that the roots of theatre are in magico-religious ritual: indeed, theatre becomes itself precisely by distancing itself from such rituals (however many traces of it might still remain).

Bibliography

The titles are given by the most accessible English edition I am aware of, when this exists. When my quotations were translated from the original, the available English edition is added in parentheses.

Alberti, Leone Battista, *Kleinere kunsttheoretische Schriften*. ed. H. Janitschek (Wien, 1877).

Antoine, André, *Mes Souvenirs sur le Théâtre Libre* (Paris, 1929).

Aristotle, *Peri poietikes (Poetics)*, ed. Leon Golden and O.B. Hardison Jr (Englewood Cliffs, N.J., 1968).

Archer, William, *Play-Making* (New York, 1960).

Auerbach, Erich, *Mimesis* (Princeton, 1953).

Bab, Julius, *Das Theater im Lichte der Soziologie* (Leipzig, 1931).

Barber, C.L., *Shakespeare's Festive Comedy* (Cleveland, 1963).

Barthes, Roland, *Mythologies* (New York, 1972).

Barthes, Roland, *Writing Degree Zero* (New York, 1968).

Baxandall, Lee (ed.) *Radical Perspectives in the Arts* (Harmondsworth, 1972).

Bradbrook, M.C., *Themes and Conventions of Elizabethan Tragedy* (Cambridge, 1960).

Brahm, Otto, *Theater–Dramatiker–Schauspieler,* ed. Hugo Fetting ([E.] Berlin, 1961).

Brecht, Bertolt, *Gesammelte Werke, 15–20* (Frankfurt, 1973). Partly transl. as *Brecht On Theatre,* ed. John Willett (New York, 1966); partly as *The Messingkauf Dialogues* (London, 1965); and partly as material accompanying the Vintage and Methuen editions of his *Collected Plays,* in progress.

Buland, M., *Presentation of Time in the Elizabethan Drama* (New York, 1912).

Burke, Kenneth, *The Philosophy of Literary . Form* (New York, 1957).

Caudwell, Christopher, *Studies in a Dying Culture* (London, 1938).

Danby, John F., *Shakespeare's Doctrine of Nature* (London, 1982).

Diderot, Denis, 'Entretiens sur *Le Fils naturel*' and 'De la Poésie dramatique', in *Oeuvres complètes,* ed. J. Assézat (Paris, 1935).

Eloesser, Arthur, *Das Bürgerliche Drama* (Berlin, 1898).

Feuerbach, Ludwig, *The Essence of Christianity* (New York, 1957).

Freytag, Gustav, *Technique of the Drama* (Chicago, 1908).

Goethe, J.W. von, *Wilhelm Meister's Apprenticeship and Travels* (New York, 1974).

Goldmann, Lucien, *Recherches dialectiques* (Paris, 1959).

Guizot, François, *Shakespeare and His Times* (London, 1852).

Gurvitch, Georges, *The Spectrum of Social Time* (Dordrecht, 1964).

Harbage, Alfred, *As They Liked It* (Philadelphia, 1972).

Harbage, Alfred, *Shakespeare's Audience* (London, 1941).

Hardy, Thomas, Preface to *The Dynasts* (London, 1930).

Hauser, Arnold, *The Social History of Art 1–4* (New York, [1962]).

Hebbel, Friedrich, 'Vorwort' to *Maria Magdalene . . . ,* in *Sämtliche Werke 11* (Berlin, 1909).

Hegel, G.W.F. *Aesthetik* ([E.] Berlin, 1965) (*Aesthetics,* Oxford, 1975).

Hegel, G.W.F. *Lectures on the History of Philosophy, 1–3* (New York, 1955).
Hegel, G.W.F. *Phenomenology of the Spirit* (Oxford, 1977).
Hugo, Victor, 'Préface de *Cromwell*', in *Oeuvres complètes* (Paris, 1881).
Huizinga, Johan, *Homo Ludens* (Boston, 1970).
Jacquot, Jean (ed.), *Réalisme et poésie au théâtre* (Paris, 1960).
Junghans, F., *Zeit im Drama* (Berlin, 1931).
Knights, L.C., *Drama and Society in the Age of Jonson* (Itarmandsworth, 1962).
Leonardo da Vinci, *Prose,* ed. Luigi Negri (Torino, [1937?]).
Leonardo da Vinci, *A Treatise of Painting* (London, 1910).
Lessing, Gotthold Ephraim, 'Abhandlung von dem weinerlichen oder rührenden Lustspiele', 'Hamburgische Dramaturgie', and 'Laokoon', all in *Gesammelte Werke,* ed. Paul Rilla ([E.] Berlin, 1954–8).
Lintilhac, Eugène, *La Comédie: Dix-huitième siècle. Histoire générale du théâtre en France, 4* (Paris, [1909?]).
Ludwig, Otto, *Dramatische Studien. Werke 4.* ed. Arthur Eloesser (Berlin, *n.d.*)
Lukács, Georg, *History and Class Consciousness* (London, 1971).
Lukács, Georg, *Soul and Form* (London, 1974).
Lukács, Georg, 'Zur Soziologie des modernen Dramas', *Archiv für Sozialwiss. und Sozialpol. 38* (1914): 303 ff. (only partially in *Schriften zur Literatursoziologie,* ed. Peter Ludz (Neuwied, 1968), pp. 261–95, and in Eric Bentley (ed.), *Theory of the Modern Stage* (Harmondsworth, 1968).
Lunacharsky, A.V. *O teatre i dramaturgii, 1* (Moscow, 1958).
Martin, Alfred von, *Sociology of the Renaissance* (New York, 1963).
Marx, Karl, *Capital, 1–3* (London, 1971).
Marx, Karl, *Grundrisse* (Harmondsworth, 1973).
Marx, Karl, *Selected Writings,* ed. David McLellan (Oxford, 1977).
Marx, Karl and Engels, Friedrich, *Ueber Kunst und Literatur,* ed. Michail Lifschitz ([E.] Berlin, 1953).
Mayer, Hans, *Richard Wagner* (Hamburg, 1959).
Müller, Günther, *Die Bedeutung der Zeit in der Erzählkunst* (Bonn, 1947).
Mumford, Lewis, *Technics and Civilization* (New York, 1962).
Nietzsche, Friedrich, *Thoughts Out of Season* (New York, 1974)
Plato, *Politics* (Oxford, 1946).
Poulet, Georges, *Studies in Human Time* (Baltimore, 1956).
Praz, Mario, *The Romantic Agony* (London, 1960).
Rolland, Romain, *The People's Theater* (London, 1919).
Rossiter, A.P., *English Drama From Early Times to the Elizabethans* (New York, 1967).

Rousseau, Jean-Jacques, *Lettre à d'Alembert sur les spectacles* (Paris, 1926) (*Politics and the Arts,* Ithaca NY, 1968).

Scherer, Jacques, *Structures de Tartuffe* (Paris, 1966).

Schlegel, A.W. *Vorlesungen über dramatische Kunst und Literatur, 1–2,* ed. G. Amoretti (Bonn, 1923) (*Course of Lectures on Dramatic Art and Literature,* New York, 1973).

Schlegel, Friedrich, *Kritische Schriften,* ed. Wolfdietrich Rasch (Munich, 1964).

Shelley, Percy Bysshe, *A Defence of Poetry ...,* ed. J.E. Jordan (Indianapolis, 1965).

Siegel, Paul N., *Shakespearean Tragedy and the Elizabethan Compromise* (New York, 1970).

Simmel, George, *Philosophie des Geldes* (Munich, 1930).

Sombart, Werner, *Der moderne Kapitalismus, 1–2.1* (Munich, 1916).

Spencer, Theodore, *Shakespeare and the Nature of Man* (New York, 1942).

Staiger, Emil, *Grundbegriffe der Poetik* (Zurich, 1964).

Steiner, George, *The Death of Tragedy* (London, 1961).

Strindberg, August, 'Author's Preface to *Miss Julie*', in *The Plays of Strindberg, 1* (New York, 1972).

Strindberg, August *Dramaturgie* (Munich, 1924).

Sypher, Wylie, *Four Stages of Renaissance Style* (Garden City, NY, 1955).

Szondi, Peter, 'Theorie des modernen Dramas' in *Schriften I* (Frankfurt, 1978).

Tawney, R.H., *Religion and the Rise of Capitalism* (Gloucester, MA, 1962).

Thomson, George, *Aeschylus and Athens* (London, 1949).

Thomson, George, *The First Philosopher* (London, 1977).

Tocqueville, Alexis de, *Democracy in America, 1–2* (New York & London, 1900).

Wagner, Richard, *Sämtliche Schriften und Dichtungen, 3, 4, 12* (Leipzig, n.d.)

Weber, Max, *The Protestant Ethic and the Spirit of Capitalism* (London, 1958).

Weimann, Robert, *Shakespeare and the Popular Tradition in the Theater* (Baltimore, 1978).

Williams, Raymond, *Culture* (London, 1981).

Williams, Raymond, *The Long Revolution* (Harmondsworth, 1971).

Williams, Raymond, *Problems in Materialism and Culture* (London, 1980).

Wölfflin, Heinrich, *Principles of Art History* (New York, 1950).

Zola, Emile, *Le Naturalisme au théâtre* and *Nos Auteurs dramatiques, Oeuvres complètes,* ed. Maurice Le Blond (Paris, 1928).

2

Brecht vs. Ibsen: Breaking Open the Individualist to Closed Dramaturgy

Correlative to the twin contextual or socio-historical axioms of illusionism and Individualism, discussed in chapter 1, is the dramaturgical construction or form of bourgeois drama. Compared to the Gothic and Renaissance *open-ended dramaturgy*, it is a *closed* one. In this chapter, I want to focus on the functions and implications of these forms, as manifested in the breaking-down and breaking-open of the closed dramaturgy in the post-Individualist achievements of the twentieth century, best represented by the dramaturgy of Bertolt Brecht.

For reasons of economical overview, I shall (with all due disclaimers for simplification, which here seems not only permissible but also indispensable) posit two 'fall guys', or idealised types simplified in regard to a general complex history as well as to their own complex ups and downs – Ibsen and Brecht. In Ibsen's case, this means taking into account only his middle phase from, say, *The Pillars of Society* to *Hedda Gabler*, which is in some ways an impoverishment in comparison to the 'epic' scope and flexibility of *Peer Gynt* (and indeed *Brand*) as much as it is an enrichment in the allusive intensity of the relationships between characters and their background. In Brecht's case, this also means concentrating on his canonic 'mature' and large-scale plays from, say, *St Joan of the Stockyards* to *The Caucasian Chalk Circle* and the not quite finished adaptation of *Coriolanus*, at the expense of the shorter *Lehrstücke* (plays for learning), which are in some ways as interesting and potentially as important. Ibsen has been often mentioned in Chapter 1, while the three plays of Brecht's just named will be discussed in separate chapters of Part 2. I shall, therefore, in fact focus here on two plays as exemplifying the closed and open European-style dramaturgy of the last hundred years: Ibsen's *Ghosts* and Brecht's *Mother Courage and Her Children*. I shall try to sketch in their use of dramaturgical time and space as well as the *dramatis personae*, and their compositional development. It would also be possible, and possibly easier, to cover their use of speech, but I shall have to forgo this perhaps crucial literary but not dominant dramaturgical level in a brief and stark overview. I shall also endeavour to link the plays' structures to their different communications with changing audiences, and end by focusing on Brecht's dramaturgy in opposition to Piscator's apparently similarly one. It will become apparent that 'open' and 'closed' are useful terms because – much as some terms in the chapter 1 – they bridge the gap between technical description and ethico-political metaphor, between dramaturgy and historical horizons.

1. Henrik Ibsen is the supreme dramatist of the Individualist nineteenth century, the one who brought to a head and a logical end its implications. Paradoxically, he is also the exemplary playwright who marks the involution and eventually the collapse of Individualist dramaturgy (already apparent in his own last phase, say from *The Master Builder* on), because he used its form for – or better, as – ideological subversion, by showing the dead-end of the closed bourgeois moral and existential universe. The basic positive tenet of Individualism – that one ought to remain true to one's innermost strivings for freedom and moral spaciousness – led in Ibsen to a depiction of bourgeois society stifling true individuality or personality. This vision was conveyed by employing the stock bourgeois form of *pièce bien faite*, the well-made play, which conquered the world as the theatrical expression of the leading (French) bourgeois civilisation. By using the careful verisimilitude of its middle-class drawing-room and characters, and its sequence of titillating sensations at the end of each act which lead to a geometrically precise dénouement, Ibsen demonstrated the ending of a civilisation with the same ideological certainty and the same forms with which that civilisation had celebrated its permanence. He turned the tools of Baconian and Cartesian analysis upon its societal originators. No wonder he was subjected to a storm of abuse, proclaimed a madman as often as a socialist. In fact, he was neither. He was a rather conservative 'Tory radical' in Rousseau's tradition, pitting the pristine ideals and libertarian arguments of the ascending bourgeoisie against the gloomy Victorian results of its conquest of the social heights.

An Ibsenian play such as *Ghosts* is bound by a wallpaper horizon and zeroes in on the central link between the individual and the Individualist society, the individual's intimate oasis and the society's basic cell – the nuclear *family*. The pivot of *Ghosts* is the woman, wife and mother, the pivot of the family, its values and its inner organisation. However, the Ibsenian family is rotten and falling apart, and the woman (for example, Nora in the immediately preceding *A Doll's House*) is leaving it slamming the door; *Ghosts* shows why she does so. More precisely, *Ghosts* does not deal merely with the family but with the *home,* meaning both the family as elementary human relationship, the house as economic and living space, and the home-owning 'line' in time. This last sense is best seen in *Rosmersholm,* the House of Rosmer standing there for home, family and dynasty in an inimitable fusion of social time and space. But it is immediately under the surface in *Ghosts:* Mrs Alving wants to expiate her 'original sin' against Individualism of loveless marriage into the Rosenvold estate by building the 'Captain Alving Orphanage' for homeless children. However, this attempt at exorcising the past is doomed: it is the children of Rosenvold, Oswald and Regina who will remain homeless outcasts. The inheritance is not to be denied: Oswald inherits the syphilitic corruption and Regina the promiscuity of their father, Captain Alving. (I shall not discuss here the Victorian variant of Fate, biological or indeed pathological heredity, which invalidates a great deal of this play by not providing sufficiently genuine objective correlatives for Ibsen's attempt at the sublimity of a Periclean tragedy: how believable is a play where venereal disease equals Destiny after the discovery of penicillin?) Inheritance is synonymous with heredity: the source of all evil is the bourgeois cash nexus or money prestige because of which young Helen was given in marriage to Chamberlain Alving. The bourgeois Individualist family thus ironically continues to be the bearer of the most relevant possible heritage – but it is the dissolution which has become relevant and not the continuity. The sins of the fathers are visited upon the sons, and the sins of the individual's youth upon his mature age – to my mind a parable on the trajectory of the bourgeoisie in history, and at any rate clearly representative for it.

Mrs Alving tries at first to blame the late Chamberlain for her misfortunes, but is eventually led to realise that her profligate husband was no more than another victim of 'the system', of society's erotico-financial hypocrisies, that he was as much sinned against as sinning. The real culprit is the stifling backround incarnated in the obtuse Pastor Manders, the ideologist and anti-Tiresias of the play. But this societal background is now itself menaced by a stronger and older background – unfeeling Nature, outraged in Oswald and visible through the windows as a distant and cold glacier and peak. As Shaw, Ibsen's clowning disciple, expressed it in the preface to his most characteristic domestic-cum-political play, *Heartbreak House*:

Nature's way of dealing with unhealthy conditions is unfortunately not one that compels us to conduct a solvent hygiene on a cash basis. She demoralises us with long credits and reckless overdrafts, and then pulls us up cruelly with catastrophic bankruptcies .... This is what has just happened in our political hygiene. Political science has been as recklessly neglected by Governments and electorates during my lifetime as sanitary science was in the days of Charles the Second. In international relations diplomacy has been a boyishly lawless affair of family intrigues, commercial and territorial brigandage, torpors of pseudo-goodnature produced by laziness, and spasms of ferocious activity produced by terror

In line with this wholly Ibsenian sanitary metaphor, the Alving family and home will, instead of raising the Alving Orphanage in atonement for the deadening of life they caused, take the path to death and destruction: a fiery *Götterdämmerung* for the Orphanage, the inner fires of syphilitic madness for Oswald, and identical prospects for Regina who will end up in the final anti-home of the play, her demonic stepfather's 'Alving Home for Sailors' alias a port brothel. There are also two projected homes as moral openings highly important in their impossibility, as the foreclosing of all alternatives: the Helen–Manders one in the bungled past, the Oswald–Regina one in the snuffed-out

future. All existing homes or social spaces are thus closed and
walled in, as in the 'well-made play', but Ibsen has the stage
look out through a glass pane on a gloomy fjord landscape
which at the end reveals a view of distant ice peaks (cf.
didascalia, Act I). The uncaring Viking, pre-bourgeois nature
(directly involved in Ibsen's earlier plays) broods over the
fragile social world; it is the same fatal Nature which
manifests itself within the bodies of the younger generation
as sterile lust and impotence, and falls as the final ironic ray
of sunshine upon the mindless Oswald. The Individualist
home is shown up as unnatural; therefore, Nature takes its
revenge as inhuman Nemesis. The space of closed drama is
on the verge of breaking down here, but the glimpse through
the pane reveals an open space whose alien indifference
paradoxically reinforces the 'no-exit' horizons (just as temporal infinity does in Sartre's play of the same English title).

The dramaturgical space of *Ghosts* is, then, *formally*
identical to that of the 'well-made play'; yet its *ideological*
orientation is inverted by means of the emotional aura of
threat and claustrophobia. But since its Individualist vision
and universe is, simultaneously, accepted as the only possible
one and rejected as totally immoral, the dramaturgical time
changes significantly. As in Balzac's *Peau de chagrin* or
generally in the generations living out the failure of the
bourgeois democratic revolutions, time lasts as anxiety, not
as the measure of acquisition but as the measure of total loss.
More importantly, the play's present is revealed as a working
out of, and in fact mask for, the past: the basic spatial
imagery of the home is supplemented by the temporal
imagery of cyclically returning 'ghosts' (*gengangere, re-
venants*). The dead hand of the past strangles any possibility
that the characters might shape their own destiny in the
present. In anguish, they are trapped in societal types and
roles that prevent them reaching for any worthwhile goal of
desire. The basis of Individualist philosophy is, as Hegel put
it, the ability of characters to act. As in Sophocles' *Oedipus
Tyrannus*, the model underlying *Ghosts*, all actions of Mrs
Alving turn against her: her son can only moan, Regina's
activity leads to no better end than Oswald's paralysis of will,
Manders' actions collapse under the sheer stupidity of his
ideology, and only the malevolent lower-class Engstrand can

succeed in his pretty and destructive plans. Oswald and Regina are condemned to reenact in an abbreviated and unalleviated form the *descensus ad inferos* of their father, and indeed social class, without any possibility of redemption. *Ghosts*, most significantly, follows the nineteenth-century compositional arch or ballistic curve (Freytag), which was:

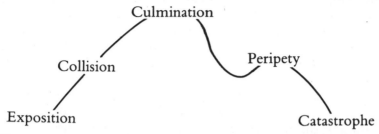

However (as Fergusson points out) the play ends in the middle. This was the clearest statement the allusive and 'apolitical' master-builder Ibsen could make: its universe is one in which the culmination is identical to the catastrophe; it is a universe with a catastrophic culmination. (This is followed by all significant Individualist drama after Ibsen, e.g. O'Neill's *Long Day's Journey Into Night*.) Concomitantly, there is no true collision, no true struggle for happiness, but only the unfolding of the past in the present. Most importantly, *there is no future*: literally for Oswald, ethically for everybody else; they are all living dead or zombies (a permanent Ibsenian motif). The final horizon of *all* significant late Individualist drama – say, Maeterlinck, the early Strindberg, O'Neill, Odets, Miller, Williams – is Death. Logically in none of them is one left with a woman capable of childbearing, of begetting a new future: Mrs Alving is too old, Regina is pledged to prostitution – both are sterilised. A necrophilic atmosphere closes in. The fundamentals of the Individualist universe and view – the possibility of characters to act, to produce gainfully in time – have been exploded.

This is why *Ghosts* provoked an enormous outrage in its audience; Shaw has in *The Quintessence of Ibsenism* collected an amusing stupidarium of the critics' frothing at the mouth. It is enough to look at its interplay of bourgeois form and anti-bourgeois message to understand that this was its major purpose and vindication. The mature Ibsen – as different from the young 1848 revolutionary – is a 'conservative anarchist' who wants (as an early poem of his has it) to 'lay the torpedo' under the whole of bourgeois society. He is not at all interested in the workers, peasants, or any other lower class. They can only be accommodated as Wagnerian gnomes, malevolent gravediggers of the bourgeoisie, as Engstrand here. Ibsen has never heard of the aristocracy or of non-bourgeois countries, civilisations and values. In the name of Individualist, Jeffersonian or *quarantehuitard* values of life, liberty and the pursuit of happiness he judges the official, Individualist, organised society to be deadly: leading to and worthy of death. But he is interested in telling that *to the bourgeoisie*, since for him there is nobody else in front of whom he might bear witness. He is flesh of its societal flesh, a son chastising the prodigal fathers in the name of ancestral values they both officially share but only he takes seriously. His basic strategy is the Romantic one of *épater le bourgeois*, but this becomes Ibsenian only by adopting all the premises of the Individualist world-view, taste, moral codes, and finally dramaturgical form – and turning them against its originators, showing its originators that they are living a lie (another permanent Ibsenian motif). Ibsen is tied to bourgeois, Individualist premises, he can communicate with any spectator, audience or age only if, when and in so far as they share those premises (at least for one evening). The twentieth-century interest in Ibsen has slumped in near-revolutionary and revived in post- or counter-revolutionary times, when there was again a point in berating Individualist relationships (for one example, in Europe from 1920 to 1950 as against 1950 to 1965).

On the other hand, and simultaneously, Ibsen cannot be accepted by completely secure and self-satisfied bourgeois audiences: they (a Dr Johnson or an Emerson) would simply walk out on him. His dramaturgy is based on communication with a class of individualists in power who hypocritically reject their past revolutionary ideals, but are at least incipiently and/or residually uncomfortable about it. The 'fourth wall' axiom of Individualist dramaturgy gives him an excellent occasion for presenting to his audience their own enclosed universe, in a way to which their structure of feeling is thoroughly accustomed, but with the value-signs reversed. Any opening in Ibsen's scenic universe would have been either a happy-end falsification of the basic relationships given in the play's theme (a way out embraced by the boulevards, Broadway, West End and Hollywood, but which is impossible for a self-respecting creator); or it would have been the glimpse of other possible universes, violating Individualist axioms. This is in fact the path taken in their different ways by writers as disparate as the later Strindberg, Chekhov or Wedekind, in the generation after *Ghosts*. But since I can here deal only with the ideal types, I shall take as the representative of open dramaturgy its best and most self-conscious practitioner, Brecht.

2. Brecht's *Mother Courage and Her Children* is a classic example of consistently open dramaturgy triumphally coping even with an historically closed situation, with the universe of total warfare. Instead of the classicist twenty-four hours of *Ghosts*, its time and composition is epical and embraces glimpses from twelve years. (Brecht was a fascinated reader of Homer and Shakespeare, and the model of the *Iliad* and the Wars of the Roses cycle is clearly present in this play, just as *King Oedipus* is present in *Ghosts*.) This gives enough scope for each of the twelve scenes (cantos if you wish) to present a different facet of the basic relationships in and around the family of Anna Fierling. As in the 'epical' narrative, the composition is paratactic (coordinated) instead of hypotactic (subordinated in the pseudo-Aristotelian 'pyramid' of acts). Each scene, and to an extent each situation of which the scenes are composed, has a certain autonomy, with a specific point being communicated. All situations and scenes eventually add up to a 'rounded' view of the dramatic universe; though the succession of scenes in fact also goes through one seasonal and even diurnal cycle, it is a vaster and more inclusive cycle, whose representativeness does not have to fit into a small, illusionistic island in societal space and natural time. However, this view has been arrived at by soliciting the spectator to approach the events by a combination of empathy and distance: empathy in so far as the *dramatis personae* represent suffering human beings enmeshed in inhuman circumstances; and distance in so far as a person's destiny is exclusively other people and their organisations, so that each person is co-responsible for the inhumanity of the circumstances. Such an 'estranged' attitude of the spectators enables them to intervene with their judgement between the situations and scenes.

The theme they are invited wonderingly to behold and to judge is: how participation in war-as-business-as-usual inevitably leads to perdition. The hyphenated syntagm is objectified on the stage in the main space-forming device of the play: *the wagon*. The wagon is the moveable house and home of this not-so-nuclear and not-so-holy fatherless family; it is their shop and business, their link with and gage of participation in war-as-business. It saves the family from starvation, as Courage is acutely aware; it also kills directly or indirectly all of her children and reduces the saucy Courage to a drained Ibsenian zombie. It is a moveable, enclosed space within the vast whirlpool of war, vulnerable and easily turned into a semi–opened and emptied space. As such, it is an inverted descendant of the Ibsenian drawing-room, which we saw losing its insulating security, its imperviousness to the great alien forces invading it from outside. The wagon is the centre of almost all scenes, the children are its drawers, and Mother Courage herself almost its personification. The spectators are expected to be acutely aware of its position, changes and dominance at the centre of the open grey horizons of this play. It is the manifestation of dehumanising destiny in this dramaturgy just as clearly as the Nature without and within is in *Ghosts*. But Brecht avoids Ibsen's dubious metaphor (icy peaks equal biological heredity, because they are both inhuman, Darwinistic Nature), leading to forced symbolism. Destiny in the Brechtian universe is, as a rule, pretty grim, but it is always man-made and potentially changeable by people (compare the symbolical black crosses as predictions of death here and in *A Doll's House*).

A *dramatis persona* too, as transposition of human personality, is not merely an Individualist indivisible atom but a contradictory and changeable 'wave package'. Courage and her children are representative plebeian Everymen. More than that, Mother Courage stands at least for the German or any other people willing to engage in the business of war and war as business investment, and possibly for humanity as a whole and the choices it is faced with in this century. As in Morality plays, she is a *Regina Humanitas* (or *Regina Germania*; one wonders how ironical Ibsen was in using this name for the only potential procreator in his play). As different from Moralities, this is only one pole of a *bipolar* stage figure, the other one being the alienated petty trader, the owner of the wagon. The greatest tension between the two poles occurs at the moment of Swiss Cheese's arrest: the famous mute cry of Weigel's Courage (see the Berliner Ensemble film) is its gestural equivalent. Mother Courage is a union of opposites; even her nickname (or man-made name) testifies to it. It was earned when she saved her little wagon business by running a corridor of gunfire. Ironically, the 'courage' came from her being more afraid to lose her profits than to face the shells. (It is, of course, a 'courage' which will lead both her financially virtuous and her ruthlessly warlike sons to face the firing squad.) As all of Brecht's main figures (Shen Te, Puntila, Galileo) she is drawn and split between the poles of generic humanity and specific class alienations. Publicly and professionally, she is a 'hyena of the battlefields' who lives off and supplies the war. Privately, and as a 'generic' being, she is a mother in the role of *paterfamilias* (much like Helen Alving) who tries to keep *her* three children out of the war and cannon-fodder status. Both of these poles or roles interact: her supplying the armies to kill other mothers' children also kills her own children.

On the other hand, as different from Ibsen, there is no moralising in Brecht's play: when her pitying daughter Kattrin (allegorically, Courage's or Germany's pitying aspect) tries to save other mothers' children, she too succeeds only at the price of death. The horizon of this play is not moralistic in the Individualist sense, it is *political – the whole universe*, in which war is a continuation of business by other means (and vice versa), is what should be put in question. No villain need be: Courage, matriarch and merchant, is a protagonist who is her own antagonist. Her children represent certain typified virtues (as explicated in the 'Song of Solomon': Eilif is also Valour, Swiss Cheese – Honesty, and Kattrin, as mentioned, Motherly Pity); all of these virtues turn deadly in the death-bringing universe. The Hobbesian universe perverts Anna Fierling's fierce bravery, commercial promptness and protectiveness. The Individualist psychology of *dramatis personae* will not do any more, it is replaced by a 'field psychology' which can encompass diametrically opposed impulses in the same person at different times and places (a feat whose mysteriousness from the Individualist point of view is the basis of Pirandello's dramaturgy). Furthermore, the war is not simply a 'natural', 'historical' background, but a process to be analysed. Therefore, particular times and places must have the character of a little play-within-the-play, or experimental demonstration: as modern cosmology has it, each is a co-variant unit within the overarching system of natural laws that define the universe. All the scenes, all the playlets within the *Mother Courage* universe or 'attitudinal field' are coordinated. They pivot around the ideologically central scene of 'great capitulation', which does not necessarily have to be a culmination in the middle of the play. It is in fact scene 4, where in the Individualist dramaturgy it would have been scene 7 or 8. The reason for this is the same as the projected inscriptions at the beginning of each scene: Brecht does not want to bludgeon the spectator into accepting his information, he gives her or him the information as early as possible and then provides him/her with data to accept or reject it on the basis of the human relations shown. Equally, the ending of the play does not have to be the final and biggest sensation in the series of sensations that constitute the 'curtain' of each act in Individualist drama (including Ibsen). The ending does not bring a tragic death or happy marriage, but only the end of the 'inner plot' or thematic question: the conclusion reached by Indra's Daughter in Strindberg's *Dream Play*, the loss of home and cherry orchard in Chekhov, the moral death of Büchner's Woyzeck and of Mother Courage.

3. Ibsen's subject-matter and audience were still mirroring each other, so that his field of battle could be an ethics common to both. After the breakdown diagnosed by him, and especially after the first world war and the first major European revolution successfully conducted not by but against the bourgeoisie (the Bolshevik one in Russia), dramatists of first significance could no longer assume, or

believe in, a homogeneity between the stage and the audience, not even for Ibsen's purposes of ethical shock. Already Chekhov's plays had suffered from a major misunderstanding which arose from this unwarranted assumption of homogeneity – of a shared structure of feeling, and therefore of unalloyed sympathy for the main *dramatis personae*. On the contrary, the conventional values of the audience are in Chekhov's plays, with rapidly increasing clarity, revealed as inadequate, grotesque, and stultifying (Serebryakov in *Uncle Vanya*, Natasha in *Three Sisters*). Finally, in *The Cherry Orchard*, the whole play amounts to an allusive debate on just what type of value is represented by the symbolic – and symbolically sterile, but perhaps renewable if collectively transmuted – orchard.

All significant dramatists had, thus, to face the fundamental theatrical and political fact that the audience was rent by violent cleavages. No longer able to please a homogeneous or at least concentrically layered audience, as Aeschylus and even Shakespeare could, major drama had to find a way of communicating with at least a part of the split audience. As the theatre-going societal groups (and in some cases whole nations) increasingly lost control over their future, dramaturgies developed to present paradoxically this paralysis as ongoing, to show what happens after the curtain of *Ghosts* (e.g. Beckett), or to imprecate at it (e.g. Artaud). But I wish here to focus on dramaturgies enacting how the paralysis may be broken. There are at least two roads to such communication, and both were developed during the fifteen years after the first World War in central and eastern Europe. They can be called *the Piscator way* and *the Brecht way* (Dort). Both are in a way open-ended, yet they communicate with different kinds of audience, and on the basis of radically different assumptions.

Piscator's 'political theatre' starts by postulating a mass 'theatre of ideas' in which the stage, suitably prepared by a master-director, would 'drag the spectator into the centre of stage events.' He maintained that 'the heroic factor of the new dramatic art' is no longer a personal destiny but 'our epoch as a whole – the destiny of the masses'. 'A man on the stage has for us the significance of a societal function,' declared Piscator. True, he noted that 'this excessive import-

ance of the political element . . . is not our fault but a result of
the present discordant societal conditions which make any
manifestation of life political'; and life in the epoch of world
wars and global upheavals lent great force to these words.
None the less, although he wanted to avoid a mere
'mirroring of the age', it can be argued that his absolute
division between personal and mass heroism, between a
sharply ideologial stage and an audience which can only say
yes or no to it, did not avoid a reified and abstract mirroring.
We ought to honour the suffering and the idealism which
guided Piscator and many brilliant contemporaries, from the
early Soviet *agitprop*, through the ventures, for example, of
the US Federal Theater, to present-day Third World
playwrights and sympathising groups, such as the Living
Theater of Miss Malina, Piscator's Greenwich Village pupil.
Surely, their work is more important for today's theatre and
future dramaturgy than all the *Hello, Dolly*s and Noel
Cowards of this century taken together. Nevertheless,
Piscator's way treats History as a force external to people, in
a Calvinist or Jacobin, rather than a humanist and Marxian,
definition of destiny. History comes from outside men's and
women's will, whether in Piscator's variant of socioeconomic mass movements or in the Living Theater variant of
projections of a collective subconscious. We, as spectators,
can communicate with it only by exulting or grieving as our
ideological interests lead us. Clearly, whatever its outward
trappings, this is an attitude demanding a lay religiousness
very akin to the medieval one: for God read World
Revolution.

Immediately before Hitler's coming to power, Brecht
passed through a 'didactic plays' phase influenced by
Piscator, the culmination of which is his great and quasi-
religious play *The Measures Taken*. Yet, though he learned
much from Piscator's way, Brecht was never entirely
comfortable in it; his dialectics demanded that every yes be
faced with a no when circumstances change. And for Brecht
circumstances were not to be comprehended except as
changing, as a contradictory process which can never come
to a full stop. Piscator's frame of mind was eschatological.
For Brecht, on the contrary, revolution could not be
envisaged as an apotheosis and cessation of history, but only

as the beginning of a truly human history. History cannot therefore descend, in an epiphany, from the stage down to the believers. On the contrary, the stage ought to permit a mixed-class audience to understand how history – without a capital – is being created by and against people like themselves. Althusser has perhaps formulated this most clearly: for Brecht, 'the play does not contain in itself the Day of Judgement on its own history, neither is the spectator the supreme Judge of the play. He too is put into question ... he is the brother of the stage figures, caught just as they are in the spontaneous myths of ideology, in its illusions and privileged forms'. We could say that the spectator has to learn to judge her/himself and her or his way of life by the roundabout way of judging the stage events. As different from Ibsen – whose commitment to didactic communication was not all that dissimilar – Brecht does this by taking into account that the *premises* of the play have also to be exposed to the spectator's scrutiny. The Ibsenian well-closed, watertight play cannot do justice to the new public and mass age; it has to be opened up into a series of coordinated paratactic situations, clearly manageable by the actor and the spectator.

Contrary to a prevailing view, no explicit ideological illuminations are necessary on Brecht's stage. As different from Ibsen's dramaturgy, they are not impossible; as different from Piscator's, they are not obligatory: it all depends on the political circumstances of the playwright's time and the ensuing verisimilitude. Twice in his lifetime, at the priviledged moments of a historical turning-point in the anti-Nazi struggle, Brecht permitted himself the luxury of such an illumination. The first time it was a resolutely puritanical one, during the last great battle the German Communists fought against Hitler in 1931–2, and it yielded Brecht's *The Mother*. The second time it was a mellower, satirical, almost ribald one, during the last great battle the world alliance of democrats and socialists fought against Hitler after Stalingrad, and it yielded *The Caucasian Chalk Circle*, defined by its Singer-narrator 'as a Golden Age almost of justice'. These two plays are personified by the great figures of Pelageia Vlassovna, the revolutionary, working-class Mother of the New, and Azdak, the disaffected intellectual and kangaroo-court judge who, by his chalk-circle decision awarding the Noble Child to the plebeian mother, becomes a Godfather of the New. But in Brecht's other major plays, the rule he enunciated when defending the cheerless ending in *Mother Courage and Her Children* holds: it is not important for *the stage figure* of Mother Courage to see that trying to make a profit out of war is wrong; she can very well remain blind, and in fact Brecht implies that, in view of recent history, to pretend otherwise would be a gross ideological varnishing or glossing-over the facts. What is important is that *the spectator watching her* (the *theoros*) should see that war is a continuation of big business, and that 'big business is not conducted by the little people.' All of Brecht's major plays deal with the little people, with a sort of plebeian Everyman, caught in the economic, class and national warfare of our century. All deal with people's alienation faced with the historical institutionalisations of their basic strivings for food, sex, friendship and knowledge. Yet all of them are also open-ended: their partisanship is not turned toward communicating recipes to the audience, but toward communicating an unsparing revelation of the audience's situation by means of a roundabout story, distanced in time or space, whose sly parables reinforce a realistic (i.e. applicable) understanding.

Brencht agreed with Piscator that the basic conflicts of our epoch are political; he once remarked that politics is when no coolie can get enough to eat (and, one would assume, also enough to love, befriend and know) without overthrowing an empire. But if politics and political economics are our destiny, Brecht never forgot, and he never wanted his audience and his actors to forget, that in the final count it is *people* who collectively shape them – that history, politics, economics and destiny are all abstractions and superstructures based on human actions, on the flux of human relationships, and on human creativity. In a poem addressed to a group of worker-actors, he wrote:

> You show us only people dragged along,
> Victims of foreign forces and themselves,
> An invisible master
> Throws them down their joys like crumbs to dogs.

And so too the noose is fitted round their necks –
A tribulation that comes from above.
. . .
No. We who are discontented
Have had enough on our low benches.
We are no longer satisfied.
Have you not heard it spread abroad
That the net is knotted
And is cast
By people?
Even now,
In the cities of a hundred floors,
Over the seas on which the ships are manned,
To the furthest hamlet –
Everywhere now the report is: *man's fate is man*.

You actors of our time,
The time of change,
. . .
Give us the world of people as it is,
Made by people and changeable.
(trans. John Berger and Anna Bostock)

Thus, in and after a Brechtian play, the spectator sees no solution on the stage. The Good Person of Setzuan remains split into Shen Te and Shui Ta; Master Puntila has found no common language with his Servant Matti; even the great intellectual searcher after the New, Galileo, though unable to suppress his itch of scientific curiosity, sits in a supervised institution occasionally enjoying a fat goose; and Mother Courage, though bereft of all her children, still runs after the army. What the spectator can gain from such plays is an insight into an encompassing reality which he shares with Galileo in so far as she is also torn between the desire to know and the desire to lead an enjoyable life; with Shen Te in so far as he likes to be good to other people and to himself; with Matti in so far as she works for a boss and with Puntila in so far as she is a boss; or with Courage in so far as he is caught in existing or lurking catastrophes and tries to save *his* little family happiness pretending the catastrophe will not smash *him*. These are all insights into what is common to all of us – if we but take the trouble to recognise it. Therefore, they do not have to split the audience on the basis of class but of socio-political receptivity – a seemingly minor, but in reality crucial difference: the difference between *predetermination* and *choice*, Destiny as transcendental or man-made.

Thus, the Brechtian way seems not only far more widely applicable than the surface polarisation of Piscator's, it also provides us with greater pleasures. Piscator can communicate with the converted, providing them with the pleasure of reaffirmation; Brecht can communicate with the sceptical but open-minded, providing them with the pleasures of discovering both what they are, and at the same time what they could be in a society where man would not be wolf to man. This is, for Brecht, on the one hand not a predetermined outcome as it was for Piscator, but a historical possibility to be freely fought for; and on the other hand, it is not the *moral* dilemma it was for Ibsen. Such a golden age or utopian society presupposes an upsurge of creativity which is, Brecht argues, incompatible both with crypto-religious orthodoxy and with the underlying system of masters and servants, of private property over the means of productivity, of markets and wars. The dilemma is *political*; the horizon of historical condition is a radical process of politics as definition and redefinition of human relationships. As in Ibsen, it is a representative (i.e. simultaneously personal and societal) salvation that is the final horizon, reason for being, and meaning of drama. But as opposed to Ibsen, salvation – whose final horizons are, of course, socialist – can be found only by breaking open the closed, acquisitive and retentive, bourgeois drawing-room: by abandoning and transcending the axioms of Individualism, its ethics and its (non-) politics.

Thus, an exemplary Brechtian play, such as *The Good Person of Setzuan*, is open-ended, but its horizon is very precise. It is a utopian or classless horizon where good people can meet with a happy ending without having to sacrifice their goodness either toward others or toward themselves. Faced with the impasse of having to choose between these two equally impossible sacrifices, the Epilogue to *The Good Person of Setzuan* exhorts:

Dear friends, dear audience, don't feel let down.
We know this ending makes some people frown.
We had in mind a sort of golden myth.

Then found the finish had been tampered with.
Indeed it is a curious way of coping:
To close the play, leaving the issue open
. . . .
Should men be better? Should the world be changed?
Or just the gods? Or ought there to be none?
We for our part feel well and truly done.
There's only one solution that we know:
That you should now consider as you go
What sort of measures you would recommend
To help good people to a happy end.
Dear friends, dear audience, in you we trust:
There must be happy endings, must must, *must!*
(adapted from John Willett's translation)

Bibliography

Only works either quoted in the chapter or providing its basic
terminology and horizon are included. They do not even approximately exhaust my debts, especially to analyses of Ibsen and
Brecht. Titles from the Bibliography to chapter 1 are not included,
though many (e.g. Aristotle, Brecht, Freytag, Hardy, Hauser,
Goldmann, Gurvitch, Lessing, Lukács, Poulet, Shelley, Szondi,
Wölfflin, etc.) are implied. Again, the titles are given by the most
accessible English edition, when one exists, and, when texts were
quoted in my translation from the original, the English edition is
added in parentheses.

Althusser, Louis, 'Le Piccolo, Bertolazzi et Brecht', in *Pour Marx*
   (Paris, 1969) (*For Marx*, London, 1977).
Barthes, Roland, *Essais critiques* (Paris, 1964).
Benjamin, Walter, *Understanding Brecht* (London, 1973).
Brandes, Georg, *Creative Spirits of the Nineteenth Century* (New
   York, 1923).
Descotes, Maurice, *Le Public de théâtre et son histoire* (Paris, 1964).
Dort, Bernard, *Théâtre public 1953–1966* (Paris, 1968).
Eco, Umberto, *L'opera aperta* (Milano, 1962).
Fergusson, Francis, *The Idea of a Theater* (Garden City, N.Y.,
   1953).
Flores, Angel (ed.), *Ibsen* (New York, 1937).
Goldmann, Lucien, *The Hidden God* (Baltimore, 1964).
Hecht, Werner (ed.), *Materialien zu Brechts 'Mutter Courage und Ihre
   Kinder'* (Frankfurt, 1965).

Hinck, Walter, *Die Dramaturgie des späten Brecht* (Göttingen, 1959).
Ibsen, Henrik, *Letters and Speeches*, ed. Evert Sprinchorn (New York, 1964).
Klotz, Volker, *Geschlossene und offene Form in Drama* (Munich, 1969).
Knight, G. Wilson, *Henrik Ibsen* (New York, 1962).
Lenin, V.I., *Tolstoy and His Time* (New York, 1952).
Lukács, Georg, *The Historical Novel* (London, 1962).
Mayer, Hans, *Anmerkungen zu Brecht* (Frankfurt, 1965).
McFarlane, James Walter (ed.), *Discussions of Henrik Ibsen* (Boston, 1962).
Meyerhold, Vsevolod, *Le Théâtre théâtral* (Paris, 1963).
Meyerhold On Theatre, ed. Edward Braun (New York, 1969).
Munk, Erika (ed.) *Brecht* (New York, 1972) (with a further lengthy bibliography compiled by D.S.).
Piscator, Erwin, *Das Politische Theater. Schriften, I* (Berlin, 1968).
Scherer, Jacques, *Structures de Tartuffe* (Paris, 1968).
Shaw, Bernard, *The Quintessence of Ibsenism* (New York, 1964).
Shaw, Bernard, *The Complete Prefaces ...* (London, 1965).
Shklovsky, Viktor, *Khod konia* (Moscow & Berlin, 1923).
Valency, Maurice, *The Flower and the Castle* (New York, 1966).
Williams, Raymond, *Drama From Ibsen to Brecht* (London, 1968).

Afterword (1982) to Part 1:
Looking Backward at Lukács

This essay was written four years ago. The author wishes to state that, at present, parts of it are embarrassing. He chooses not to say which parts. 'Take what you want and leave the rest.'

No, I hasten to explain the above quote is not mine, nor is it invented. I found it in the Journal of Chinese Philosophy *(1978), introducing an article by a Mr M. Teitelbaum. And no, it does not fully apply to this book, since I have deleted or recast the most embarrassing parts of the first two chapters, written in the 1960s. It just seemed a wittily relaxed way, worthy of the splendid Chinese tradition of amateur erudition, to introduce the necessarily less witty considerations to follow in this afterword to Part 1, pertaining to our less relaxed world. For, if one were to believe that works of criticism (or indeed of fiction) were perfect, self-enclosed globes containing in themselves the reason why they were so and not otherwise, organic works of art paralleling divine creation, in one word* products finished once and for all, *then the clause just coming up would be strange or indeed damning for its author: I have serious doubts about chapter 1. More than is the case for the other chapters, its wisdom is partial or onesided. Besides its general tone, there are two crucial crystallisation points I am dubious about. The first is its yardstick of 'generic humanism', postulating an absolute final horizon of what pertains to the genus* homo sapiens *as such, which is of Feuerbachian provenance and stems from Marx's* Economic and Philosophic Manuscripts of 1844. *It is not necessarily simply wrong, and to my mind it cannot be simply evacuated from the text. Indeed, it is partially right – even if abstract, Rousseauist, and petty-bourgeois – in so far as it is a provisional shorthand or code for formulating a deep-seated and wholly justified horror at the degeneration of life (and culture) under bourgeois hegemony. But it seems clear to me today that it should be sublated into Marx's (and Brecht's, Benjamin's, Bloch's, . . .) maturer, better differentiated approach hinging on the commodity as mystified ideology, an approach grounded in his* Grundrisse *and* Capital. *(Let me also hastily add that such a dialectical incorporation does not involve a split between Marxian humanism and Marxist science à l'Althusser, which is merely a 'cold' obverse of the petty-bourgeois humanism and which I have always strongly rejected.)*

The second crucial yet questionable focus of the first essay is its uncritical reliance on an excessively Hegelian conception of monolithic world-historical epochs (of clear religious lineage), in this case the bourgeois epoch or age. My materialist obedience to the historical material at hand then logically (and correctly) but uneconomically and inelegantly led me to veer between this monolithic monad and the numerous nonbourgeois exceptions I had to postulate. While retaining the strengths of such soteriological simplification (without which history is simply meaningless, a supremely inelegant hypothesis in culture), I would, again, today wish to subsume such veering under a more differentiated model fitting the artefacts and the human relationships which are to be explained much more closely. Rather than static this would be a dynamic model of several societal groups, traditions, ethics, and ideologies coexisting in conflictual tension and permeation within the same epoch, in spite of its hegemonic element. Such a dynamic model would follow in the footsteps of Bakhtin, Gramsci, Raymond Williams, and some others, including prominently the names mentioned earlier in this Afterword. It would very probably entail differentiating the necessary overarching notion of an epoch's 'drama' (and/or 'theatre') into class, national, and even genre traditions.

However, my justification for retaining the first essay of the book is that I do not believe works of criticism are finally finished products: they are rather momentary notations of an ongoing process, three-dimensional cuts in the Minkowskian space/time continuum effected for practical reasons and evaluatable by their practical usefulness. Thus, it is not at all for sentimental reasons that I would be loath to part with a record of my first orientation, which came about under the heady influence of the early Lukács, the one from 'Zur Soziologie des modernen Dramas' to History and Class Consciousness. On the contrary, I have not hesitated to partially cut or change some of the more replaceable passages in this chapter. However, its basic profile and vocabulary cannot be satisfactorily cleaned up. Its only alternative would be a new underlying *hypothesis on bourgeois drama, for which I do not yet feel ready.*

At any rate, I believe it is much more useful to focus – as I do in chapter 1 and in the rest of the book – on epistemological and ethico-political axioms that underlie and explain major 'structures of feeling' (R. Williams) of given societal groups and conditions as well as major shifts in their reconstruction of reality, than to focus on 'realism' (later Lukács). The assumption of one hegemonic nineteenth-century tendency to a transcendental principle and value is in a number of ways quite stultifying. First of all, this can explain neither products of other ages (e.g. the medieval Mysteries, or twentieth-century dramaturgy from Jarry or Chekhov to Brecht, Beckett, and beyond – not to speak of Asian theatres) nor the non-hegemonic genres of the supposedly 'realist' age (e.g. fairy-tales, Shakespeare's romances, or para-literature from the roman-feuilleton to science fiction). Second, the canonisation of realism is strongly tainted with the illusionist tendency (of undoubtedly bourgeois provenance) mystically to equate fiction with fact, and narrative space, time and personae with empirical environment and people. Finally, this leads to taking a specialised fictional construct, such as a play, as a magic casement opening on a 'real' reality (whatever that may be). The logical obverse and complement of this view – and also an inherent antinomy in it – is that the Work of Art is then also taken as privileged, an enclosed self-sufficient world, a Second Reality 'mirroring' the first in arbitrary ways. Interminable and necessarily inconclusive debates on this quaint 'mirroring' follow, attempting to conciliate Art and Science in ways vitiated from the outset by such reified concepts, here indicated by the capital letters (see also chapter 4).

Illusionism leads, in fact, at least as easily to an élitist l'art pour l'art consumerism as to political commitment; these two spell each other in history roughly according to whether the bearer and addressee of illusionism (as well as of Individualism) is a waxing or a waning class. The mystical foundation of illusionism brings in its train the whole alienating entourage of empathy and aestheticism. Any theory that wants to connect such an unruly entourage with society and history has to reintroduce these as a 'context' – which in the final instance means political factors that inevitably function as highminded gendarmes policing those unreliable aesthetical wrigglers, the 'texts'. Lukács's trajectory from soulful ethical formalist to unhappy and sniping fellow traveller of Stalinism is, in retrospect, a quite logical possibility if not probability. Though any approach can only be used according to the critic's talent and the conjunctures around her/him, I hope the one used here opens at least a chance for avoiding such a trajectory, which is cognitively inadequate at both its ends, though costlier in blood and tears at the latter.

Learning (negatively) from Lukács's fate hinges, thus, on recognising first that narrative form *(i.e.* fiction *in the sense of fictiveness or fictivity) is the absolutely central category for understanding literature (and culture); and second, that form is most intimately, intrinsically, and immanently sociohistorical: no policeman need be. Form is explainable only, and explainable sufficiently, by means of axioms which go to shape a structure of feeling—such as Individualism and illusionism. They mediate between (or perhaps question the distinction of) 'text' and 'context' because they partake equally of what Lukács called aesthetics and ethics, and what I would today propose to call the* agential-cum-chronotopic discourse *(fiction, i.e. stories with narrative space, time, agents and action—literature, spectacle, the plastic arts)* and the discourse of opinion *(doxology, i.e. stories without clear space/time and agents/action—philosophy, science). Ideally or potentially, discourses are neither unruly school boys to be slapped down by an authoritarian master ('... as the cockney did to the eels when she put 'em i' th' paste alive. She ... cried, "Down, wantons, down!" ',* King Lear *II. iv), nor balloons disappearing above our dark sublunary regions. Ideally and potentially, they are self-policing (autonomous though not independent) social practices. To recognise that they are such could harness the great strengths and avoid the limitations of Balzac-style realism, or should one call it determinist materialism, and of the critical approaches arising from it. Its strengths are the connections it makes between the material environment and actions of societally precise* dramatis personae. *Its limitation is the sleight-of-hand identification between the fictional and the empirical verisimilitude.*

Looking back, then, at chapter 1 and its methodological implications, I would hope that it is not uninteresting both as a negative and as a positive experiment. Negatively, it teaches that a Marxian methodology cannot be achieved simply as the sum of Feuerbach (radical humanism) and Hegel (salvational holism), respectable—and in principle superior to most other methods—as this early Lukácsian stance may already be. Positively, I still think that the basic strategy assumed, that of differentially opposing the Elizabethan (and the Periclean) dramaturgy to the bourgeois one by means of the already mentioned pair of axioms, of confronting the giant Renaissance parent with the degenerate Individualist offspring, is useful. However, noblesse oblige: *we need an approach capable both of broad overviews (indispensable for salvational horizons) and of a flexible espousing of actual dramaturgic movement (indispensable for explicative credibility). And this, as I learned, is a tall order. It is scant comfort to me, as to any of us – but perhaps a second justification for even fragmentary approaches such as the present ones – that nobody has delivered the goods yet.*

PART 2

3

Politics, Performance and The Organisational Mediation: The Paris Commune Theatre Law

To be radical means to grasp things by the root. And the root for man is man himself.
(K. Marx, *Toward a critique of Hegel's Philosophy of Law* , 1843)

And the root for theatre is people showing forth human relations to people.
(A corollary, 1969)

1. General: Politics and Performance (and Organisation)

In a certain sense, politics – the organisation of people's living together – is always implicit in theatre performance, whose one defining trait is the presence of figures showing forth human relations in the 'holy circle' of the stage. The only matter of special interest here would be to find out when, why and how the normative framework of human relations on the stage begins to differ so radically from a code acceptable to the audience that the performance has to explicate, thematise, and make programmatic its new and strange ethics and politics. In modern history – say, from the French Revolution on – this explication has been connected with the revolutionary upheavals of the body politic. In such cases, theatres as institutions and as creative ensembles have had to abandon their dream of a homogeneous audience which shares a common ethics with the stage and is at the same time representative of the society as a whole.

By logical extension, some institutions and ensembles have at moments of sufficient social tension been led to intervene more directly in everyday politics. Sometimes a theatre

83

performance was supposed to be a spark for action on the
world stage (as a rule in a capital city): Shakespeare created a
paradigm for the mechanics of such a play within a play in
Hamlet's Mousetrap. A memory of *Richard II* with its
abdication scene being similarly used by Essex's rebelling
faction might well have gone into the making of the Players
in *Hamlet* and the antecedents and effects of their little play,
right up to the doctoring of the text by the politically minded
patron of the performance. If Piscator (as we keep hearing
from his pupil Miss Malina) really thought that the performance of Auber's *La Muette de Portici* – a rather stuffy opera
about Masaniello's revolution in Naples – which sparked the
1830 Belgian revolt was the only instance of a theatre's
effectively participating in historical events, one must charit-
ably suppose that this was a manifestation of his Greenwich
Village blues rather than of his knowledge of theatre history.

Piscator was right, though, if he was speaking about the
last hundred years. With the growth of population and of
urban and informational density, the thousand or so people
gathered in a theatre have become far too small a percentage
of the whole to be directly effective; the play-within-the-play
dwindled to one marginal item in the mouths of Osrics. With
the appearance of new media supplanting the classical pulpit,
forum (club or coffeehouse), and stage – that is with the rise of
the mass press, mass socio-political organisations, and
especially cinema, radio, and television – theatre, as an
institution, found itself relegated to a sometimes prestigious
but certainly marginal and almost élitist position in social life.
The groups wishing to exert a direct political influence could
no longer be satisfied with the Shakespearean forms of a
Macbird! or *The Screens* (Websterian or Fordian forms in this
case). The generation which had produced the short-lived
but extraordinary spectacle hybrid of Happenings went easily
outside the 'holy circle' and into the streets of New York,
Paris or Chicago. The cause sanctified every street corner and
made a backdrop of any wall – and that is where the audience
was, too, mostly looking through the camera eye (by
courtesy of sensationalist commercial television corporations
out of Dziga Vertov and John Dos Passos).

Such a movement may be logical, and perhaps even
necessary, but it tends to pull *theatre* as known in the
European tradition (i.e. based on an organised fable) back

again into the sturdier and more primitive *spectacle* form. Perhaps this is instinctive wisdom – the crab of drama pulling its tender and vulnerable braincase back into the symbiotic shell of spectacle. The street-corner mime and storyteller has survived the worst civilisation crashes in history; in the earthquakes to come, the light-travelling 'guerrilla theatre' species may be the only chance for the survival of the theatre genus. Yet the term 'theatre' would then have to take on a meaning quite different from the present-day institutional-ised symbiosis of drama and spectacle: the acting ensemble would contract out of the sessile institution; drama would be left to libraries or bonfires as the case may be; and spectacle revert to gesture and music, with such minimal verbal elements as are needed for minimal information and not for the cognitive and poetic, which demands redundancy.

Any modern actor is an intellectual in direct proportion to his making sense as an actor. Now intellectuals in our time generally, and with some historical justification, distrust organisations (when they don't kow-tow before them). But for that factor it seems obvious that much more attention would already have been paid to a third aspect of the field of politics and performance. This third aspect is neither politics in performances nor performances in politics, but the *organisational mediation* between politics and performances. What kind of organised ensembles (groups of performers) can and should exist if theatre art is neither a platonic idea in a timeless heaven nor a profit-oriented business in measured time? How can a performing group be organised when a coherent tradition of performing together for several years is necessary for *any* significant spectacle? Such an organisational mediation is crucial for both classical (ruling-class) and anarchist (plebeian) theatre, for drama and 'mixed media' performing. For example, the excruciating incoherence (in their own terms) of most Happenings is surely due to the one-shot nature of their performing groups. Or, to employ what seems a clinching argument, somebody like myself who does not at all believe that classical dramatic theatre has outlived its usefulness and ought to be jettisoned, can be as interested in this field or theme as somebody who believes the opposite. The field might be called the politics of organising significant performances.

This theme has a general and a particular aspect. Its general aspect merges with an intelligent theory and practice of politics *tout court*, or, if you wish, with a critical anthropology: what kind of organisation of human relations is required (counter-indicated, optimal, etc.) for a given kind of spectacle? Or better: what kind of a society and social ethos is correlative to a given kind of spectacle, since it provides the spectacle with audience, themes and points of view? Yet parallel with our general thinking about this general aspect (as citizens) we are (as people connected with theatre) directly faced with the *particular* aspects of spectacle organisation, and we cannot wait for society in general to straighten itself out and hand us solutions on a platter. 'Theatre now!' may be as impossible as 'Freedom now!' in any full sense: yet without such an endeavour there would be no Theatre (or Freedom) tomorrow either. Organisational liberation is a necessity of life, and a liberating theatre organisation is a necessity of theatre life. This necessity can only be met by a coherent and significant methodology.

2. Particular: On Modern Types of Theatre Organisation

Significant theatre in our civilisation has, until the last hundred years or so, always had an individual patron susceptible to lapsing into good taste or at least tolerating it. In western Europe, individual, aristocratic patronage collapsed in the eighteenth century; in central and eastern Europe it lasted until the mid-nineteenth century; while in the USA it never had a chance. Individual capitalist management began to collapse at the end of the nineteenth and beginning of the twentieth centuries. The new breed of monopolists (Shuberts in the USA, Tennent and Littler in Britain) not only quickly grew into impersonal enterprises but also ceased to support significant (cognitive, poetic) theatre. The big corporations in primary production have always practised patent hoarding and suppression of new processes on a mass scale; yet they never could do it quite as completely as did the theatre monopolists. Bound up with language, most theatre is commercially safe from international competition; some Craigian scenography and, of course, the Stanislavskian directing and acting which is the crowning achievement of nineteenth-century theatre, could be incorporated here and there in prestige productions without causing a real and permanent lapse into twentieth-century significance. On the other hand, theatre monopoly had a huge investment in obsolete productive forces to protect: these 'productive forces' embrace the god-awful buildings in the capital cities (especially New York) and the provinces as well as the organisational rules and customs of production in theatre industry, including prominently the Fuehrer principle and the carrot-and-stick (sell yourself or starve) incentive. Modest innovations in some aspects of production organisation, such as the Group Theatre, quickly failed because of their compromising modesty; potentially deeper going ones, such as the Federal Theatre, were quickly hounded out of existence. Nevertheless, these two groups and their echoes account for most of the significant US theatre in the 1930s and 1940s.

All this can, of course, only begin to suggest some main diachronic lines leading up to the argument (which deserves book-length development) that in our time no form of direct financial patronage which exerts power over theatre institutions and ensembles is capable of producing a significant theatre in any temporally consistent or spatially embracing sense: anything more, in fact, than the odd flash in the pan – a fortuitous meeting of text and actor or director which is statistically bound to happen even at the worst of times.

In a somewhat more systematic and synchronic form, the argument would run as follows. The three main roads which today seem open to the theatre as institutionalised art are: (1) monopoly control (commercialisation), (2) state control at various levels (nationalisation or municipalisation), and (3) self-management guaranteed by an economic and political democracy working upward from community level (socialisation).

Commercialisation implies, in sociological terms, the ideological rule of the economically dominant class. In aesthetic terms it means, in a technologically obsolete industry, the rule of the *ancien régime* in theatre arts: conservative Individualism, inert illusionism, and the sentimental pieties of the more-or-less well-made play. It is at best limited to and by the pre-1914 taste, however refurbished (for example Stanis-lavski plus psychoanalysis).

The effect of *nationalisation* depends on the historical role and present character of the state in various countries. In conjunction with conservative control over repertory and style, it can be instrumental in preventing the break-up of bourgeois (usually Victorian) tastes – for example, in the Soviet Union after the 1920s, or in Teutonic-influenced *Mitteleuropa* where those tastes were until the 1960s not seriously threatened within the state and regional theatres. In other cases, enlightened nationalisation (especially at the municipal or regional level) can be beneficial, in so far as it may give a relatively free hand to various *de facto* self-managing ensembles, usually grouped round a well-known figure (e.g. the first Soviet decade with Vakhtangov, Meyerhold, Tairov, Mikhoels, etc.; the Berliner Ensemble; Vilar and Planchon in France; the Piccolo Teatro in Milan, etc). Yet in all cases, sooner or later, the creative element of the ensemble will come into conflict with the dominant state, regional, municipal or even foundation bureaucracy, since it will be unable to respect the limits of the bureaucratic taste without becoming a museum such as the Comédie Française or the Vienna Burgtheater. That is why, in our day, people like Vilar and Strehler came to a dead-end and had to resign.

Finally, only a socialised theatre, a *system of associations of creative theatre workers,* has a historical chance of achieving a coherent and significant body of theatre for our age – much as the Elizabethan cluster of theatres achieved it for their age between the time of Marlowe and that of Jonson. This follows of necessity if one accepts the strong argument for identifying the enjoyment specific to our age with a scenically organised insight in, and understanding of, con-temporary *possibilities* – latent as well as actual – for human relations. (See Brecht's *Short Organon* for a first theoretical formulation; but the whole of modern theatre juxtaposes what is with what could or should be.) Since these possibilities are startlingly variegated and new, they have to be searched for by a coherent group of theatre workers united by a common structure of feeling and view of people in the world, by common working ethics. (This does not necessar-ily mean a common ideology or lay religion, though it often turns out to be the none-too-happy case, e.g. the Living Theatre).

Now any well-trained Individualistic (Broadway) actor can follow standard rules of empathising with the *known* human relations by studying different roles each time in a different theatre, and trusting that their stereotyped nature and the director will coordinate discrepancies; and of course the star-system is even easier, since the discrepancies between the star and the rest of the cast do not have to be ironed out. But there is no possibility whatsoever of delving for the New, of dialectically juxtaposing actual and latent possibilities on the stage, except by long co-operative work. The ideal Broadway actor is an interchangeable Pawn ready to leap into any role at a moment's notice; and the Queen (star) is always the Queen just as the Castles (co-stars) are always flanking her. Since the Pawns must also be self-propelled, they are promised that those which survive the move in and out of different squares (role statuses) into the end-game will get a 'break', i.e. a chance at becoming a Queen – if you are not gobbled up in the hotly-contested final square. Or to change this from the chess into the biblical imagery, the (few) righteous hardworking Marthas who also turn out to be God-favored Marys will enjoy a revelation, a favourable Judgement Day when they shall finally sit at the right-hand side of the *New York Times*, yea even in televised flesh and not seen as through a mere missing fourth wall darkly. For theatre people encoded in such a mystical way, an intelligent search for the New is institutionally precluded.

To take the first example that comes to mind: *Waiting for Godot*, if one is to believe the critics, failed to find four top-grade commercialised actors in US theatre who would know how to play Beckett (apparently, there was one lucky throwback among them). That is no reflection on anybody's potential talent, but simply on everybody's educational context. How can you play *Endgame* if you don't know whether you are a Pawn or a check-mated King? Much less Brecht who also wants you to know *why* you are a Pawn and not a King! A full range of actors for Brecht (or, say, Genet) thus seems still unachievable for commercial theatre. In other words, no US Brecht or Genet could be performed by the commercial theatre, while the 'regional' theatres, such as the

Guthrie or the Arena, though trying for a co-operative significance, have not fully established a viable alternative. Albee and Williams, reporters of the hysterical breakdown of Individualistic relations, remain the best Broadway can give today; and the undoubted talents of authors of *The Glass Menagerie* and *Who's Afraid of Virginia Woolf* (both early but unsurpassed works) are in turn profoundly inflected by the theatre for which they write. Paradoxically, a self-managing collectivism turns out to be the only way back to really free, personal creative competition.

The conclusion seems inescapable that if there is any future for significant theatre (dramatic and other) it lies in theatre groups organised on the basis of socialised self-management: run by the ensemble itself, with certain modalities of responsible interplay with the communities from which the audiences are drawn. (This is not community control, except in so far as the community may be thought of as an association of theatre-goers, parallel to the theatre group as an association of theatre-makers – the boundaries between these two groups are becoming rather fluid by now anyway.) Significantly, if one looks at the organisational forms of spontaneous new ensembles founded by the young in the last fifty years (from the Soviet TRAM through European student theatre of the 1940s and 1950s, to the Living and subsequent US groups), a more or less socialised self-management is their one common hallmark. All the ways lead to Rome – and highwaymen lurk on all of them.

The central discussion, then, into which I cannot now enter but which I would hope to see evolving among the people practically concerned, would not concern whether? but how? – what forms of self-management, and most importantly what interplays with what communities, are to be sought? As a critic from afar, I can decently contribute only methodological comment on certain practices, and historical examples and lessons which might prevent the battering at some (at least cognitively) open doors. The first contribution I tried briefly to approach above; and I may perhaps record that it is based on twenty or so years of intimate acquaintance (as theatre-goer, theatre critic, member of theatre boards, and artistic advisor to a festival) with state, commercial and self-management theatres. The second

contribution – a crucial historical example of organised discussion on theatre organisation – I propose to approach next
through a brief survey of the 1871 Paris Commune law on
theatres.

3. Individual: The Paris Commune on Theatre Organisation

Do not expect from the Commune more than from yourself!
(Brecht, *Days of the Commune*, 1949)

My purpose is not to discuss the 1871 Paris Commune, or
even its brief practical endeavours to re-organise theatres as
self-governing associations which would play for mass,
popular audiences. Of course, such endeavours are implied in
the debate which follows and form by themselves a very
significant link in a vision and yearning as old as theatre and
human creativity. That vision was resurrected in the theories
of Diderot and Rousseau, in the practice of the 1789
Revolution, in utopian-socialist thought down to 1848, and
Wagner's essays on theatre written under that impulse. After
1871, it was to inspire Romain Rolland's and Firmin
Gémier's concepts of 'théâtre populaire', Nietzsche's revalua-
tion of Greek theatre, and most importantly the Soviet
post-revolutionary theatre. Through these channels it has
flowed into the mainstream of a worldwide twentieth-
century debate on the rebirth of theatre. However, it is
possible here to explain only the immediate contexts
necessary for understanding the debate on theatre organisation in the Council (or Assembly), the highest body of the
Paris Commune.

The Rhetorical Tradition Behind the Debate
To begin with, these are only the *minutes* of the debate, and
anybody who has ever read the minutes of any meeting that
did not strictly deal with facts and figures will appreciate how
impossible it is to present creative thought in the best of
digests. Second, the *Council members* (sixty-four in all; no
attendance record for this session was available to me) were
strongly influenced by the French middle-class nineteenth-
century political oratory and journalism. They were of

preponderantly petty-bourgeois origin: 'clerks, physicians, teachers, lawyers, journalists', as their colleague and historian Lissagaray observes. (Of the speakers in the debate, Vaillant and Rastoul had been physicians, Urbain a teacher, the chairman Régère a veterinary surgeon, and Cournet, Pyat and Vésinier – alas – journalists.) True, twenty-five members of working-class origin also sat in the council – a proportion unheard of in any bourgeois democracy then or since – but they were overwhelmed both in number and, more importantly, in political style. Only a few, such as in this debate Langevin and, notably, Frankel, spoke with a distinctive voice. Ideological allegiances cut across social origin and divided the Council into a rainbow majority composed of 25–30 'radicals' interested primarily in political and not social change (e.g. Urbain and Régère) and 15–20 followers of either 'Blanquist' or 'neo-Jacobin' terrorist voluntarism (Pyat being the most pernicious phrasemonger among them). Sincere adherents of a 'democratic and social Republic,' this majority was under the sway of First Republic – especially Jacobin – rhetorics and forms, quite heedless of a very different situation. They liked theatrical gesture, posed as continuators of 'our forebears' of 1789–94 (even the realistic Vaillant did not escape this cliché), and were often as touchy as stars or, worse, hopeful understudies. Many of them were dominated by a magniloquent extremist phraseology from journalistic and political combats of the 1860s, falling easily into such contradictory, bohemian stances as a demand for political terror but economic and institutional *laissez-faire*. The minority – revolutionary socialists of all shades, doctrines and degrees of clarity – consistently opposed the extremist political violence of the majority and demanded thoroughgoing *societal* changes. Though never organised formally, members of the Workers' International Association supplied the backbone of this minority and indeed of all socioeconomical measures of the Commune, as evidenced here in the endeavours of Vaillant, Frankel (the only one who could be called a Marxist) and Langevin.

For these reasons, most (though not all) speakers used (and possibly the stenographing summariser helped this along) in moments of such stress and lack of time as during this debate, going on amid heavy military operations, a certain political jargon which is always difficult to translate because it is bound to sound faintly ludicrous out of context. (The benevolent reader should just imagine how the minutes of a US Senate Committee or indeed of the executive of any English-language radical group would sound in French!) For example, a term such as 'la pensée' should probably, in this context, be rendered as 'creativity', and not as 'thought', but I have hesitated to foist interpretations on an historical document whenever not strictly necessary for an intelligible translation.

The Politics and Ideology of the Conflict Over Theatre

The debate on theatre was sparked by a provisional draft decree submitted by Edouard Vaillant, the delegate for education ('enseignement': but the term was applied in a very wide sense corresponding probably to what we would today call cultural affairs, i.e. both education and the arts). A delegate was chairman of one of ten Commissions or Delegations to which the Commune – rejecting the division into legislative and executive branches – had delegated day-to-day executive power. Each was therefore composed of about half a dozen Council members acting as a collegiate body which fused the functions of a parliamentary committee and a ministry. Though a Delegate might often be a person of considerable prestige, all decisions were reached by majority vote.

Vaillant's general policy was to assist a process of theatre socialisation as against its earlier commercial or court regimes. His delegation, and the Council as a whole, had already entrusted the Paris Artists' Federation, chaired by the eminent painter Gustave Courbet, with the organisation of expositions such as the annual Salon, and with running the galleries and museums. It had thus implicitly accepted – without prejudging the role of Commune supervision – the aims of the Artists' Federation, defined in its statutes as 'the government of the art world by the artists' with the purpose of 'a preservation of the treasures of the past; a showing forth and valorisation of all elements of the present; and a culture-induced regeneration of the future.' Yet, the immediate occasion of Vaillant's draft decree was a struggle on his 'second front' inside the Council itself, against authoritarian, state control by the Delegation for General Security (also referred to as 'Societal Security') – in practice, leaders of the Commune police and intelligence service under the redoubtable Rigault and his lieutenant, Cournet.

On 8 May Cournet had fired the manager of the Paris Opéra for sabotaging the instructions of the Commune, and appointed in his stead not only a new manager (an opera singer) but also a board of six members of whom four were security functionaries. Since theatre was at that time a great popular favourite and moulder of attitudes, any change in its state led to sensitive political reactions. Cournet's clumsy act had an immediate adverse effect on the Paris circles connected with the theatre, and Vaillant hastened to introduce a bill delimiting the jurisdictions of police and culture. However, any such bill also had to spell out the principle of self-management or association in the theatres, which then superseded the rights of individual proprietors. (These rights had dwindled fast in the 1860s: some privileged theatres had remained court-controlled, while others were being swiftly gobbled up by powerful outside trusts such as the Société Nantaise; private property had already been to a considerable degree divorced from personal creativity.)

Vaillant's proposal was warmly seconded by Urbain, a member of the Delegation for Education. As soon as openly challenged, even Cournet – although palpably offended by references to the high-handedness of his police (of 'Societal Security', as he rectified pedantically) – curtly agreed that theatres should be under the jurisdiction of the Education Commission. Vaillant's groping for an arrangement which would conciliate self-management by theatre artists with an overall accountability to his Delegation was thus attacked principally from another side. For in the Council, balancing the extreme of authoritarian *étatism*, there was a much stronger anarchoidal extremism, insistently represented in this debate by Pyat. Following Proudhon's posthumous book on art (*Du principe de l'art et de sa destination sociale*, 1865) whose basic thesis was that no government had the right to deal with art because any such contact would corrupt art, Pyat let loose two long diatribes (I calculate them at about forty minutes each) whose repetitive tenor – often garnished with generalisations from dubious facts, such as the one about Molière's theatre – went squarely against not only governmental but any organised societal intervention into art matters by means of law or public subsidy. In that spirit, Pyat's ideological ally Vésinier countered Vaillant's motion with one of his own, which was eventually reduced to the amendment about abolishing 'all subsidies and privileges'. This finally became part of the Commune decree, although the abolition of subsidies (as Frankel pointed out by his question to Vésinier) was contradictory to the decree's aim of favouring self-managing theatre associations.

Although Vaillant had not worked out a mechanism for gearing single self-managing ensembles to an overall policy on theatre as a public service – a problem admitting anyway of no solution without large-scale practical try-outs over many years, or even decades – his basic approach was quite clear: 'Our revolution has the duty to ensure the means of labour and production to the worker,' and 'theatres should belong to associations of artists': this is the vantage point from which he refused both 'state art' *and* freedom for proprietors (of buildings in his day; also of copyrights and investment capital in ours) to dictate to creative workers. Pursuing a very interesting line of thought (also to be found in Marx), he observed that 'exploitation in art... is perhaps even more intolerable than in a factory,' and ended by noting that even singers and actors are people: not instruments for and objects of consumption but subjects of economic needs and human justice. Theatres are 'not only throats but also stomachs', a witty counter-parable to Menenius Agrippa's one of the body politic. (This was to be picked up, from here or from the common basis in socialist doctrine, as applicable to plebeians in general in Brecht's adaptation of *Coriolanus* – see Chapter 7.)

The clearest and most consistent exponent of a socialist 'golden mean' between *étatism* and anarchy in this debate was Léo Frankel, a revolutionary worker-cum-intellectual (a prototypic 'organic intellectual' in Gramsci's sense) from Hungary. Tactfully prefacing his remarks by declaring he agreed both with Vaillant (on self-management) and Pyat (against state control), Frankel in fact rejected both Pyat's intellectual anarchism and some of Vaillant's inconsistencies.

He pleaded for a full self-management by theatre workers' associations, including their right to elect the theatre manager. At the same time, he recognised the right and duty of 'the state as ensemble of individuals' (i.e. of a societal totality truly representative of public will rather than of a professional administrative apparatus, bureaucratic or parliamentarian) to deal with theatre and the arts generally. His attitude is the closest prefiguration of subsequent European socialist and revolutionary practice, most notably in the Soviet Union in the 1920s and Yugoslavia in the 1950s and 1960s.

The Time Context

An indication of the Paris Commune's tendencies of development can be found in the fact that after the Theatre Law was adopted at least one general meeting of opera artists (singers, musicians, dancers and technical staff) was called to consider measures necessary for 'substituting for the exploitative regime in the theatre a regime of associations.' The newspaper of the future historian and Council member Lissagaray, *Le Tribun du peuple*, demanded that other 'interested citizens' from outside theatre (librettists, composers, etc.) should also be allowed to participate in the meeting. This brought up a promising possibility of reconciling general public interests and particular self-governing rights. Vaillant himself – as this debate shows – also envisaged that eventually a Delegation for Art, delimited from school matters, would be set up. As one can see from the session chairman's remarks about dance vs. education, such an idea would have had further supporters in the Council. But it was already too late. The debate itself, held on 19 May, had had to be interrupted after Urbain's speech for urgent military considerations. Two days later, on the day the Theatre Law was published, the Versailles government army broached the defences of Paris. The final remark by Dr Rastoul, that he regretted two hours spent on theatre, was thus pragmatically right, and this almost Arcadian discussion while the long knives were being sharpened on the doorstep was to a certain point Quixotic. But from a non-pragmatic, cognitive point of view, Don Quixote is at least as right as Sancho; and this touching idealism is also a measure of the Paris Commune's historical significance. Its best people were fanatically determined to introduce into human relations, regardless of practical roadblocks, 'Freedom now'–a system of free association of all producers.

The history of theatre in the last hundred years turned into different channels. Instead of a time for general assemblies of theatre workers, the next seven days (May 21–8) became the infamous 'bloody week', when between 15,000 and 40,000 (the exact number is still unknown) Communards were executed in the Paris streets. This solved the question of theatre organisation for quite a while. But even in strict theatre or drama terms, there was a price to pay. Towards the end of the century, the tolerant liberal critic Emile Faguet sighed publicly: 'Every evening all Paris theatres play the same piece under different titles. All of us in France feel we are rotting away. This general malaise has been felt more or less clearly since 1815; but it has turned into anxiety since 1870. What will come of this? A renaissance or a final disaster?'

The Personal Context

Individual and at the same time representative or typical (see 'Cast' below and the remarks on 'bipolar characters' chapter 2):

Only two points will be noted here. First, parallel with its class composition, the Commune Council had an age composition quite different from established political norms. The Versailles government's youngest member was 53, its head, Thiers, 74, and its average age 63 years. Only 5 of the 64 Commune Council members were over 60 (including Pyat); the average age of its two subsequent supreme bodies, the Executive and the Committee for Public Safety, was 38. Of those taking part in the debate, Vaillant was 31, Régère 55, Cournet 33, Pyat 51, Vésinier 48, Frankel 27 and Rastoul 36.

Second, the protagonists – Vaillant, the mostly silent Cournet, Pyat and Frankel – were members of the Executive Council and/or Delegates: they were *representative* figures of the Commune and of its ideological cross-currents. That is perhaps what gave the following debate, beneath its specific verbiage, a classical clearness and dramatic rhythm worthy of Shaw – or should we say Racine?

4. Exemplary: The Debate on the Theatre Law of the Paris Commune, 19 May 1871 (Uncut Text of Minutes)[1]

Cast (in order of their appearance)
Edouard Vaillant (1840–1915): engineer, doctor of sciences, physician, studied in France and Germany, Blanquist, member of the International and of the Central Committee of the Paris National Guard. Member of the Council's Executive Commission and Delegate for Education. Condemned to death after the Commune, took refuge in London, politically active, left the International as 'insufficiently revolutionary' after its 1872 Congress. Newspaper editor in France after the 1880 amnesty, from 1893 Member of Parliament for a plebeian suburb of Paris, from 1901 in the United Socialist Party. For all his vacillations into extremes, Vaillant was one of the most interesting and significant figures of the Commune and of French politico-intellectual life of the last third of nineteenth century. (See M. Dommanget's biography.)

Raoul Urbain (1836–1902): private teacher, political orator, one of the most extreme and controversial members of the 'majority,' member of Delegations for Education and for War. Condemned to perpetual hard labour after the Commune, after the amnesty worked as an obscure clerk in the Paris prefecture, far from politics.

Dominique-Théodore Régère de Montmore (1816–?): chairman of the 19 May session, veterinary surgeon, political orator, member of the 'majority' and of the Delegation for Finance. After the Commune sentenced to deportation to a fortress, whence history loses him.

Frédéric-Etienne Cournet (1838–85): clerk in commerce, then newspaper editor, several times imprisoned as Blanquist, fought in the Prussian siege of Paris. Member of the 'majority,' of the Executive Commission, of Delegations for General Security and for War, Delegate of Security (head of police) 24 April–13 May. Condemned to death after the Commune, took refuge in England, Blanquist delegate to the 1872 Congress of the International. After the amnesty, journalist and Blanquist activist in Lyons and Paris.

Félix Pyat (1810–89): journalist, also writer of social

problem plays, such as *Le Chiffonnier de Paris*, 1847, active in the 1848 revolution, radical deputy in the Second Republic, refugee after 1849 in Belgium and England. Returned to France in 1869 to pursue energetic anti-government journalism, fined and imprisoned, fled again to England. Returned to Paris after the fall of Napoleon III, founded the newspaper *Combat* and, when that was suppressed, *Le Vengeur*. One of the best-known opposition journalists in Paris, he seems however to have taken no part in the insurrection which proclaimed the Commune, and he disappeared as soon as street fighting began in May. A leader of extremist 'Jacobins' in the Council, member of its Executive Commission and later of the Committee for Public Safety. Condemned to death after the Commune, lived in exile, re-entered political journalism after the amnesty, Member of Parliament in 1888. Pyat was 'typical of the ineffectual, idealistic, and bombastic revolutionaries' (Mason), 'a good pamphleteer but detestable politician, without clear ideas, without programme' (Bruhat-Dautry-Tersen). His attitudes and his taste for long-winded oratory are well exemplified by this debate.

Camille-Pierre Langevin (dates unknown): metal-turner, a leading member of the Paris section of the International, imprisoned in 1870, sergeant in the Paris National Guard; member of the 'minority' with vaguely Proudhonist leanings, member of the Delegation for Justice. Emigrated after the Commune, returned in 1880 and devoted himself to organising workers' consumer co-operatives. A good representative of the workers' rank and file in the Commune. Brecht's Langevin in *The Days of the Commune* seems to fuse the real prototype with Fränkel and the author's imagination.

Pierre Vésinier (1823–1902): journalist, exiled after 1852, became the secretary of Eugène Sue. Expelled from several countries for anti-Bonapartist writings. Member of the London section of the International, returned to France in 1868 as political journalist and speaker, imprisoned, then fought in the Prussian siege of Paris. Edited the newspaper *Paris Libre* and later also the *Journal Officiel*. 'Jacobin' member of the 'majority' and of the Delegation for Public Services, assistant secretary of Council. Condemned to death after the Commune, took refuge in London where he quarrelled with almost all other refugees and wrote venomous attacks against them. Returned to France after 1880, seems to have abandoned radical politics. Another unfortuante example of the journalistic 'radical bohemians' in the Commune.

Léo Fränkel (1844–96): born in Budapest, became a socialist while a student in Germany, imprisoned with Bebel in 1864, exile in England and friend of Marx, founded the Lyons section of the International in 1867. Jewellery worker in Paris, condemned with Langevin in the 1870 trial, after the fall of the Second Empire reconstituted the French Council of the International. One of the most realistic 'minority' members, Delegate for Labour, Industry and Exchanges, 'in fact, with 27 years, the first minister for labour of the first workers' state' (Bruhat-Dautry-Tersen), introduced a series of pioneering labour laws and measures. Wounded in the final fighting, condemned to death, refugee in London where he continued to work for the International. Returned to Hungary in 1876 and was one of the pioneers of the Hungarian socialist movement. Imprisoned 1882–4 after a strike, moved to Vienna and worked for newspapers. Returned to Paris and participated in the 1889 founding Congress of the Second International as well as in its subsequent congresses. Lived in penury as correspondent of a German socialist newspaper, died from pneumonia (read exhaustion). His final wish was to be buried at the Père Lachaise cemetery of the Commundards, in a red flag. An exemplary nineteenth-century socialist. (See M. Aranyossi's biography (Berlin, 1957).)

Dr Rastoul (first name unknown; 1835–75): physician, political orator, member of 'minority' and Delegation of Public Works, concerned primarily with the ambulance service. Condemned after the Commune to deportation to an island, drowned while attempting to escape.

Minutes
Citizen Vaillant, Delegate for Education: I am asking the council to reach a decision in the matter of delimitation of functions.

The theatres are up to a point within the jurisdiction of [the Delegation for] Security, whose duty it is to supervise the premises and to ensure the maintenance of morality. But theatres should primarily be looked upon as eminent educational organisations, and in a Republic they should be looked upon as such only. Our forebears thought of them in this way, so that the Convent by its decree of Germinal, Year II, decided the supervision of theatre should be entrusted to the Commission for the People's Education. The [Delegation for] General Security should still be entrusted with supervising the premises; but we should not forget that, just as the Revolution of 1789 gave the land to the peasants, our Revolution of 18 March has the duty to ensure the means of labour and production to the worker.

Theatres should belong to associations of artists, and it is to that end that the Delegation for Education has thought it necessary to assemble all artists. I am asking the Council to ratify by its decision that theatres are within the jurisdiction of the Delegation for Education. Let the Delegation for Security exercise a strict supervision, especially in the circumstances of war in which we now find ourselves. But the [Delegation for] Security has just appointed the director of the Opera; this fact seems to prejudge [the conduct of] Council policy.[2]

I am therefore asking the Council for a favourable decision, and I hope to obtain it.

Citizen Urbain: Citizen Vaillant has already proved his competence in the educational field, but I must add to this that the power of the police over theatres should be limited exclusively to keeping order during performances. As fas as the putting on of plays is concerned, the best we can do is to put the theatres under the jurisdiction of Education. Theatres are the widest and best means of the people's education. The former governments made theatre into a means of teaching all the vices, we shall make it a means of teaching all the civic virtues. We cannot tolerate any more the vile spectacles in theatre, we shall transmute a nation of corrupt people[3] into a nation of citizens! (*Cries of 'very good!'*)

* * *

Citizen Chairman[4]: Citizen Vaillant asked at the beginning of our session that we solve the theatre problems; he insists that a discussion be opened on this matter.

Citizen Cournet: I believe that theatres are a means for the education of the people, and that they should be transferred to [the Delegation for] Education.

Citizen Chairman: I must confess that I personally do not

quite see the connection between education and choreography. Still, I shall read Vaillant's motion:

'In accordance with the principles outlined by the First Republic and expressed in the Law of Germinal 11, Year II,

The Commune decrees:

Theatres belong under the jurisdiction of the Delegation for Education in all matters of their organisation and administration. The Delegation is mandated to put a stop to the system of theatre exploitation by a manager or by a group of entrepreneurs, and to substitute for it in the shortest possible time a system of association.

Édouard Vaillant.'

Citizen Félix Pyat: I do not understand citizen Vaillant's proposal, nor do I understand citizen Cournet's. I cannot tolerate the interference of the State into the field of theatre nor into the field of literature. In a State which is still in napkins, theatres need the patronage of a Richelieu, of a Maecenas; but in a free country, which proclaims freedom of personality and freedom of thought, putting theatres under the tutelage of the State is un-Republican. You have a right to supervise the carrying out of the thought's faculties, but to outline its path – that is tyranny, not only unbearable but also fatal for thought.

It is the glory of French theatre that it freed itself from tutelage. When Molière founded his theatre, an officially licensed theatre already existed, but this was not the theatre of Molière. Molière founded his theatre just as a contrast to the one subsidised and patronised by the State.[5] In this moment, I am not opposed to an attentive supervision of theatres, but I stand for an absolute right of individual thought to express itself in the form it wishes to.

Citizen Vaillant: Citizen Pyat has perhaps not grasped the import of my proposal. The First Republic did not think of the freedom of theatre in the way we think of it today. It managed them in a somewhat dictatorial way. For example, it ordered them to stage a given play three times a week. But bear in mind that when one acts justly, one always acts in the name of freedom. And when the State is the Commune, it is its duty to intervene often, to intervene [into matters of art] in the name of justice and freedom.

I think that this is a field of major interest for the State, where intense political activity is called for. More than that, it is in our interest that the police should not meddle in societal matters. We have [instead] to try building up socialist institutions everywhere.

A specific feature of the nineteenth-century revolution is that wherever a product exists [it demands that] the producer should be fully remunerated. The product of [work to] the worker – this axiom of truth is applicable to all; this truth must be applied to the artist in equal measure as to any other producer.

In art, exploitation is perhaps even more intolerable than in a factory; all theatre personnel are exploited from top to bottom. A dancer has to sell herself in order to live. In a word, this was robbery from beginning to end.

It is indispensable to institute in the theatre a regime of equality, the regime of association. The duty of the police is only to deal with guarantees of morality and with security measures.

I demand the formation of a special Delegation for [jurisdiction over] works of art; but it is clear that the police has no place in such a Delegation, which should properly be within the framework of the educational system.

It is the duty of the general theatre administration to change the present regime of property and privilege into a system of associations which is wholly in the artists' hands.

Citizen Cournet: Theatres did not fall within the jurisdiction of the police, but of the [Delegation for] General Security – this is the first error I want to point out.

The second error is to believe that General Security has prejudged [the conduct of] Commune policy by appointing the director of the Opera.

Citizen Felix Pyat: I am very happy to see that citizen Vaillant has agreed that theatre problems are a matter of association. Association is better than management, especially management by one man. But allow me to note that you cannot forbid that private enterprises should possess managements. You cannot declare that no Paris citizen has a right to open a theatre.

I come now again to your point of view: if you want to institute association in the theatres supported by the State, you have that right since you are paying. But I am first of all asking: what is the use of the state having a theatre, of Berry[6] farmers paying for opera dancers? To my mind, that is absurd.

We are communalists and federalists; we have already proclaimed this. Let the Paris Commune, then, if it wishes to spend funds for an opera theatre, abstain from forcing the farmers from Beauce[6] to participate in it, let it not manifest tyranny compelling them to pay taxes so that a theatre might exist on one of the boulevards of Paris. I protest against an opera theatre paid for by the whole of France so that it might operate in Paris.

Later on, if you find it useful to create a communal opera [in Paris], a thing I do not agree with, then let the Commune pay for its keep. Then, but only then, will you have the right to prescribe for your actors the organisational form which pleases you.

As far as any patronage and influence on art are concerned, I find that this would be an assault on the freedom of human thought; at the same time, it would be illogical for you to do it. There should be no State literature or State science, just as there should be no State religion. The academy of medicine and the academy of music should completely disappear in their present form; they personify in art, science, literature a tyranny identical to the tyranny of religion.

I have in these matters the experience of what I saw in other countries, and I do not hesitate to declare that if French science is retarded, if its genius yields pride of place to the genius of other nations, the reason for it must lie in such an unhealthy patronage. What important work have we produced since French theatre, since the Comédie Française came under the governance of courtiers? It has borne only insignificant fruit, a kind of artistic stillbirth.

Does England, the homeland of Newton, have academies supported by the State? Not at all! Their academies are always local and independent, and functioning in a federative way they draw their advantage from their freedom.

I raise my voice therefore against the patronage system which is being proposed to you because I am deeply persuaded that, if our literature and science are dead from the eighteenth century on, they can – regardless of all your good intentions – be renewed only in full freedom.

Citizen Langevin: I do not share the opinion of citizen Pyat. If the theatre is an educational instrument, I propose that the Commune should exercise a strict and serious supervision over this branch of education. I believe that the reason for the halting progress of literature should not be sought in exessive supervision but much rather in a tolerance shown to bad literature. Therefore, I am in favor of the Commune's control over theatres.

Citizen Vésinier: I shall read a draft proposal:

'The Commune decrees:

1.   All subsidies and monopolies in the theatre are abolished.

2.   Theatre is completely free.

3.   Any misdemeanour or crime in theatre is a misdemeanour and crime in common law, and is to be repressed and punished as such.

Vésinier'

There are no misdemeanours or crimes of theatre, of press, of literature just as there is no crime of thought. There can be crimes caused by theatre plays; but they are normal crimes in common law, pertaining to normal legal procedures.

We strive for freedom, for the right to do whatever does no harm to anybody else, but we do not wish a regulated freedom, subject to special laws. That is why I put before you the above draft proposal.

Citizen Vaillant (Delegate for Education): Citizens, we should deal in politics rather than in metaphysics. While not wanting to make any attempt upon freedom, we are faced with the practical task of carrying through a thorough re-organisation. Theatres – that means not only throats but also stomachs. In them, there are people who earn disproportionately much and people who do not earn enough. Therefore, it is necessary that the Commune regulate certain situations of a moral and material character. Clearly, we do not want a *State art*. The only thing [as far as supervision goes] which should be done at this moment is to ensure public security and morals. An end should be put to all forms of exploitation. Who is to do this? A Delegation whose special task this is, until the time you create a General Delegation which will put an end to the old society. My proposal is thus an organisational measure.

Citizen Vésinier: I withdraw my proposal, and I ask that it should not be published in the *Journal Officiel.* While we are being shot at is not the time to talk about theatres.

Citizen Félix Pyat: I know that in a time of fighting, just as in Year II [of the First Republic], there can exist a full right of deciding about all manifestations of thought, regardless of its form – be it the press, the theatre or the painter's brush. If you use it for the purpose of stirring up civil war, you will be suppressed. But as far as the future is concerned, I stand by what I have said. (*Cries of 'Let's vote!'*)

Citizen Chairman: Here is the proposal of citizen Vaillant. (*Reads it aloud.*)

Citizen Vésinier: I wish to propose an amendment to the proposed decree of citizen Vaillant. I propose the following: 'Theatre monopolies and subsidies are abolished.'

Citizen Félix Pyat: But Vaillant's[7] proposal will impede a manager who wants to open a theatre, since he will think only associations can open theatres.

Citizen Léo Fränkel: I agree with the opinion of citizen Vaillant as well as with that of citizen Pyat. Let me explain. Truly, the fact that theatres depend upon any delegation seems to me extraordinarily detrimental to the cause of socialism which we want to further. The management must depend on the members of the association: it is their right to elect the manager. On the other hand, I do not agree with citizen Félix Pyat when he affirms that the State must in no case further the associations or intervene into matters of theatre. The State considered as a power which incarcerates thought into a hothouse, as in the time of Napoleon III, has no business intervening into the affairs of the people, which are foreign to it. But when the State can be considered as the ensemble of individualities, it is its duty to enter into matters of literature as well as into matters of education. We have heard here that thought must be free, that reason should have no protectors. But I shall cite here the example of two Frenchmen: of Diderot, who was supported by Russia, and Voltaire, who was supported by Frederick of Prussia.

Summing up, I think that theatres should be put under the surveillance of the Delegation for Education, which would further the associations by all possible means.

Citizen Chairman: Citizen Vaillant has withdrawn a part of his draft proposal. None the less, he is still maintaining the organisational paragraph, which in my opinion he could also drop. In these circumstances, I think the decree can be put to the vote.

Citizen Vésinier: May I remined you that I submitted an amendment?

Citizen Fränkel: I ask citizen Vésinier whether he would include under the term of 'subsidy', which is in his amendment, a credit given with the aim of furthering associations?

Citizen Vésinier: Yes. Associations can be furthered. But any association can be formed freely, without granting to it any subsidy or monopoly.

[The decree of citizen Vaillant with the amendment is put to the vote and adopted.]

★ ★ ★

Citizen Rastoul: I regret that we spent two hours on discussing theatres.

After this the debate on theatre matters was closed, and the Commune adopted the decree in the following form:

'The Commune of Paris, in accordance with the principles outlined by the First Republic and elucidated in the Law of Germinal 10, Year II, decrees:

— All theatres are within the jurisdiction of the Delegation for Education.

— All subsidies and monopolies in theatres are abolished.

— The Delegation [of Education] is given the mandate to end the regime of theatre exploitation by a manager or a group of entrepreneurs, and to substitute for it in the shortest possible time a regime of associations.'[8]

Notes

[1] I have attempted to translate this debate as faithfully as possible. However, a number of passages are elliptical, and I have supplied the missing parts in parenthesis. More complicated is the case of a number of other passages which are imprecise and sometimes unclear. Whenever it was not possible to translate them literally, I have used my best guess according to the context of the

argument. A real critical or 'diplomatic' treatment of these minutes was not possible here.

It should be noted that in the session of 21 May (or of 1st prairial, Year 79) – reproduced in the *Journal Officiel* of 22 May 1871 (facsimile reprint·Paris, Maspéro, 1970), as well as in the Bourgin-Henriot edn cited, pp. 470–2 – several Council members protested against the truncated accounts of the debates reproduced in the *Journal Officiel*, the official daily. Two of them, Régère and Rastoul, had been participants in the debate on the Theatre Law. Indeed, Régère's protest referred directly to it:

Thus, in what concerns the Vaillant proposal on theatres, I would have liked to see reproduced [in the *Journal Officiel*] the developments given to this question; this would have proved to our enemies that we are not so afraid of their menaces that we would not have time to deal with questions of this kind and to preserve our independence of language. – In particular, some very lofty meditations by citizen Félix Pyat have not been published; I demand the reproduction of these passages cut in the *Officiel*.

However, the interventions of Vaillant were also truncated. In this latter session, Vaillant explained he had authorised Vésinier (who edited the *Journal Officiel*) to cut them. But there was more to this: the cut was apparently demanded by the Committee of Public Safety, the supreme body of the Commune at the time, who might have felt the argument otiose at a time of heavy combats.

None of this, dealing as it does with cuts in the newspaper condensation, affects these minutes. I am sorry to say that a suggestion questioning the minutes on the basis of this was none the less tacked on to the French translation of my article in *Travail théâtral* no. 2 (1971), 82, without consulting me, by the editors (reportedly by M. Emile Copfermann).

The first publication of this chapter, in *The Drama Review* no. 44, was accompanied by photographs of the speakers and of some other aspects of the Commune, which proved financially too costly for book use; I refer the interested reader to them.

2 Cournet's ordinance of 9 May, published in the *Journal Officiel* of the following day, revoked the manager of the Paris Opéra because he had sabotaged a benefit performance for war victims and musicians. It appointed another provisional manager and, what is more important, a commission of six members 'to watch over the interests of musical art and artists' – an ambiguous formulation giving the Security people a bridgehead in the arts

susceptible of indefinite expansion. Vaillant's draft Bill and the debate on it efficiently scuttled this strategy, providing incidentally an excellent example for socialists in power of how to deal with their own police bureaucracy: by prompt and public challenge.

3 Urbain's reference to 'vile spectacles', as well as Vaillant's later reference to economic and sexual exploitation of theatre people (especially women), were based on theatre life during Napoleon III's reign which favoured not only frivolity but a systematic voyeurist eroticism that was, in the government's opinion, a good channelling of energies which might otherwise have been more dangerously employed. A dancer, for example, was supposed to provide all of her many indispensable dresses herself, which practically meant that all dancers had to be mistresses of rich Parisians; the situation of singers and leading actresses was not very different. There is a great deal of evidence about this, perhaps the best known of which are novels such as Zola's *Nana*.

4 The chairman of that session was D.T. Régère; the present member of the Executive was Eugène Pottier, a designer and also member of the executive of the Paris Artists' Federation – who was a few weeks after the session, while hiding from the Versailles terror, to write the words for the *Internationale*.

5 This is a prime example of Pyat's shallow demagoguery. Soon after settling in Paris, Molière's company became 'patronised by the State' just as its rivals: it received a building for performances and an official court name ('troupe de Monsieur'). As for subsidies, according to the company's own precise books (*Registre de la Grange 1658–1685* [Paris, 1876]), it varied in the 1660/1 to 1672/3 seasons between 3500 and 25,500 livres yearly, or between 7 and 38 per cent of total receipts. Of course, Pyat's ideological 'free market' premise is as shaky as his theatre history.

6 Both Berry and Beauce are rural provinces in the heart of France, presumably very far – geographically and in tastes – from caring for or benefiting from a Paris theatre, especially opera. The argument is, of course, demagogic and specious.

7 I have changed 'your proposal' into 'Vaillant's proposal' because Pyat was obviously not referring to Vésinier's amendment but back to the mainstream of the debate.

8 The French text may be of interest:

'Les théâtres relèvent de la Délégation à l'Enseignement.
Toute subvention et monopole des théâtres sont supprimés.
La délégation est chargée de faire cesser, pour les théâtres, le régime de l'exploitation par un directeur ou une société, et d'y substituer, dans le plus bref délai, le régime de l'association' (The

Paris Commune *Journal Officiel* of 21 May 1871, p. 622. The rest
of the minutes are to be found in *Procès-verbaux de la Commune de
1871*, éd. critique par Georges Bourgin et Gabriel Henriot [Paris,
1945], 2: 413–14 and 425–30.)

Bibliography

Deservedly the most famous history of the Commune is the one by
its member P.O. Lissagaray, *Histoire de la Commune de 1871*
(Bruxelles, 1876), reedited many times later in France and
elsewhere. To my mind still the most illuminating sociopolitical
comment is K. Marx's *The Civil War in France*, (London, 1871 – of
which the best edition with pertinent companion pieces seems to be
the French one at Ed. Sociales [Paris, 1953]), as well as V.I. Lenin's
in various articles culminating in *The State and Revolution* and in
The Proletarian Revolution and the Renegade Kautsky (both Moscow,
1918). The following list has been established strictly for its
informational usefulness, although I find that the organizing
ideologies in a number of the books are rather inadequate and
prevent a full understanding of the subject, from anti-socialists such
as Mason to Stalinists such as Bruhat, Dautry, and Tersen or
anarchists such as Ollivier.

The debate of the Council of the Commune has been taken from
its minutes in the *Procès-verbaux de la Commune* 2: 413 ff., éd.
critique par G. Bourgin et G. Henriot (Paris, 1945).

1. General

d'Almeras, H., *La Vie parisienne pendant le siège et sous la Commune*
(Paris, s.d. [ca. 1935]).

Anon. [M. Vuillaume, H. Bellenger, and L. de Marancour],
Hommes et choses du temps de la Commune (Paris-Geneva, 1871).

Bourgin, G., *Histoire de la Commune* (Paris, 1907).

Bruhat, J., Dautry, J. and Tersen, E. *La Commune de 1871* (Paris,
1960 – with a huge bibliography).

Danilin, Iu., *Parizhskaia kommuna i frantsuzkii teatr* (Moscow,
1963 – a pioneering work on the Commune and theatre, to
which this article is much indebted).

Fabre, M.A., *Vie et mort de la Commune* (Paris, 1939).

Guesde, J., *La Commune de 1871* (Paris, 1934).

Jeanneret. G., *Paris pendant la Commune révolutionnaire de 71*
(Neuchâtel, 1872).

Jellinek, F., *The Paris Commune of 1871* (London, 1937) (with a
dozen pages of further bibliography).

Kerzhentsev, P., *La Comune di Parigi* (Rome, 1951) (Russian original, Moscow, 1940).
Koechlin, H., *Die Pariser Commune in Bewusstsein ihrer Anhänger* (Mulhouse, 1950).
Kundel, E. (ed.), *Tagebuch der Pariser Kommune* ([E.] Berlin, 1971 – with the correspondence of Fränkel and Marx).
Labarthe, G., *La Theâtre pendant les jours du siège et de la Commune* (Paris, 1910).
Lavrov, P., *Parizhskaia Kommuna* (Geneva, 1880).
Lefrançais, G., *Etude sur le mouvement communaliste à Paris 1871* (Neuchâtel, 1871).
March, T., *The History of the Paris Commune of 1871* (London, 1896).
Mason, E., *The Paris Commune* (New York, 1930).
Molok, A., *Parizhskaia kommuna v dokumentakh i materialakh* (Leningrad, 1925).
Ollivier, A., *La Commune (1871)* (Paris, 1939).
Rihs, C., *La Commune de Paris* (Geneva, 1955).
Vésinier, P., *Histoire de la Commune de Paris* (London, 1871; translated later into English).

2. Biographies

Dommanget, M., *Edouard Vaillant . . .* (Paris, 1956).
Aranyossi, M.A., *Leo Fränkel* ([E.] Berlin, 1957; Hungarian original, Budapest, 1952).
Lur'e, A., 'Leo Frankel', in *Portrety deiatelei Parizhskoi Kommuny* (Moscow, 1956).
Tersen, E., 'La Carrière militante de Léo Frankel', *Cahiers internationaux*, no. 16 (1950).

4

The Mirror and the Dynamo: On Brecht's Aesthetic Point of View

> The time has come to give art, by a pitiless method, the precision of the natural sciences. But the principal difficulty for me is still the style, the indefinable Beauty resulting from the conception itself.
>
> (Flaubert, *Correspondence*)

In the preface to his most famous theoretical essay, the *Short Organon for the Theatre*, Brecht in part retracted his early vituperations against aesthetics, which in the 1920s had led him to ask (as the title of an article of his goes): 'Shouldn't we liquidate aesthetics?' With the growing maturity and complexity of his poetry and plays, the feedback from practice to theory which was a permanent feature of Brecht's work led him to recognize that those vituperations – which he never wholly abandoned – were directed at 'the heirloom of a depraved and parasitic class' (*GW* XVI:662),[1] and not at a philosophical and sociological discipline dealing with the pleasing and the beautiful (mainly in art), as such or as a whole. For, by the end of the 1930s, Brecht had in his lyrics and dramas, as well as in his theoretical writing,[2] recognised that his own work was also pleasurable – if pleasure were no longer opposed to learning. This assumed a redefinition of aesthetics which refused to recognise the divorce between entertainment and learning, between the aesthetically pleasing and the intellectually cognitive functions of artistic signs (*GW* XV:285ff), but on the contrary insisted that aesthetic standards were linked to the cognitive adequacy of a work of art. Such a new aesthetics involved a radical departure from any attitude of indifference to practical experience. It posed anew questions concerning the relationship of a pleasure-provoking object to 'external reality'. The new aesthetics redefined imagination as creative, the aesthetic attitude as a significant *activity*, and the aesthetic response as a constructive and interpretive event. Cognitive meaning was thus recognised as a no less important element of 'style' than, say, sensuous surface.

Within such a context Brecht felt that his 'theatre of a scientific age' could take up its abode in aesthetics. Even natural sciences, he explains somewhat curtly in the *Organon* preface, create an aesthetics of their own, and he quotes approvingly Oppenheimer's dictum about a scientific stance 'having its own beauty and being well suited to man's position on Earth'. Brecht concludes this preface (in the dignified first person plural which he affected as a semi-humorous form of acknowledging his mistakes): 'Let us therefore, probably amidst general sorrow, revoke our intention to emigrate from the kingdom of the Pleasing, and let us, probably amidst even more general sorrow, manifest our intention to take up our abode in this kingdom. Let us treat the theatre as a place of entertainment, as proper in aesthetics, and let us examine which kind of entertainment suits us!' (*GW* XVI:662–3).

In this chapter I wish to demonstrate, first, that this attitude of Brecht's should be taken seriously, and that the distinctive values of his work and its enduring qualities are to be found in the ambitious formation of a specific Brechtian beauty, pleasure or aesthetics. His work can therefore be analysed using – and where necessary modifying – some classical aesthetic categories. Second, I wish to show that the most significant of these categories is a *look backward* from an imagined golden future of justice and friendliness to his (and our) cold world and dark times. Brecht's central aesthetic device, the technique of estrangement [*Verfremdungseffekt*], and the whole estranging arsenal of Brechtian poetics flow logically out of such an angle of vision.

1. The basis of Brecht's world-view is a Marxian horror at our present state and a firm orientation towards changing it: '[Einstein said] that he has, ever since his childhood, thought only about the man hurrying after a ray of light and the man in a falling elevator. And just look how complicated this grew! I wanted to apply to the theatre the saying that one should not only interpret but change the world' (*GW* XVI:

815). The references to Einstein and to Marx's eleventh thesis on Feuerbach locate the starting-point as well as the all-informing stance of the new aesthetics. Beyond this, an awareness is implied of *what* needs to be changed (an alienated world) and of *how* theatre could represent the changing of the world (by understanding the work of art as a 'symbolic action' or as a de-alienating pleasure-in-cognition). They represent two closely connected aspects of Brecht's vision: a theory of human reality, and a theory of art as an autonomous understanding of that reality. Both of these may have been aspects of an artistic vision rather than systematically formulated doctrines, and the term 'theory' should doubtless here be taken primarily in its etymological sense of *theoria*, an understanding look or viewing (see the Appendix to chapter 1); none the less, they were constantly informing Brecht's aesthetic practice. It is a measure of his relevance that these are the foundations upon which *any* radical renewal in aesthetics has to be based.

Brecht's mature aesthetic *theoria* presents us again with the problem of the relationship between Art and Nature, known in aesthetics as the Aristotelian question of mimesis. From the very beginning of *Poetics,* where Aristotle defines most poetry and singing as mimesis, this central concept is susceptible to three principal translations: *copying, representing* (performing) and *expressing*. Though Aristotle's use, in spite (or because) of his professional pleasure in neat definitions, oscillates between these meanings, the above example indicates what has also been found by Koller's examination of the use of the term in Aristotle's time (say in Plato or Lysias): that the central meaning of mimesis includes an active relation of the *mimoumenoi*, the 'representers' or 'performers', to the model.[3] It is sufficiently clear that singing about an event, or dancing it, cannot be taken as a straight copy of that event, but only as an expression according to autonomous musical (or choreographic) conventions. The central position of the term *representation* for mimesis can perhaps be clinched by Aristophanes' use in the *Thesmophoriazusai*, where Mnesilochus wants to meet Euripides as the protagonist of his latest play, *Helen,* and sets about performing a little play-within-the-play, dressed as Helen: 'I'll *represent* [Euripides'] brand-new Helen.'

The changing fortunes in the use and abuse of mimesis, from Sophocles and Plato to, say, Stanislavski and Zhdanov, offer material for fascinating studies in the history of aesthetics, philosophy and politics, which would (together with the equally fascinating history of catharsis) explain why Brecht persisted in calling his dramaturgy 'non-Aristotelian'. From all that emerged in this long debate we are here concerned simply with the fact that even in Aristotle's time mimesis fundamentally meant *representing* (in theatre: performing, showing). This means that both the model to be represented *and* the ways of representing it (technologically, in a given medium, and culturally, in given possible conventions of representation) were – and were admitted to be – co-determining elements of the mimesis. Throughout the centuries, creators and theoreticians of art not wholly blinded by ideologies have seen that art was no magic window opening on reality but itself a specific reality – neither a photographic nor a symbolist copy of Nature but a representation of processes in reality, parallel to scientific or philosophical ways of representation, and interacting with a changing world. In this light, Brecht's formulation of a modern Marxian or Einsteinian epistemology 'merely' took up and refashioned the mimetic tradition dominant from tribal performances through Indian, Chinese and Japanese plays to the Renaissance, which bourgeois aesthetic practice and theory had interrupted. This also underlies Brecht's affinity for the (largely plebeian) Asian, medieval and Elizabethan dramaturgies. However, as already noted, this classical mimetic tradition underwent in its turn a major inversion of its horizon and *telos* at his hands. In the words of Marx, which became the basic orientation of 'The Philosopher in the Theatre' (as Brecht liked to call himself), this is: 'Philosophers have only *interpreted* the world in various ways, the point is – to *change* it.'

Or, as one might formulate the position of Einstein (whom Brecht also took as an exemplary figure, liked to compare himself with, and was preparing to write a play on): there is no specially favoured coordinate system or reference point; each coordinate system has its own time dimension; yet the general laws of nature are equivalent for all reference systems. In other words, though the old notion of an eternal, essential identity of reference systems has to be abandoned, yet through modification – which can in each case be analysed and grasped – general principles of Nature (read: history of human relationships) remain valid in a new dialectical way for all reference systems. Marx's disdain for the old ways of interpreting the world as something given – as a text to be reproduced by an indifferent actor of the World Play – and Einstein's insistence that though Nature was not chaotic there was no absolute perspective from which all events were scaled up or down, both represent fresh strategies of grasping reality, closely akin to Brecht's own. (One could also place within that kindred family of visions those of Picasso or Eisenstein, but that would be matter for another essay.)

By the nineteenth century, bourgeois aesthetics had wholly forgotten the traditional implications of mimesis – reacting with a sterile denial of any relation between art and nature. As discussed in Part 1, it rested on the twin axioms of *individualism* – conceiving the world from the individual as the ultimate reality – and *illusionism* – taking for granted that an artistic representation in some mystic way directly reproduces or 'gives' Man and the world. Against this, Brecht took up a position of productive *critique*, showing the world as changeable, and of what I shall for want of a better term call *dialectics*: conceiving the world as a process and man as emergent. In contrast to the idea of a one and only Nature – and Human Nature – to be found in or beneath existing relationships, Brecht's work is based on an emergent human history within which all variants of Nature – and of Human Nature – are specific societal achievements and simultaneously alienations. All existing societal relationships (including the ones in the first Communist states) are historically unique and yet cautiously commensurable; none are final or perfect. All of them are therefore to be met by dialectic critique, keeping in mind the possibility and necessity of change. Art is not a *mirror* which reflects the truth existing outside the artist: art is not a static presentation of a given Nature in order to gain the audience's empathy; Brecht sees art as a *dynamo*, a vision or organon which penetrates Nature's possibilities, which finds out the 'co-variant' laws of its contradictory processes, and makes it possible for critical understanding to intervene into them. This attitude attempts to raise art to an ontologically – or at least epistemologically – higher plane of creative significance than illusionism. The estrangement [*Verfremdung*] of ways of speaking, for example, 'makes it easier to translate the natural into the artistic [*ins Künstliche*]; moreover, [it] translates according to the meaning' (*GW* XV:370): to Brecht, art is a Meta-Nature with its own language, yet not in the sense of a negative of nature (in the *l'art pour l'art* fashion) but participating in the meaning of reality. Art is no beautiful platonic lie, but an autonomous, 'artful' (*Künstlich* is a pun uniting 'artistic' and 'artificial') reality; and its productive stance is analogous to that of modern cosmology and anthropology. It is experimental, testing its own presuppositions – in theatre, by feedback from the effect in practice of its text-performance. Seeing the world as sets of changing possibilities, it is a reflection *on*, not *of* nature – including human nature, developing within history and as history.

Borrowing a Brechtian method of exposition (which he took from German philosophy), Table 4.1 may be useful. The 'mirroring' attitude corresponds to the alienated reality which was characteristic of the nineteenth century, but which lives on tenaciously (among other places, on all the Broadways and *boulevards* of the world). The 'dynamic' attitude corresponds to the twentieth-century tendencies toward de-alienation, although some of its champions may also be found in a long tradition: since, say, Epicurus and Lucretius, and including, notably, isolated oppositional figures in the nineteenth century such as Marx, Büchner, and Rimbaud – all of them, logically enough, Brecht's favourites.

2. The basic strategy of 'dynamic' aesthetics is to observe the possibilities realised at any given time and compare them with a fuller realisation of the same possibilities – looking at the present from a point of comparison located in another epoch. 'The "dreams" of the poets are merely addressed to a new spectator, who relates to them differently from heretofore', wrote Brecht in a planned conclusion to the *Messingkauf* dialogues: he followed this with the statement that poets themselves are men of such a new epoch. From this position, 'The question of the didactic becomes an absolutely aesthetic

Table 4.1

Illusionist and Individualist aesthetic attitudes (The Mirror)	*Critical and dialectical aesthetic attitudes* (The Dynamo)
Reality is seen as an ensemble of visible and calculable commodities (including Man)	Reality is seen as interacting processes in an experience of painful humanisation.
Nature – including Human Nature – is universal, eternal and unchangeable; surface differences are so much local colour.	Nature – including Human Nature – is historically conditioned and changeable; different forms of behaviour result from tensions between a humanising possibility and specific societal alienations.
Mimesis copies Nature as the only reality; art (theatre) is a reflected, purified Nature, a *Pseudo-Nature*.	Mimesis brings forth a specific reality; art (theatre) is a simile of and alternative to Nature, a *Meta-Nature*.
The work of art suggests the existence of previously known objects.	The work of art proves its own existence as a creative vision and object.
Art (theatre) transmits insights into a subjectively reflected objective reality.	Art (theatre) creates insights into the subject–object relations in possible realities.
Ideas and ideology are the basis of aesthetic being: philosophical idealism.	Material practices are the basis of aesthetic being: philosophical materialism.
The universe is monistic and deterministic: growing awareness leads to tragedy, lack of awareness to comedy (Ibsen, Strindberg, O'Neill).	The universe is pluralistic and possibilistic: growing awareness leads to comedy, lack of awareness to tragedy (Shaw, O'Casey. Brecht).
Man is seen as a 'three-dimensional' *character* revealed psychologically through conflict with environment; the unity of such a character is a metaphysical axiom.	Man is seen as a contradictory *ensemble* of several possibilities and qualities, intersecting in his actions; the unity of such an ensemble is a datum of social action.

Table 4.1 *(Contd.)*

Illusionist and Individualist aesthetic attitudes (The Mirror)	*Critical and dialectical aesthetic attitudes* (The Dynamo)
Highest ideal: eternity (Nirvana); fulfilment in noble dying.	Highest ideal: liberty (classless society); fulfilment in productive living.
Patriarchal, authoritarian strength.	Power-sharing, liberating suppleness.
To feel a magical aesthetic illusion fully is to penetrate into an eternal human experience.	To understand a critical aesthetic showing fully is to gain insight into the possibilities and societal limitations of human experience.
The 'well-made' play's *closed form* is composed of a chain of situations linked by deterministic causation and moving to a climax on the same plane.	The well-made play's *open form* is composed of fixed points of a process distributed in various planes with a climax calculated to happen beyond it, in the spectator.
Indispensable arbiter: Policeman, Royal messenger *(Rosmersholm, The Inspector General).*	Indispensable arbiter: Judge, Wise Fool *(Saint Joan, Caucasian Chalk Circle).*
Ideal synoptic point of the play: a look through the eyes of main characters (the presuppositions of the play are given).	Ideal synoptic point of the play: a look at all characters from outside the play (the presuppositions of the play are tested).
Ideal onlooker: he to whom all unfamiliar things are familiar, because he sees their eternal essence through surface appearances – God.	Ideal onlooker: he to whom all familiar things are unfamiliar because she looks for the unrealised potentialities in each stage of human development – person of blessed classless Future.

question, solved, so as to speak, in an autarchic way' (*GW*
XVI:3*). From the vantage point of this projected new
world, a scientifically questioning look at human relations
sees the present as an historical epoch: all of its events
(especially the most 'normal' ones) are remarkable. 'As
empathy makes an everyday occurrence out of the special, so
estrangement [*Verfremdung*] makes the everyday occurrence
special. The most general happenings are stripped of their
tiresome character by being represented as unique. No longer
does the onlooker escape from the present into history; the
present becomes history,' says Brecht (*GW* XVI:610). And
further: 'He who has looked with astonishment at the eating
customs, the jurisprudence, the love-life of savage popula-
tions, will also be able to look at our eating customs, our
jurisprudence and our love-life with astonishment': only the
spiritually impoverished Philistine sees everywhere an Everyman adaptable to all roles: 'Like Lear, he has reaped
ingratitude, he has raged like the Third Richard. He has
sacrified all sorts of things for his wife, like Antony for
Cleopatra, and he has treated her more or less like Othello.
Like Hamlet he hesitates to wipe out an offence in blood, and
his friends are Timon's kind of friends. He is absolutely like
everybody, and everybody is like him' (*GW* XVI:574–5). If
this petty-bourgeois is wrong in his empathising, if his
motivations are not eternal nor his standpoint and epoch
normative, then it is *his* actions and *his* world which are
shown to be catastrophic and savage:

> I am a playwright. I show
> What I have seen. At the markets of men
> I have seen how men are bought and sold. This
> I, the playwright, show.
>
> How they step into each other's room with plans
> Or with rubber truncheons or with money
> How they stand and wait on the streets
> How they set snares for each other
> Full of hope
> How they make appointments
> How they string each other up
> How they love each other
> How they defend the spoils
> How they eat
> That is what I show.

I see avalanches appearing
I see earthquakes advancing
I see mountains straddling the way
And I see rivers overflowing their banks.
But the avalanches wear hats
The earthquakes have money in their vest-pockets
The mountains have alighted from cars
And roaring rivers command policemen.
That is what I reveal.
         (*The Playwright's Song* – GW IX:789–90)

If such a 'slaughterhouse' period as ours obviously cannot be historically privileged, then all its surfaces are 'period', historical exhibits before the evoked jury of spectators 'differently related to experience' – that is, *posterity* (*die Nachgeborenen*, to whom Brecht's possibly most significant poem is addressed). Another poem is entitled 'How Future Times Will Judge our Writers': those times and generations are the supreme arbiters of the Brechtian world. Friendly and inexorable, they sit in judgement on this age, like the plebeian Shades on the great Lucullus, consigning its vivid criminals into nothingness (where Mother Courage's actions also consign *her*); they judge, accuse and condemn, like Azdak judging the rapacious Natella Abashwili, like Shen Te accusing the cruel world and the bland gods, and like Galileo's scientific 'I' condemning his weak empirical self. The central, informing model of Brecht's dramaturgy is the tribunal.[4]

In still another fragment of the *Messingkauf*, Brecht himself openly indicated that the external standpoint of his approach is in the future: the key for understanding any figure in his dramaturgy lies 'not only outside the sphere of the figure, but also further forward in evolution. The classics have said that the ape is best to be understood starting from man' (*GW* XVI:610 – a reference to Engels' essay on human evolution through labour). He repeated this view in the *Organon*: the proper estranging way of playing a role is as if the character 'had lived a whole epoch to the end and were now, from its memory, from her knowledge of future developments, saying those of her words which had proved important at that point of time – for important is as important becomes' (*GW* XV:367).[5] Perhaps the most effective way of putting this is again to be found in a poem, whose date (about 1926) makes it a document of the moment when the look backwards from a happy future crystallised in the young Brecht. The poem is called 'This Babylonian Confusion' and shows how the author wanted 'slyly to tell a story' about a grain dealer in Chicago:

> To those who have not yet been born
> But will be born and will
> Live in quite different times
> And, happy they! will no longer understand
> What is a grain dealer of the kind
> That exists among us.

The impulse for this poem is biographical:

For a certain play [it was to be called *Wheat* or *Joe Fleischhacker from Chicago* and to play at Piscator's; studies for it were later transmuted into *St Joan of the Stockyards*] I needed the Chicago grain market as background. I thought I would acquire the necessary knowledge by a few quick questions to the specialists and people in that field; but the affair was to take a different course. Nobody, neither well-known economists nor businessmen – I travelled from Berlin to Vienna to meet a broker who had worked his whole life on the Chicago exchange – could give me a satisfactory explanation of the happenings at the grain market... The projected play wasn't written – instead of that I started reading Marx.[6]

But from this true story, Brecht in his poem ascends into allegory and an Erewhonian dialogue with yet unborn listeners. The listeners, however, show no understanding, ask unanswerable questions about the world which boasted of grain dealers, and finally put the writer off:

> With the calm regret of
> Happy people. (*GW* VIII:149–51)

From this vantage point of an imaginary just and friendly future of happy people, where 'man is a helper to man' (*An die Nachgeborenen*), the poet can in his plays and verse practise the classical (Marx's, Bellamy's, Morris's) anticipatory *look backward* into his own bloody, empirical times, taking in the reality of this age of strife between classes and nations, of mankind divided against itself in the societal alienation of the capitalist mode of production and consumption. In this way of looking there is no sharp division between the epic and the dramatic in the sense of Aristotelian or (better) Schillerian poetics. If the aesthetic uniqueness of such an attitude lies in confronting man as changeable in time, then 'Schiller's distinction that the [epic] rhapsodist has to treat occurrences as wholly past, and the [dramatic] mime as wholly present (letter to Goethe of 26 December, 1797) is not quite exact any more' (*Organon, GW* XVI:684). For if people are not temporally fixed points in Newtonian space but future-oriented vectors in Einsteinian time/space, they are not to be encompassed either by a mimic, dramatic present or by a rhapsodic, epic past. Looking at them from the author's imagined future, they are objects in the past, to be shown by epic narrative. Looking at them, simultaneously, from the author's present, they are subjects in the present, to be shown by dramatic presentation. The new view of them will therefore consist of a precisely graded mingling of the 'epic' and the 'dramatic', of people as an object of cool anthropological cognition *and* as a subject of passionate dramatic sympathy. As compared with 'Aristotelian' Individualist poetics – especially as understood by the German nineteenth century from Hegel and Schiller to Freytag – this kind of performing was not 'pure' drama, it was 'epic'. In fact, however, it fused 'dramatic' presentation with 'epic' narration, embodying this in the alternation of action with narrators, songs, titles, etc., and in a special behaviour of the dramatic figures. The whole arsenal of estrangements is the aesthetic working-out of such a new epico-dramatic, dialectical mode of dramaturgy. When estranging had fully worked itself out in Brecht's practice, he was able to recognise that, although his theatre was 'epic' compared to orthodox quasi-Aristotelianism, this term did not render it justice: 'We may now abandon the designation "epic theatre" for the theatre we had in mind. This designation has fulfilled its duty if the narrative element, always present in theatre, has been strengthened and enriched ... creating a basis for the particularity of new theatre' (*GW* XVI:925). The proponents of the designation 'epic theatre' had too readily assumed that it was, 'naturally', epic compared to the existing drama and theatre: they had fallen in the trap of looking at Schiller's or Reinhardt's dramaturgy as *the* dramaturgy, forgetting in the heat of the battle their own basic estranging standpoint, and mistakenly conceding drama to the enemy.

The strategy of the look backward, then, presented dramaturgic situations simultaneously as 'human, all too human' history for our sympathetic involvement and as inhuman, alienated pre-history for our critical understanding. It created tension between a future which the author's awareness inhabits, and a present which his audience inhabits; this tension is at the root of the most significant values of Brecht's work. It is because the golden age is yet to come that man in this iron age cannot be good, try as he may, without being pulled apart either from within, as Puntila, and from without, as Shen Te:

> Your bidding of yore
> To be good and yet to live
> Tore me in two halves like lightning. I
> Don't know why: I couldn't be good to others
> And to myself at the same time.
>> (*The Good Woman of Setzuan*)

3. Brecht's central aesthetic and historical standpoint of looking backward can be analysed in his practice into two principal estranging components, which can be called *the view from below* and *the view from above*. The view from below is the anarchistic, humorous 'Schweik look' of plebeian tradition; it is inherent in the stance which Brecht's (and Hasek's) Good Soldier assumes in facing the world. Its richness stems from a constant juxtaposition of the official and the real, the sentimental and the naive, the ideological and the practical. Figures like Azdak are obvious protagonists of this comic look. The view from above, on the other hand, is the rationalist 'Diderot look' of intellectual tradition; it is inherent in the stance which the author of *Jacques the Fatalist* (or of *Candide,* or of *The Persian Letters*) assumes in facing the world. It critically illuminates the most intimate structures of bourgeois life and art. Brecht, as Chiarini has noted, is the last great pamphleteer of the bourgeoisie, who, however, turned against his own class (as he himself said in the poem 'Kicked Out with Good Reason', [*Verjagt mit gutem Recht*]), 'baring its secrets to the people'. The Diderot look meets the Schweik look in the politics of de-alienating the human animal.

The Schweik element in Brecht's work is evident at first glance. Equally important, however, is the patron saint role of Diderot (in the 1930s Brecht even tried to found a Diderot Society for the study of theatre). Like Diderot, Brecht started from the assumption that human reason can understand and master even the most unreasonable instincts, even the most complex circumstances, even the bloodiest contradictions of this stockyard world. Like Diderot, Brecht was interested in how art relates to a new concept of nature, man and society, to a new aesthetics. Like Diderot and his fellow theoreticians, Brecht asked from the actor 'that his tears flow from the brain'. Like Diderot, he wanted a dramaturgy which could give the *homme moyen sensible* of tomorrow insights into human relationships and the relations behind those relationships (*GW* XV:256–60). Like Diderot, Brecht thought of himself as of a 'philosopher in the theatre' (with the distinction of having advanced from Shaftesburian to Marxian optimism). No wonder that the following fragment might have come from either of them: 'In the great play, the play of the world, the one I always return to, all emotional souls occupy the stage, whereas all creative people sit in the orchestra. The first are called mad (alienated); the second ones, who depict their follies, are called sages (philosophers). The eye of the sage is the one which lays bare the follies of various figures on the stage'.'

Brecht's opus might be most usefully divided into three phases: the early and the middle 1920s; the late 1920s and early 1930s; and the mature phase from the middle 1930s on. The first two phases – to speak of them within the framework of this essay – abstracted and made absolute the views from below and from above. These two at last coalesced into the dynamic look backwards of his final great plays.

The first, anarchist phase – the phase from *Baal* to *Mahagonny* – is marked by a tendency towards *absolute non-consenting*[8] or a self-indulgent nihilism. The author distances himself from reality without having open historical horizons or new values in sight. The estrangement takes the form of a *reductio ad absurdum,* and operates by isolating banal elements from reality. Critics have not been slow to notice that *The Threepenny Opera* works by equating the gangsters to the bourgeois (as Gay's play and much of the literature of that age did too – see Fielding's *Jonathan Wild the Great*), implying that therefore the bourgeois are gangsters too. Perhaps it has not been as clearly stated that this 'opera' also *delights* in such asocial bourgeois gangsters. The gangster – bourgeois equation is, therefore, an object of uncritical admiration at least as much as of social criticism. Possibly it is just the delight in such an unsolved incongruity which led to its huge success with all shades of the middle-class audience. Brecht himself, craftily truthful, proclaimed it was still a 'digestive' play where the bourgeois dream is both realised and criticized (*GW* XVII:991). That is also why in his next phase he so strenuously tried to change it when rewriting the scenario for the Pabst film and even more notably when writing *The Threepenny Novel*.

Most critics would probably agree that Brecht's plays of the first phase do a far better job at the destruction of bourgeois values than at setting up any – even implicit – new values. They do not deal in transvaluation but in devaluation, similar to much that was happening at the time in Central Europe, from the Dadaists to, say, Pirandello. Therefore this phase of Brecht's vision foreshadows some essential traits of the later grotesque or 'absurd' playwrights such as Beckett or Ionesco. At least one of his early plays, *The Wedding* [*Die Hochzeit*] is almost pure Ionesco *avant la lettre*. What is here, however, perhaps most significant is that Brecht soon outgrew this uncritical non-consenting attitude. By the end of the 1920s, he was sufficiently above his 1919 playlet to change its name to *The Petty Bourgeois Wedding* [*Die Kleinbürgerhochzeit*]. This apparently slight change is symbolic. Where Ionesco makes a given *condition humaine* into *the* human condition, Brecht locates it in a precise anthropological and societal context. He denies it eternal status by tying it down to an alienated socio-cultural system, with whose change the historical human condition would change too.

The second, rationalist phase – from *Man Is Man* to *The Mother,* the phase edges being, as always, blurred – is marked by a tendency towards *absolute consenting* or a self-indulgent didacticism. If the first post-World War One, phase was given to apolitical ideologising, the second, which came about in an atmosphere of fierce political struggle in Germany, was given to political ideologising. This finally resulted in a kind of Mystery play, as exemplified by *The*

Measures Taken. Whereas the absolutely non-consenting phase tended to deny society in favour of the individual, this play implies that the individual should deny himself in favour of the society. He should disappear into a collective *ad maiorem Dei gloriam,* it being then of secondary importance whether this God is identified as such or laicised into, say, the World Revolution. The apology of an *ecclesia militans* may have been quite understandable at that high point of tension in Germany, but it has to be seen as such when looking back at Brecht. Such a play is a poetical expression of a lay faith whose aims are of this world but whose methodology is fundamentally religious, even though not theistic but political. It is interesting to note that at the time it was first produced, this play was acclaimed by some Christian critics as a great crypto-religious tragedy, and severely taken to task by some Marxist critics, although written as a glorification of what Brecht conceived the Communist Party was (or should have been) like. Certainly, such uncritical consent is more Jacobin or Anabaptist than truly Marxian.

The final, mature vision of the sequence from *The Good Woman of Setzuan* to *Life of Galileo* came when the playwright had seriously (and joyously) accepted practical corrections against over-confidence in either plebeian anarchy or lay clericism. In the 1930s it became obvious that the gangsters of *The Threepenny Opera* led *also* to Nazism, and that the fanatics of *Measures Taken* led *also* to Stalinism. Therefore, constantly on the alert for feedbacks from lived human history, yet holding on to the significant standpoint of a future friendly humanity, Brecht fused the strengths of both the view from below and the view from above. From the plebeian view, he took a disrespectful, critical attitude towards everything that claims to be an eternal value, especially towards societal power structures. He also took the parodic forms used to such effect in plays like *The Threepenny Opera,* based on the puppet theatre, on street ballads and pamphlets, on fair-barkers and penny arcades, and distilled through the traditions of Büchner's revolutionary bitterness, Wedekind's provocative bohemianism, and the goon-thinking of Nestroy, Valentin or Karl Kraus. The rationalist view taught him to search for clearly defined values which make out of understanding and cognition a pleasure, an aesthetic principle, and which were used to such efect already in plays like *The Mother* or (in the richest prefiguration of his later masterpieces) *St Joan of the Stockyards.*

The mature Brechtian vision then, used both kinds of estrangement, the nihilist 'Schweik' one and the rationalist 'Diderot' one, and fused them into one method, which finally understood itself as dialectical. In a very noteworthy passage of Brecht's *Dialogues of Exiles,* the interlocutors come to agree that Hegel's dialectical method is a great humorous world principle, because it is based on switching between different levels of understanding, just like humour or wit. Thus this dialectical Brechtian vision is a new link in the classical chain of wits, the bitter or smiling debunkers going back to Lucretius and Aristophanes, Rabelais and Cervantes, Fielding and Swift; and perhaps one might mention also Brecht's favourites outside literary discourse: Breughel and Picasso in painting, Chaplin and Eisenstein in film, and Marx.

Using the language of dialectical estrangement to master the alienated world, Brecht's mature aesthetic is not based on pure idea. It is in a permanent two-way relation of theory to practice, and it therefore overcomes ideological dogmatism. That is how he could also overcome the weaknesses of its components – the primitive and insular aspect of anarchism, still peeping out in *Schweik in the Second World War,* and the aprioristical and monochromatic aspect of rationalism, still to be found in a play like *The Days of the Commune* (both, however, were left unfinished, and have to be considered as first drafts only). The open-ended character of Brecht's aesthetics led to a methodology of experiment or 'essays', and he accordingly called all his works after 1928 *Versuche.* What he meant by this is perhaps clearest if one looks at the successively richer (though to my mind not finally resolved) versions of *The Life of Galileo.*

To the dramaturgic representation of people on the stage in their interrelationships, Brecht's mature aesthetic vision says at the same time yes and no. It says yes to them as human potentials, looking back at them from the vantage point of the future; from the same point of view, it says no to them as instances of *homo duplex,* the cleft human of this specific perverted period. All of his plays together, the ambitious if unfinished *summa* or *Comédie humaine* of Brecht's, might borrow the title of one: *Der Jasager und der Neinsager [He Who*

Says Yes and He Who Says No]. They were always strategies of de-alienation, of a striving towards an integral humanity, towards people who would be students and masters of what Brecht called the greatest art – the art of living. Liberating aesthetics finally found its foundation in firm ethics, understood as a basic need on the order of food, sex, sociability or knowledge: and the demand for cognition as an ethical imperative led to the recognition that theatre 'must be allowed to remain something wholly superfluous, which, to be sure, means then that one in fact lives for the superfluous' (*Organon, GW* XVI:664). This is Brecht's final vindication of aesthetics in terms of the Marxian jump from the realm of necessity to the realm of freedom (or in terms of its prefiguration). The (ironically) superfluous commodity, the supreme good that one can rightly live for, is on that side of the boundary between necessity and superfluity, which turns out also to be the boundary between death (or a death-in-life zombiedom) and life. Trickily, Brecht's term *Ueberfluss* (here necessarily translated as 'the superfluous' in order to echo the preceding *Ueberflüssiges*) also means plenty or abundance, indeed even excess and exuberance, literally 'overflow'. One lives for plenty, exuberance, overflow. In another *Organon* passage Brecht praises the untrammelled societal pleasure in the magnificence of even anti-social activity, such as that of a river in flood, provided society may master it (*GW* XVI:673). Thus the collective rationalist has looped the loop, incorporating into his rationalism the anti-social magnificence (of Mauler, of Coriolanus or, best, of Azdak) as a bearer of the Renaissance principle of fullness and plenty – or indeed the Dionysian (Nietzschean?) principle of raging excess. At this dynamic and utopian convergence point and vanishing point, Judge and Wise Fool met with the Princely Child: the German Chalk Circle closed.

Notes

[1] All quotations from Brecht have been taken from his *Gesammelte Werke* Suhrkamp edition (Frankfurt, 1973); all translations are mine. They will be indicated in the text by a *GW* in brackets, with the Roman numeral indicating the volume and the Arabic the page number.

² This is already clear in one of his fundamental essays. *The Street Scene* (1938; *GW* XVI:546 ff.) with another landmark, *Theatre for Pleasure or Theatre for Learning?* (1936; *GW* XVI:262 ff.) marking the visible transition towards it.

³ Cf. H. Koller, *Die Mimesis in der Antike: Nachahmung, Darstellung, Ausdruck* (Bern, 1954).

⁴ First argued in Mordecai Gorelik's unjustly neglected *New Theatres for Old* (New York, 1940; 1962).

⁵ Compare the Swiss playwright Max Frisch's discerning diary observations from the time of his acquaintance with Brecht in 1948: 'Brecht relates to a projected world which doesn't yet exist anywhere in this time, visible only in his behavior which is a lived and inexorable opposition, never daunted through decades of external toil. Christians related to the other world, Brecht to this world.' (*Tagebuch 1946–1949* [Frankfurt, 1950], p. 287.)

⁶ Brecht's note, quoted in H.J. Bunge-W. Hecht-K. Rülicke-Weiler. *Bertolt Brecht* ([E.] Berlin, 1963). p. 40, transl. D.S. Elisabeth Hauptmann, Brecht's collaborator at that time, wrote in her diary of July 1926 about Brecht's work on *Joe Fleischhacker*, a play planned as carrying on the series of 'the coming of mankind into the big cities' begun with *In the Jungle of Cities:* 'Finally Brecht started to read national economics. He asserted that money practices were obscure, he had to see now what money theories were like. But even before he came to important discoveries, at least for himself, he had concluded that the old (great) form of drama wasn't fit for representing such modern processes as the international distribution of wheat, the life stories of people of our times and generally for all events with consequence.... During these studies he drew up his theory of "epic drama" ' ('Notizen über Brechts Arbeit 1926', *Sinn und Form. Zweites Sonderheft Bertolt Brecht* (1957), p. 243; transl. D.S.)

⁷ Diderot, *Le Paradoxe du Comédien*, ed. E. Dupuy (Paris, 1902), pp. 96–101 (transl. D.S.).

⁸ The term has been taken from Brecht's own use in such plays as *The Baden Learning Play on Consenting*. 'Consenting' was one of the key terms of post-war German sociology which Brecht seems to have been quite well acquainted with, especially through Fritz Sternberg and Karl Korsch (see Sternberg's memoirs *Der Dichter und die Ratio* [Göttingen, 1963], and the discussion of Brecht's correspondence with his mentor, Korsch, in Wolfdietrich Rasch, *Zur deutschen Literatur seit der Jahrhundertwende* [Stuttgart, 1967]). Compare Max Weber's chapter 'Einverständniss' [Consenting], in *Über einige Kategorien der verstehenden Soziologie* [Max Weber, *Soziologie – Weltgeschichtliche Analysen – Politik* [Stuttgart, 1964], pp. 126–40).

5

Salvation Now, For All Flesh!: Structures of a Slaughterhouse World (Saint Joan of the Slaughterhouses)[1]

1. Cosmology and Diegetics: The Ups and Downs of Salvation

The universe of Brecht's play *Saint Joan of the Slaughterhouses* is divided into what one might call (with a retrospective use of his *Schweik in World War 2*) *upper spheres, lower spheres* and a *limbo* or *no-man's land in between.* The upper spheres are those of politico-economical power and decision-making. They are constituted by the meat-packers at the Chicago stock exchange, culminating in Mauler; however, he becomes the head of the vertical cartel only because he is connected to a larger mysterious universe or Empyrean of high finances and presumably ultimate, unquestioned capitalist power – the hidden 'New York' opposed to this play's manifest microcosm of 'Chicago.' The lower spheres are composed of the stockyard workers and marked by powerlessness in the face of a destiny that comes from above 'like the rain' (674, 720).[2] That destiny, their 'misfortune', is composed both of inclement nature ('the terrors of cold Chicago', (669) and of the politico-economic climate created by the capitalists in their Hobbesian system of mutual preying. Marginally, the lower spheres involve also the cattle-raising ranchers from the 'Missouri' prairies, and, at the lowest rung of the ladder, the cattle led to slaughter.

The topology of *Saint Joan* is a fusion of the robust oppositions of German Leninism with a simplified version of the medieval, Dantean salvational vertical. The basic opposition between two classes, taken from European sociopolitical reality after the first World War and the Bolshevik revolution as interpreted through *The Communist Manifesto* via the Leninist storm and stress of the 1920s, is expressed through the image of huge masses standing against each other as armies with front-lines. The Black Straw Hats marching with drums and flags as 'Soldiers of the Lord' (684) 'everywhere where unrest prevails' (674) is only a particularly explicit case of the general militarisation of life under Imperialism (as was their prototype, the 'Salvation Army' which Brecht studied attentively), an example of the front-like divisions within society:

> [...] built up
> In giant squadrons facing each other
> Employers and employees
> Battling fronts: irreconcilable.
> Run round between them, reconciler and mediator
> Of use to neither, and perish completely. (725)

In classical urban insurrectionary language, front-lines in a civil war are barricades:

> *Slift:* The main thing, where do you stand, man? This side or that side of the barricades?
> *Snyder:* The Black Straw Hats stand above the battle, Mr Slift. Therefore this side. (721)

Such a front-line or barricade is permanent, since economic warfare never ceases. It is an intensification of the 'border of poverty' (756) which exists not only as a financial statistic but in the actual topography of the city's Packingtown slums, which recall Sinclair's *The Jungle.* (In classical American idiom, which Brecht did not use here, it separates the right from the wrong side of the railway tracks.) In moments of acute conflict approaching civil war, such as the attempted general strike, it is a front on which an actual army actually employs machineguns and tanks (752, 753, etc.). Therefore, the workers' only weapon is their number, organisation and solidarity (741, 749, 758, etc.). That is an indispensable condition for counter-violence, for a counter-army in the process of formation (741, 749, 751, 758, esp. 753). The imperative of organisation into a tight 'net' (742, 759) is also decisive for Joan's final role and failure, of which more below.

In this basic Leninist opposition, a sociological stratification of upper (oppressor) and lower (oppressed) class (718, 723) is on the verge of being collapsed and resolved into a *secessio plebis,* into a strategic horizontal of two opposed enemy formations. However, in *Saint Joan* this collapse (prophetically, for German reality) does not come about, and the momentarily threatened hierarchic vertical remains dominant, powerfully reinforced by a Dantean moral topology. Grim Chicago with its 'omnipotent cold' (679), its rains, and – as their conjunction – its snowstorms attacking the huddled poor (722, and later), the 'wind in the depths' (778), is not too far from the nethermost circle of Hell congealed by Lucifer's fanning; and the correlation of the physical 'depths' of hunger attendant on the cold, rain and snow (711, 732, etc.) with the moral depths of 'cold skinning' of man by man (710) can be compared to *Inferno* episodes such as the Ugolino one. However, such a vertical cosmology of 'Heaven and Hell, up and down' (762) differs strongly from Dante's, not only because it is dramatically foreshortened but, more significantly, because its upper spheres of socioeconomic power are throughout the play a sardonic anti-paradise of pre-established disharmony. They are characterised in great detail right up to Joan's final prophetic maledictions which sum up the pertinent oppositions:

The Packers and Ranchers (very loud, so that Joan is drowned
out):   If the building shall rise high
         Top and bottom must apply.
         Therefore keep each in that place
         God has given him in this race.
         Pace by pace
         Have him work his proper measure:
         Should he rather take his pleasure
         'Twould our harmony displace.
         Down below the low are right
         The mighty are throned on heights.
         . . .

Joan: But those who are down are kept down
         So those on high can stay high
         And the baseness of those up high is beyond all
             measure
         And even if they got better, that would
         Not help, for unmatched is

The system they made:
Exploitation and disorder, bestial and so
Incomprehensible. (780–1)

The earlier quotation about Joan as 'reconciler and mediator' (725) indicated that between the two front there is – as befits this slaughterhouse world – a category of 'middlemen,' ideological rather than commercial. They are identified openly as such in that dialogue because both Joan and the Black Straw Hats are such ideological middlemen who are, at that point, splitting apart. With the intensification of the gulf between high and low, the Black Straw Hats are openly aligning themselves with one 'side of the barricades' and Joan with the other. This no-man's land between the front-lines is also somewhat like the Dantean Limbo where dwell people who have not had sufficient fortitude even to commit their own sins, and therefore bear the brunt of Dante's deepest contempt. It is characteristic of this play, however, that these people in the middle – an artistic transformation of the middle classes between the capitalists and the workers – are the focus of interest. In a strange way, Mauler with his lofty and base souls, and the close links to Joan, can also function as a mediator between up high and down below, but only in the interests of up high. (More will be said of such communications in the third section of this chapter.)

Thus, the basic oppositions in the universe of *Saint Joan* are vertical (upper–in between–lower), with secondary oppositions in each of the three horizontal layers: the war of each against each between packers, the alternative orientations of the middlemen, the different degrees of consciousness between workers, strike leaders, and ranchers. An understanding of the diegetic unfolding of such oppositions seems indispensable for all subsequent discussions. It is briefly summarised in Tables 5.1 and 5.2.

The play is clearly divided into two parts plus the ending. Up to and including scene VIII the stage figures, as well as the action, shift between the various spheres: Mauler goes to open a hospital, the poor workers and ranchers are taken to the stock market and to Slift's house, the packers visit the Black Straw Hats, while Joan circulates freely through the whole system. Between scene VIII and IX, a good director will locate his single interval. In the long scene IX, the

Table 5.1: Oppositions (Paradigmatic)

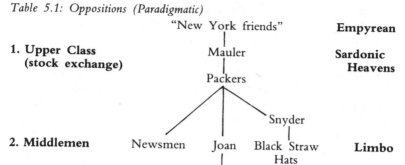

Table 5.2: Unfolding of Oppositions (Syntagmatic)

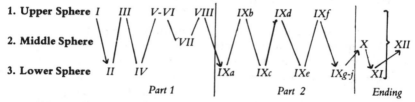

secession of the workers is existentially (though not ideologically) a *fait accompli:* the action shifts between the upper and lowest spheres; they are juxtaposed directly without intermediaries, but the figures can no longer cross the gap (except for the newsmen who function as camouflaged scouts in enemy territory, and for Mauler's 'crossing the border' toward the end). The ending (scenes X–XII) consists of Mauler's illumination and the grand finale. (Scene XI is compositionally dubious and would probably gain by being – as in the earlier versions – amalgamated with scene IX.) In the finale all figures meet for the first and last time under the aegis of a victorious Mauler in the 'canonisation' of Joan.

Within such a division, *Saint Joan* develops following several interlocking rhythms. In the upper, primary politico-economic domain, it follows the *unfolding of the crisis cycle or spiral* marked by the letters from New York detailing the phases of the cycle in scenes I, VI (but scene VI refers back to V), IXb, X.[3] The four phases of the 'terrible cycle' (704–5), freely adapted from Marx, are its beginning (over-production – scenes I–IV), rise (speculation – V–VIII), culmination (crash – IX–X), and stabilisation on a higher level of cartelisation with the workers bearing the costs both as labourers and as consumers (X).

In the central, ideological domain (central both in the vertical scheme of the Tables, and in the sense of holding the centre of the spectators' attention), the three scenes in which the action shifts from the highest to the lowest sphere (II, IV and IXa) are also Joan's three 'descents into the depths.' This whole aspect of the play reposes on a metonymic system of vertical positions and tendencies. In her *first descent,* Joan recognises the degradation of the workers – 'the lowliest' (672) are 'going under' (673), and it's no good preaching to them a spiritual uplift ('strive up, don't strive down,' 674) and reprimanding their striving after 'lowly pleasures, ... this little bit to eat and pretty apartments and movies' (675), while they are starving and freezing:

> That rises no higher than the rim of a bowl....
> Living from minute to minute uncertainly
> They can lift themselves no longer
> From this lowest ground.... (677)

In her *second descent,* Joan recognises that this degradation's ultimate cause is not ethical but economic – the workers cannot afford a goodness or a just anger whose price would be starvation in cold Chicago: 'Don't you see that it rains on their wickedness?' (696) After she has tried the appeal to the good capitalist's conscience (scenes V and VI) and moral indignation against the bad capitalists (scene VII – 'you up here doing such things,' 707), Joan realises in her *third descent* that the workers have to help themselves against the upper class and the religious middlemen. However, she is deterred from becoming a consistent participant in such self-help by cold, credulity, and pacifism – basically, by not having shared the existence of a worker, which leads to a failure of imaginative sympathy and thus to her downfall:

> [A violent person] is surely
> Full of deceit against his fellow men
> Outside of all bonds
> That are customary among men.
> No longer belonging, he would find

Himself, in a world no longer familiar
No longer at home. Above his head
The planets would run no longer
By the old rule. Words would
Change their meaning for him.
. . .

Three days in Packingtown in the morass of the slaughternouses
Joan was seen
Stepping downward step by step
To clear the mud, to appear to
The lowest. Three days downwards
Striding, weakening on the third and
Swallowed by the morass in the end. Tell them:
It was too cold. (754–5)

Finally, Joan's death (scene XII) is a *last descent* into the depths. Her downfall is inexcusable and irredeemable ('The stone does not excuse the fallen,' 758–9). It is therefore only very ambiguously negated within the play, which has no happy end. Not only is the canonization by the massed choirs of capitalist consensus a consciously false uplift:

Snyder:	Arise, Joan of the Slaughterhouses
	Intercessor for the poor
	Comforter of the lowest depths! (778)
	. . .
The Butchers:	Climbing means: on others climbing
	And this heavenly upwards-striving
	Also must be downwards-trampling. (781)

– but even Joan's own belated uplift is still theoretical and reactive, couched in and imaginatively tied to the dominant class terminology of socio-ethical up and down, and therefore perceivable as despairing and somewhat hysterical:

And those who tell them they can rise in spirit
While stuck in mud, their head should also be
Smashed on the pavement. (782–3)

This should prevent the careful spectator from investing her, even at the end, with the saintly and therefore infallible character of Shaw's Saint Joan – from staging his own sentimental, middle-class, Individualist canonisation. But it

does not at all lessen the validity of most of her insights –
certainly not of those supported by the general drift of the
play. Her final realisation in scenes XI–XII is that it is
necessary and possible to change the world radically, and that
this will inescapably have to be done by solidarity and force:

> I for example have done nothing.
> For let nothing be counted good, no matter how it looks, but
>   what
> Really helps, and let nothing be held honourable but what
> Changes this world finally: it needs it! (780)

Joan's descents into the depths are thus harrowing, but they
do not lead to any radical, salvational Harrowing of Hell,
only to an understanding how desperately that is needed:

> Fast disappearing from this world fearlessly
> I tell you:
> Take care that when you leave this world
> You were not only good but left
> A good world! (780)

The Workers are subject to iron laws of political economy;
Joan wanders around trying to understand them and the laws
they are subject to. Oscillating between the upper, central,
and finally also the lower level, *Mauler's line* is the third and
final rhythmic determinant of *Saint Joan*. As mentioned,
Mauler is also an intermediary. As 'the contemporary stage
of the Faustian Man' (4*) he has two souls: the base, business
soul, striving toward *Fleisch* (the only half-translatable pun
on 'flesh' and 'meat' on which so much of this play reposes),
belongs to the politico-economic domain; but the lofty,
sentimental soul striving toward *Geist* (spirit, mind or
ideality) belongs to the ideological domain and makes of him
the *animus* of Joan's *anima*. Mauler is physically present in the
whole first half of the play, except for scenes IV and VII
which, however, show the result of his actions. In the second
half, after being in the centre of action in the upper sphere
scenes, he – most interestingly – in scene IXh 'crosses the
border of poverty' (755) into the lower spheres, symbolically
shedding his riches, wiped out in the crash, by letting go his
detectives (who protected him in those spheres in the
prefigurative scene IIb). His experiences in that theologico-

political hell or purgatory, his 'humbling' (scene X) lead to his final ascent or 'exaltation' (765). That ascent and enthronement – which is Mauler's real Assumption into the Heavens of full power as opposed to the window-dressing of Joan's canonisation – is due to a double illumination of his. In the ideological domain, he has recognised (in scene X, at the Black Straw Hats, where he realises the drowning have to clutch at straws) that salvational beliefs too are manipulable, with an effect even greater than the manipulation of politico-economic information he has been so adept at. After this, he was able to recognise in the politico-economic domain that the ideologically subjugated workers are potential consumers, not merely producers (this recognition is a bent development of Joan's urge to raise their moral and economic 'purchasing power,' (705)). Thus, Mauler's journey into the dark and cold nether regions is the obverse of Joan's: ready to lose all, he gained all. Where Joan's single-minded search, high and low, for goodness availed her nothing, Mauler's double soul proved able to valorise all the twists and turns that happened:

Misfortune downs the down and out
It lifts me up, by spirit's route. (757)

Therefore, in the ending of *Saint Joan,* Mauler fuses his dramaturgic function as protagonist with that of undisputed arbiter, indeed the *metteur en scène* of this world play. He, the perfect capitalist, can keep both souls – the spiritual (lofty) one serving the business (base) one, of course. 'At the end of *Saint Joan of the Slaughterhouses,* those up high ascend one more step, whereas those down below descend to the same amount.'[4]

Such an insistent use of a medieval or Baroque cosmology with its moralised vertical, as well as the innumerable biblical structural elements testify to the salvational character of *Saint Joan.* One of the recurrent biblical references – even though within the play's chronology it is quite inaccurate – is that to the seven days of a malevolent creation (722, 733, 761, 763); another is the various temptations of both Joan and Mauler on their different *viae crucis.* The play's black or atheist variant of Dantean cosmology, straining but failing to turn into a Leninist horizontal Armageddon, is similar to medieval Mysteries through its vertical, and to Shakespearean histories and problem plays through its horizontal aspects. Like a (Left or Feuerbachian) Mystery play, it alternates between moral and power statuses; like, say, *Troilus and Cressida* or *The Merchant of Venice* (but translated into class warfare), it alternates between opposed camps, with some go-betweens and renegades. This cosmology and composition are eminently supple, suited to showing matters of both global and indeed cosmic import (as in the middle ages) and intense figures, representative of clashes between opposed camps, which are sometimes internalised within the same figure (as in the Renaissance). Of course, the ideology and world-view would be diametrically opposed to that of the great dramaturgies of European class civilisation. One could think of Brecht as of a Mystery playwright who was (as Blake said of Milton) of Satan's party, or as of Thersites writing *Troilus and Cressida:* 'die Dramaturgie wird durchforscht werden' [dramaturgy will be investigated], to coin a Brechtian slogan. The destiny of Man is Man (i.e. other people), and salvation will not come from above, but through political economics and ideology:

> Only force helps where force rules, and
> Only men help where there are men. (783)

2. Anthropology: The Political Economics of Fleshly (Slaughterhouse) Existence

The basic vertical configuration of the *Saint-Joan* universe allows for several lines of communicating things and ideas between its constituent classes: from up downward, from down upward (both can be established directly or by means of middlemen), and horizontally within each class. Those power-lines are, as discussed above, of two main kinds – *politico-economic* (material power) and *informational* (ideological power). This section discusses the politico-economic interactions.

There are further exchanges transacted in the play than just those of the stock exchange where cattle are turned into profit and speculation. This is in effect also a labour exchange, where the labour power and indeed the brute existence of labourers (workers and ranchers) are also bartered for. The axiological backbone of this play is Marx's labour theory of value (i.e. that all values created by production of goods flow exclusively from the action of labour on the natural raw materials – so that all other autonomous functions in the process of production, primarily that of the capitalists, could be dispensed with). In that light, it is not only Mauler who is a modern Faust, with Slift as his Mephistopheles: in a way, Humanity as a whole – represented by the workers – has also entered upon a losing pact with the devil of Capitalism. It is thereby animalised and reduced to the position of cattle slaughtered by the jungle predators and bloodthirsty devourers of raw meat. A second strain of imagery, fleshing out the skeletal topology of vertical and horizontal, is a turning of *cattle* and *men* into *flesh*, bloodied, bought and sold, renewed (through food: meat for the rich; soup for the poor), or lacking such renewal (in hunger). This second pattern will serve to discuss the political economics of raw existence, the 'reproduction of immediate life',[5] in *Saint Joan*.

The actual topography of this play is, of course, based on the opposition of *stock market* and *stockyards*. The stock market subsists on the exploitation of workers to the point of freezing and starvation; the stockyards subsist on the slaughtering of cattle. One basic relationship of the figures in this play (let us remember that in an earlier version Brecht had choruses of oxen, swine and workers in the finale!) can, with due prudence and confirmation by the subsequent discussion, be formulated as *Packers:Workers = Men:Cattle*. The power-wielders deal with the lower, powerless class in analogous ways: the lockout and subsequent actions of Packers against Workers cancel their 'human face,' it is a kind of bloodless, 'cold' slaughtering (which can, however, in a crunch turn to actual bloodshed, a 'hot' slaughtering, by the army and police – 'bashing [their] heads in,' (745)):

> *Mauler:* I want to tell you my true opinion
> 　　　　Of our business:
> 　　　　So naked, only buying and selling

> Each man coldly skinning the other man
> It can't go on; there are too many that
> Howl in misery, and there'll be more
> [That fall] into our bloody cellars .... (710–11)

The 'many', the deliberate ambiguity of '*Was da* in unsere blutigen Kellern fällt', equates workers and cattle. Complementarily, Joan's weighty passage from the finale identifies the disjunction between the upper and lower human spheres as an almost biological or geographical one, with not only different knowledge and value-measures, but even different languages, and concludes with the same reified pronoun ('Und *was* Menschengesicht trägt/Kennt sich nicht mehr'):

> For there is a gulf between those up high and those down below,
>   bigger than
> Between the Mount Himalaya and the sea
> And what goes on up high
> Is unheard of down below
> And unheard of up high what goes on below.
> And there are two languages high and low
> And two measures for measure
> And whatever wears a human face
> Can know itself no more. (780)

Brecht's primal vision of 'a jungle of cities' (not a lush but a cold jungle, a tangled thicket frozen by the winds of exploitation and alienation that blow across the Luciferic wastes of Lake Michigan), his constant preoccupation with a Social-Darwinist bestiary, expands in *Saint Joan* into a complex set of references to the bestial, carnivorous Slaughterhouse World. There, the lower class is butchered by the upper-class predators, whose internecine struggles are thereby reduced to a fight over the spoils. The function of the strike leaders and stockyard activists (the rabble-rousers) is, in fact, rousing the rest of the workers from a cattle-like stupor to an active, human if violent, intervention into their own crassly alienated destiny (see the quote at the end of the first section above, p. 140).

Especially striking in this 'world like unto a slaughterhouse' (672) is the *parallel between oxen and men*. 'Cattle' [*Vieh*] in the collective form is used in *Saint Joan* only in connection with buying and selling, marketing and pricing in the stock market [*Vieh-börse*] operations (678, 699, 700, 708, 726–27, etc.). But oxen are often almost persons, pathetically equipped with feelings although not with articulated speech. The play opens with Mauler's lament for the 'blond ox,' 'looking dumb to heaven,' being slaughtered, and with his resulting aversion for this 'bloody business.' Explicitly, Mauler associates the ox and himself: ' 'twas as if it [the blow] was meant for me' (667); 'such oxen's achings/Shut up no more within this breast' (668). Later, this sentimental identification is doubted by his competitors. They know his 'business soul,' buying 'anything and everything that even looks like a hog or an ox' (716), better:

> *Slift:* He saw the poor ox die and decided
> Instead of this poor ox
> He'd slaughter rich man Cridle. (686; see also 682)

But Mauler, strengthening the identification of oxen with innocence, gives them even precedence over the workers Joan pleads for:

> Oxen I pity, Man is bad.
> For your plan, men are not ready.
> First, before the world can change
> Man must change. (688)

– as well as against the packers:

> You brazen butchers, howl in your mothers' laps
> When the tormented creature ceases screaming!
> Go home and say, one amongst you
> Could hear no more the oxen screaming
> And chose your screaming over theirs!
> I want my money and peace for my conscience! (699)
> . . .
> *The Packers:* You filthy butcher! Here, take *our* flesh, cut your
> part out from it!
> *Mauler:* He who is an ox may not wonder that one gets
> hungry looking at him.

> So, Graham, now I demand to have your cans!
> You can stuff yourself into them.
> I'll teach you the meat business [*Fleischgeschäft*].
> (740)

Mauler is also at his most Shakespearean, one of the wholesale butcher-barons bearing 'the yoke of responsibility' (769), when speaking about oxen and *Fleisch*. The parallel to Shylock's pound of flesh can also be found in this Merchant of Chicago's earlier 'Would you have the nerve/To carve your meat from such misery?' (698). In keeping with Brecht's double-soul theory of Hamlet,[6] echoes of his vacillation can also be heard in a moment of lucidity:

> But this is a business in which it is
> To be or not to be, that is: am I
> The best man in my class or shall myself
> The dark road to the slaughterhouses take. (730)

Mauler and the packers are not alone in insisting upon such a metaphoric fusion. In the first chorus, the workers already do protest too much:

> Who do they take us for? Do they think
> We'd stand here like oxen, ready
> For anything?
> . . . .
>
> Why aren't you open already, you skinners. Here
> Stand your oxen, you butchers, ready! Open up!
> (*They knock.*)   (669–70)

Luckerniddle, who fell into the bacon boiler, is referred to by the young worker as 'Uncle Bacon all dressed up in his tin can' (690), and his bosses as 'butchers' by his wife (691) (the frequent use of this appellation is, in the Slaughterhouse World context, to be taken as something more than a dead metaphor). Mrs Luckerniddle, having gone hungry for two days, begins to 'devour' the hush-money food 'like a beast' (695); Brecht uses here, as often in the play, *fressen,* another word-play on brutalised human but also properly bestial eating: e.g. *gefrässig* (678) and *Fressgier* (706) for the workers, and *die Fresse,* 'the bloody snout' (701), for the speculators. It is made quite clear that Mrs Luckerniddle has been reduced to such a sub-human status by the political economics of the stockyards and the existential pressures of the Slaughterhouse World upon human as well as bovine flesh.

Therefore, when in the development of the play, by scenes V and VI, and then especially in the stock market dealings in IX and X, 'oxen' begins to be used alongside 'cattle' for business-deal purposes, the oxen have already been associated with suffering humanity in and of the stockyards and slaughterhouses. Obversely, those in power are not only butchers, skinners, knackers or grinders – i.e. fleshers; they are also – as Joan, the conscience of this play, realises – wild beasts:

Have you no respect at all for the human face? Then it could be that they [the poor down below] don't look at you as men either any more, but as wild beasts that simply must be slain in the interest of public order and safety! [....] Yes, don't look so dumb, one shouldn't treat men like oxen, but you're not men, get out and be quick about it .... (723)

It is for this specific reason of inhumanity and bestiality that Joan proceeds to drive the money-changers from the Temple (see for another biblical association in connection with oxen the reference to 'muzzling the kine that tread the corn', 707–8). Further, in her parable of God calling on Adam in the Garden of Eden, the hind is an Edenic cow, from a time when animals had not differentiated into domestic and wild (this is even clearer in the German term *Hirschkuh*, literally 'hart-cow'): 'Adam ... has his hands so to say up to the elbows in a hind again, and so he hears the voice of God full blooded ...' (728). The parable applies not only to Mauler's sensibility about oxen but also to Joan, who will die, as well as to the workers whose alienation from humanity will continue and grow as a result of Mauler's actions. Finally, when Joan comes to the cattle-market with the poor, she chides the Packers for 'making meat more and more expensive' and recounts an *exemplum* about Judgement Day:

...how will you look then, when our Lord and Saviour lines you up and asks with his great eyes: Where are my oxen now? What have you done with them? Did you make them available to the public at accessible prices? ... then the oxen behind you will scream in all the barns where you've hidden them so that their prices should rise into the wild blue yonder, and with their screaming they will bear witness against you before the Almighty Lord. (703–4)

Here it is Christ's mute question and great eyes that identify him as the Lord of the Oxen, who can therefore appeal to him 'blond and huge an looking dumb to Heaven' (667; such an identification is well prepared by the traditional association of Christ with meekness, suffering, the ox present at his birth, etc.).

Slaughtered, skinned and gutted, oxen are transformed into *flesh (meat) and blood.* This, of course, applies to all cattle – as can be seen from the graphic account of new 'self-service' swine-slaughtering (681). I have already commented on how much of the force of the constant punning on 'flesh' and 'meat' – which not only identifies dead cattle with living humans, but can bring in many other allusions, from Shylock to sex – is blunted in English. None the less, the constant references to it (there are about fifty in *Saint Joan*), together with the perpetual mention of slaughtering, butchers, the bloodiness of business in general (and of Mauler in particular, 670, 678, 685, 686), analogous to bloody warfare (714, 765–67), establish a powerful, dense atmosphere reeking of the stockpens and slaughterhouses. The play's events are causally connected to and coterminous with a constipated meat-market (*Fleischmarkt*, 667, 770); the strike leaders call the packers 'meat-people' (*Fleischleute,* 741); the *Fleischgeschäft* is *meat* business in relation to packers (the *Fleischring*) who sell the canned meat and in relation to the cattle within the meat cans (668, 697, 719, etc.), but in relation to the workers who cook the 'filthy soiled meat' in their 'shit-holes and slop-kitchens' (670) yet cannot buy it because of low purchasing power (705), it is a *flesh* business, cannibalistic in implication:

Of course, if everyone has to hack up his neighbour with an ax just to have a piece of ham on his bread ... how could then any sense for higher things not choke within the human breast?! (705)

It is from the workers as producers, consumers, tenants (see

676), and so on, that Mauler, the meat and flesh king (*Fleischkönig* (670, 671, 719); and see also the Shylock references above), draws the stuff for his black transmutation: 'From ruined houses he draws rent, from rotten/Meat gold.' (680). He himself has the 'weakness' of boggling at the slaughter but profiting from its results, graphically materialised in his consuming the raw meat, the bloody steak (711) which immediately and magically restores him to his senses. This striking stage metaphor reposes to a significant degree on the notion of an unholy communion with the flesh of the sacrificial ox that he has recognised as not only man-like in its suffering but higher than man in its innocence. Its evil transubstantiation enables Mauler to grow into an Atlas, who bears on his shoulders a whole world of *Fleisch* (713). This personification is then cosmographically expanded – using Voltaire's proportion from *Micromégas* – to a stockyard porter of the larger planet and deity of Saturn, and the buyer of all the cattle from the still larger star of Sirius (716). Finally, at the end of the play, the *Fleisch* is cut down, both by burning one-third of all cattle (meat) and by locking out one-third of the workers (flesh) whose wages are also lowered by a third (771). The result is that the 'dark time of a bloody confusion' is replaced by 'law and order' (771–2), which means a higher price for meat (776). The harmony of the meat market, the proportions of fleshly and bloody power and existential exploitation which form the body politic of this microcosm, is re-established:

> Now take a breath! The market now gets well!
> The bottom point has once more lost its spell!
> ... And once again the world whirls in the right course.
> (*Organ music.*) (772)

3. Ideology: Communications, Informational Exchange

Thus, the Marxist political economics undoubtedly present in *Saint Joan* (the labour theory of value, and the crisis theory) happens in the flesh and blood of the workers and packers, Mauler and Joan. Political economics determining the existential destiny of all strata of society represent here a first,

basic exchange-system or code. But there is a second code or
system of interaction and exchange too, composed of the
informations passed or suppressed through various communicational networks.

The informational interaction works on three lines.[7] The
first is an extremely well-developed and manipulated net-
work of communications *within the upper class*. Mauler is, if
not at its fountainhead (which is in 'New York', literally behind
the scenes), at least at its first cataract or dam (see Joan's dam
parable, 704); in the microcosm of the play he controls the
flow of crucial information. Because he receives it just a short
time before anybody else, he can bend the events. He
witholds the economic information from New York
from other packers while acting through Slift, but in
the climactic fourth message, Mauler communicates it to
them as his trump-card for reorganising the meat trade into a
vertical cartel. *A fortiori*, all such information is withheld
from the workers and the general public, who are misin-
formed through the press. This first line of informational
interchange is one of *privileged information*, that classic
weapon of all ruling groups. By means of it, Mauler
manipulates the stock exchange (which is itself a system of
financial information, among other things). As discussed in
the first section, this also shapes the rhythm of *Saint Joan*.

The second line is a truthful, but extremely precarious,
informational system *within the working class*. (There is no
hint of a system which would link the 'Chicago' workers
with the 'Missouri' ranchers or similar groups.) It is a 'net'
(742, 759) whose meshes are improvised and therefore liable
to slippage. Joan becomes such a crucial mesh which gives
way: the information does not circulate in a closed system, its
truth seeps out and is lost. With it, this struggle in the cause
of social justice has also been lost. Parabolically, this
functional failure and not the final scene is Joan's death.

As different from these two *horizontal* lines of communication within the opposed spheres and classes of the stock
market and the stockyards, the third and dramaturgically
central line of information flows vertically, *between the
capitalists and the working class*. Its medium is all the
middlemen in the play – the economic middlemen who
appear very briefly in scenes, V, IXf, and in the finale being

the least important among them. The important bearers of the communicational vertical are the Black Straw Hats, Joan (who splits off from them), and Mauler with his command of the press and his personal descent into the depths. The Black Straw Hats are the professional middlemen who deal in lifting up the souls of the workers, and at the same time in counteracting any this-worldly (up)rising of the nethermost class, which would flatten the whole vertical structure. By Brecht's definition, they therefore function from above downward. As Mauler finds out, their pervasive metaphor of helping the sinking people from drowning in the morass or sea of troubles is predicated on their being the indispensable straw to be clutched at; no drowning, no need for straws – that is the basic vested interest and blind spot of clerical charity-mongering or political reformism:

> ...Man is
> For you what helps you, so too for me
> Man was only what was prey. But even
> If man meant only that: who is helped
> 'Twould make no difference. Then you'd need drowning men.
> For then your business would be
> To be straws. So goes everything
> In the great circulation of commodities and planets. (764)

Superadded to the static vertical of up and down there is in *Saint Joan* a dynamic vertical of upward and downward which indicates these 'mediating' relationships (see the discussion in the first section), as in this early speech of the Black Straw Hats' Lieutenant Dark:

> But how do you expect to move upward, or what with your lack of understanding you call 'upward'? Through brute force? As if force had ever turned out anything else than destruction. You think if you rear up on your hind legs, then there will be Paradise on Earth. But I tell you: that way one makes no Paradise, that way one makes chaos. (675)

Other quite effective forms of communication between the capitalists and the workers are the falling wages with which the play begins and ends (669, 771), the 'rising misery' balancing the 'rising profits' (748–9), and the 'putting-down' of the general strike (772) by the military. Further, the battle between the capitalists on the stock market is fought by means of the ups and downs of the foreign tariffs and various prices. Finally, personal destinies can also be described in those terms: Luckerniddle 'falls into the bacon boiler' (689); 'Lennox has fallen' (literally, 'has been felled,' (682)); 'careless questioners' such as Joan, asking uncomfortable questions about earthly affairs, 'From step to step/Groping downwards to the answer never given/ ... vanish into filth!' (679).

At the end of the play, the Black Straw Hats find that the 'up' in whose service they operate means Mauler rather than God. They are thus identified as bearers of a specific, long-range informational or ideological system, communicating values predicated upon the existence of an upper and lower class in the scheme of things. Mauler's henchmen in the press are, complementarily, bearers of a specific, short-range informational system, communicating primarily bits (bytes) of 'hard' news which turn out to be 'soft', non-factual (such as the news of the factories' opening, spread to break the strike). Through all of these helpers, Mauler operates in the same downward direction as the Black Straw Hats, only starting from a greater height and descending to a deeper humbling in, and understanding of, the depths. He and Joan are equal masters at communicating a public image, and the only non-lower figures who have an ear for and a certain insight into the basic fact about the lower spheres: their undeniable and persistent existence. Mauler can therefore take up Joan's idea of them as not only labour-power but also purchasing-power. Thus he combines a long-range or basic insight with short-range improvisations, old alienations with new. It is therefore logical – or better, congruent – that he can incorporate the Black Straw Hats into the overall scheme of his vertical and downward cartel as natural allies (see Table 5.3).

The only attempts at communication and pressure going from below upward come from Joan and the strike leaders (Communists). The ideological failure of the former and the pragmatic failure of the latter are complementary; the reasons for that complementarity are not explained in the universe of *Saint Joan*, and would have to be inferred from the larger context of Brecht's opus. Beside the general Leninist doctrine

Table 5.3: *Directions of Interaction*

Spheres

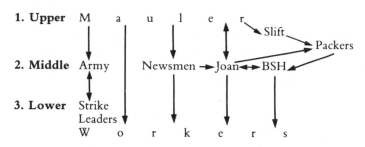

1. **Upper** M   a   u   l   e   r

2. **Middle** Army   Newsmen →Joan↔BSH

Slift

Packers

3. **Lower** Strike
Leaders
W   o   r   k   e   r   s

of the allies necessary for a working-class revolution, one
might speculate that the implications in Brecht's mind were
very similar to those that, at the same time, led Gramsci to
formulate the concept of a new 'historical coalition' and a
new type of class hegemony.[8] Joan might be characterologi-
cally a naive religious girl from the provinces who has just
entered the large city (there are no clear indications as to that
in *Saint Joan*, but the genesis of the play seems to point that
way). However her behaviour and sociological function
between the blocks of capitalists and workers are those of a
petty-bourgeois intellectual. She is an intellectual because her
basic motive – like that of Brecht's prototypic intellectual
Galileo of whom she is a first sketch – is 'I want to know' and
'I must know it,' a refrain she repeats half a dozen times (first
in scene IId). Prefiguring Galileo, she formulates, or at least
implies, in the course of the play a series of cognitions or
discoveries. But she is also a petty-bourgeois idealist, failing
at the crucial moment when it was necessary to abandon the
mediating role and throw her lot totally in with the cold,
starving and lonely lower class. (In that respect, she might be
thought of as a sympathetically-drawn obverse of Mayakovsky's Menshevik or Reconciler in *Mystery Buffo*.) Therefore, her final cognitions about leaving a good world, about
the bestial system which must and can be destroyed by the
same means it is maintained (i.e. by men using force) are, for
Brecht, as valid as Galileo's final self-accusation. But those of
Joan's actions and utterances that retain the images of the
intellectual as pivot and mediator should be taken more as
characterising her debilitating ideology than as the upshot of

the play's logic. One would mention here such masterly and quotable passages as Joan's vision of the columns marching through Chicago (734), with clear echoes of the 'Chicago Commune' chapter from Jack London's *The Iron Heel*. This vision, as evidenced in the whole metaphysical imagery, the final confession ('What happens then, I don't know'), and the incomprehending reaction of the workers, is a direct prelude to her failure in the climactic scene IX. But to my mind the clearest example is the famous 'seesaw parable' (749). Though it correctly identifies the capitalist system as the unity of an opposed 'up' and 'down', and can therefore be taken as a step in Joan's development, it still postulates an unmoving fulcrum – which is homologous with her own vantage-point in the social middle. A seesaw is defined by the *balance* between *opposing ends*. The vision of the opposing ends is thus a recognition of indestructible class contradictions: '... those who are up/Only stay up because these stay down/And only as long as these stay down.' But it is at the same time the recognition of a fixed balance between mutually dependent ends; and the whole image is itself a static balance between recognition of facts and value-judgement.[9] As Marx remarked, the recognition of class struggles is not an invention of his, but of a clear and conscious bourgeois historiosophy; one can very well recognise them and still draw value-judgements diametrically or significantly opposed to those of the working-class movement. This is precisely what Joan does immediately after her seesaw speech: 'Yes, it seems almost like a play to me, therefore/Unworthy, if I stay here' (751). A seesaw is, after all, a plaything, a children's game, and Joan's position here that of a spectator, exactly as a few moments earlier:

Joan: ... I am for your cause, heart and soul.
The Second Strike Leader: Our cause? Well now, isn't that your cause? (742–3)

Thus, Joan found out that the Black Straw Hats' system of communications works only one way; and as a religious genius she tried to become her own autonomous ideological middleman with a two-way system (just as the historical Joan of Arc had her own communications both with God and with the French people). Yet she never adopts the truly radical, revolutionary perspective of another, horizontal system of interactions which would abolish classes, and render unnecessary any communication between upper and lower humanity – whether one-way or two-way. Therefore she functions, Mauler's Mephisto recognises this, as an 'ethical' reformist and can finally be used by an ideologically and organisationally updated, but structurally unchanged, vertical slaughterhouse system:

> *Slift:* That's our Joan. She's just in the nick of time. We want to bring her out in a big way, for through her humanitarian effects upon the slaughterhouses, her intercession for the poor, even through her speeches against us she's helped us to get through some trying weeks. She's to be our own Saint Joan of the Slaughterhouses. We want to set her up as a saint and spare her no respect. On the contrary, just that she's seen with us should prove that humanity holds a very high place in our esteem. (778)

It should be mentioned that there is a third code or exchange-system conspicuous by its absence in *Saint Joan*, that of erotics. This absence is by itself a significant given of the play. The sparse hints, such as Slift's little speech about denying that Mauler slept with Joan (726–7), merely point out how totally the erotics are overwhelmed by economics, by the dire necessities of personal and class survival. Emblematic of that dehumanisation, which turns flesh into meat and food, is the case of the Luckerniddles. There is no possibility of writing a play about erotics as long as survival-economics and destruction (including brainwashing, destruction of true information) loom so large in the present world, Brecht concluded in the mid-1920s.[10] Much later, he tried to integrate erotics and existential politics: in *The Good Woman of Setzuan* he dodged around such a synthesis a bit, and only in *The Caucasian Chalk Circle* did he discreetly succeed. To may mind, the almost successful fusion of erotics and existential politics is another reason for thinking of *The Caucasian Chalk Circle* as Brecht's most significant play (see for some other reasons, the chapter 6). But in *Saint Joan*, he deals basically with the *mutual relationships of the politico-economic and informational exchanges* or interaction systems between the *dramatis personae.*

These two systems or codes, so powerfully present in the play, relate to each other as basis and superstructure. However, though jobs, work, hunger and meat prices, are clearly shown as basic, Brecht manipulates this well-worn and slippery metaphor much better than most Marxists. True, the information (and misinformation) is ideology. Yet ideology is extremely important; in fact, it turns out to be crucial for the outcome of the politico-economic interactions. Mauler's first reaction, when found by the packers in the Black Straw Hats' mission and asked to save the market, is to ask how many 'such Bible shops' are around (scene X). He knows that the stock market has crashed and that troops had to be called in, yet his first order of business is not police or credits but consolidating the 'Bible shops' in a proper and efficient spirit. This exemplifies Brecht's profound under-standing of the relation between ideology and economics, so much more sophisticated and in advance of his age than has been generally realised. In fact, on the strength of this play alone, it becomes clear that he was one of the great pioneers of the theory of communications and its socio-political function. Unfortunately, his theory is for the most part not explicit but implicit in his plays, his interest in radio and film, and his other writings.

4. The Seesaw Structure: Time-Horizons and Elective Affinities

Thus, through this whole play, there runs a counterpoint between the 'existential' (or politico-economic) and the 'image-building' (or ideological) domain or theme: how does one programme the consciousness of people, especially the working classes, so that they will accept Mauler? Right at the beginning there is again an exemplary situation when the newsboys cry: 'Chicago Tribune, noon edition! Meat-king and philanthropist Pierpont Mauler attends the opening of the P. Mauler hospitals, world's largest and most expensive!' Yet oh the stage one sees that he is accompanied by two private detectives to keep him from being 'knocked off' (scene IIb) – a classic estrangement-effect arising from the clash of the infrastructure and the superstructure. This kind of counterpoint of reality and image grows with the play and culminates in the canonisation of Joan, which is a *locus classicus* of image-building. It would deserve extensive study as such, in comparison with the finales of Schiller's *The Maiden of Orleans* and Goethe's *Faust*, which Brecht chose to invert satirically just because they also deal in image-building.

Homologous to this thematic counterpoint are the relationships on two deeper structural levels of *Saint Joan*. The first is the complementary use of politico-economic and salvational *time-horizons*. These time indications are sometimes not so much complementary as simply alternative, since Brecht uses them with equal nonchalance to linear causality or logic as Shakespeare uses his anachronisms (e.g. it is impossible to establish a precise chronology of the events in *Saint Joan*). The second is the main dramaturgic peculiarity of this play, the Mauler–Joan relation, including the relation between Mauler's 'two souls.'

Politico-economic time is quantitative and equivalent to money: it deals with wages, prices, payments and business deals. It is, of course, present in its pure form in the deals on the stock market, especially in scenes V, VI and IX. It includes precise clock time tied to contractual deadlines, from Mauler's two minutes to decide about buying all the cattle in Illinois (716), through the five days' grace to Cridle (683), to the 40 months' rent the packers offer the Black Straw Hats (724) where the equivalence of time and money is even semantic. It culminates in Graham's quasi-Homeric account of the stock market crash (765–7), and – in a sudden widening of the play's horizons – in the various loudspeaker news flashes which go from 'The Bank of England closes down for the first time in 300 years' to 'The Five-Year Plan in four years!' (783), and which should indicate the collapse of this whole time-horizon. The workers, directly dependent on the stock market, are also under the sway of this time-horizon which works in meat and flesh; their time-horizon is determined by wages and working time:

At least we demand
The old wage, which is anyway too little, at least
The ten-hour day and at least . . . . (670)

This dependence is paradigmatically shown in the *exemplum* of Mrs Luckerniddle, who drops enquiries about her husband – in effect sells them – for twenty lunches: 'I have, you know, not eaten for two days' (694). The zero-level of human existence, including human time-horizons, is marked in *Saint Joan* by the locked-out workers' cold and hunger, a cluster mentioned with the same obsessive frequency as the oxen–meat–blood image cluster. As Joan concludes, surely Mrs Luckerniddle would have

> ... asked about him who gave her support
> For yet some time, as is proper
> But the price was too high that amounted to twenty meals. (696)

At the other end of the spectrum of societal time,[11] the Black Straw Hats initially pretend to be exempt from politico-economic time, to be the bearers of a qualitative, *salvational* time-horizon. They work for practically no money, they preach that earthly, politico-economic uprising and wages are to be forsaken for the more sublime vertical of Heaven and, to combat hunger and cold, they distribute some warm, but fatless, soup. Soup is a characteristic or trademark of theirs and of their relation to the workers: the Black Straw Hats dole it out; the workers drink it. The exchanges should ideally stand at a saved soul for a soup bowl. (Conversely, Mauler eats steak; Joan as middleman eats some not identified leftover food of Mauler's, and later, with the workers, 'snow,' i.e. nothing.) But soup, as well as rent, soon runs out without the packers' money, and Paulus Snyder, the successful clerical *apparatchik*,[12] has to accept their politico-economic horizon, reducing the salvational pretence of the Black Straw Hats to a conscious 'opium of the people' (scene VII). Joan, on the other hand, parts company with them because she is the other half of this famous but often truncated definition of Marx's: 'the heart of a heartless world.'[13] Beginning with a general and abstract though already exceedingly powerful sketch of the time correlative to the Slaughterhouse World:

> In a dark time of bloody confusion
> Ordered disorder
> Planned arbitrariness
> Dehumanised humanity
> ...
> We want again to introduce   God. (671–2)

– she insists throughout the play on the necessity of a
salvation, of a new creation. Her references to the seven days
of snowfall (722) and her Martin Luther King-like dream of a
protest march through Chicago, 'Showing our misery's
whole extent in public places/Calling upon whatever looks
like Man', which she dreamed, significantly, 'Seven days
ago' (734), are pertinent examples. Such a new creation is
qualitative and equivalent to human lives. It would also be a
Judgement Day upon the old one, as is clearly shown by the
parable discussed earlier about the abuse of the oxen revealed
on Judgement Day (703–4). But Joan comes to recognise that
salvation must work through jobs, wages and prices, and
tries to persuade the packers and then public opinion to adopt
her views. Since the whole system is 'Exploitation and
disorder, bestial and so/Incomprehensible' (781), and since
she fears a world of radical change, 'no longer familiar' (754),
she does not succeed in fusing the salvational and politico-
economic time-horizons. Nobody does in this black play.
But Pierpont Mauler succeeds in yoking them together
forcibly.

In fact, Mauler's 'two souls' can be defined not only as
tending spatially up and down, or thematically to sentiment
and business, but also temporally to salvation and profit: 'I
want my money and peace for my conscience!' (699). He is a
master at manipulating the two time-horizons against each
other. The play begins with his wish to end seven (biblical)
years of servitude to political economics:

Ever since I went into this business, therefore seven
Years I've avoided it [visiting the slaughterhouse], Cridle I can
No longer: e'en today I'll give it up, this bloody business.
You take it, I'll give you my share real cheap.
. . .

So fast
Must now this Lennox fall, for I'm myself
Quite intent on becoming a good man. (668)

But his goodness is purely self-seeking, and he is very willing
to use political economics without allowing for, say, the
change from 'good times' to 'bad times' when his contracts
are questioned (682). His spiritual soul knows that the
salvation of one human being is more important than ten
million dollars (762), and that 'Seven days I held/This city of

Chicago by the throat' (763); yet his business soul tries to use
money, the congealed form of politico-economic time, for a
fake salvation:

So go and tell them that money is coming, it will be there on
Saturday night. Mauler is getting it. Even now he goes to the cattle
market to get it. (729)

Though Joan sees through him in this particular instance (the
fake Sabbath will be achieved at the expense of the
locked-out workers in the snow), at the end Mauler succeeds
in keeping both souls and both time-horizons – the lofty,
salvational one serving the base, politico-economic one by
staging a false salvation, a blasphemous canonisation. Mauler
refurbishes the falling building of capitalism, an image he
develops in two remarkable speeches. The first, 'On the
Necessity of Capitalism and Religion' (scene VIII), scolds Joan
for denying money, the paramount means for holding
together a stable societal edifice in 'the disfavour of the
planet':

For otherwise everything would have to be completely torn
    down
And the plans changed from the ground up, according to a quite
    different
Unheard of, new evaluation of man, which you don't want
Nor do we, for this would happen without us and without God.
    (731)

At his nadir, after the crash, Mauler retracts:

And about that thing made of sweat and money
That we've built up in these cities:
It's already as if one
Made a building, the biggest in the world, and
Most expensive and practical, but
By oversight and because 'twas cheap used
Dog shit for material, so that staying
There would yet be difficult and in the end his fame
Just that he'd made the biggest stink in the world. (757)

But that depression does not last, and in Mauler's triumphant
finale the politico-economic building and time-horizons are
reaffirmed, having bent to their purposes Joan's initial,
powerful but insufficiently precise need for salvation:

In a dark time of bloody confustion
Dehumanised humanity
...we want
To make possible the order-promoting work of you Black Straw
  Hats
Through generous outlays of money. (771–2)

Money, which was earlier identified with shit, has now transmuted Joan's concern with God into the Black Straw Hats' concern with keeping the shitty vertical building in 'order'. A Swiftian, scatological image is fittingly applied to an axiologically empty world.

Finally, the anthropological as well as cosmological centerpiece of *Saint Joan* is the tension between high and low incarnated in Mauler, in Joan, and in their mutual relationships as their personal strivings or 'souls'. Even without Brecht's explicit reference to 'the Joan–Mauler-type,'[14] it is clear there are deep *elective affinities* between the 'double-souled' industry captain and the salvationist girl. They are the only figures who partake of all levels of the play. Their wanderings through its topography are almost symmetrical and inverse: Mauler's curve of power descends to its lowest point in scenes IX and X and ascends again to its zenith at the end (if we forget the loudspeaker reports); Joan has – as the newsmen tell her at her high point in scene IX – 'a great success, but now the affair is over' (754). In scene IX Mauler falls too, but his insights and the backing of 'New York' permit him to rise again. Joan's insights come too late, and she has no power base; an alliance with the strike leaders might have achieved it, if they themselves had a better system of communications as well as a better grasp of the seductive power and necessity of salvational propaganda, and the workers a consciousness resembling theirs. But such conditions do not obtain in this microcosm. The precarious state of the workers' 'net' of communications, of their class consciousness, and of Joan's late maturing are all of a piece: they are dramaturgic correlatives of Brecht's basic diagnosis for Germany and the revolutionary movement of that time. True, as always, his plays are open-ended and permit the spectator to imagine other outcomes should a sufficient number of conditions be changed: a diametrically opposed outcome will be explored in Brecht's following play,

The Mother. My point is that the conditions to be changed would include the entire atmosphere of *Saint Joan*. That is why tinkering with Mrs Luckerniddle to make her into a Communist Party adherent in later versions is not too convincing. Thus, Joan's death can counterbalance Mauler's victory only outside the play: by leading to an increment of understanding in the spectators, and making them – with the help of changing economic and political conditions revealed at the end of the play by the loudspeakers – into Joan's continuators and improvers. As usual, the culmination of a Brechtian play lies outside, not inside it.

Looking backward at Joan and Mauler from Shen Te and Shui Ta as well as *a contrario* from Grusha and Azdak, it becomes clear that they are in some crucial ways two halves of a hermaphroditic whole, who might be called the superior, idealistic or farsighted bourgeois man of action (almost a Nietzschean superman). Mauler despises the run-of-the-mill capitalists possibly more than Joan does, and is delighted when she expels them from the 'Temple'. When Joan finally tries to do something for the workers against Mauler, she cannot accomplish it. Mauler readily takes over her initial idealistic diagnosis of 'the dark world of dehumanised humanity' and finally uses her even in her death. Indeed, his double nature or 'two souls' are by a whole system of correspondences (primarily, their upward and downward strivings) connected to his relationship with Joan, who is, as it were, his externalised sentimental soul – *Mauler: Joan = Meat-King:Oxen Pitier*. Just as Mauler is one rung above an orthodox meat-king and has an almost god-like function for this world, so Joan is not the pitier of oxen but of workers (the 'next rung' category in the vertical topology of suffering and powerlessness in *Saint Joan*).[15] Further, both the upward and the downward striving are perverted in comparison with the norm of a fully humanised union of reason and emotion. Mauler's reason is used only as a 'scheming brain' (668) in politico-economic warfare, Joan's develops too late; Mauler's muddled, sentimentalised emotions serve his schemes, Joan's subjugate and fragment her understanding. In certain subtle, but strong ways, the 'two souls' and the Mauler–Joan relationship correspond to the basic class and topological dichotomy of this world, within a time-hallowed 'world's body' metaphor.

It follows that Mauler is a significant creation only in so far as he is not a conscious hypocrite[16] but, intermittently, a sincerely sentimental philanthropist (philobovist?) who becomes a complete cynic only when (in scene X) he has recognised that 'true penitence' cannot replace money. Brecht's point here is that sentimental philanthropy and religiousness are especially pernicious when sincere – in Joan as well as in Mauler.

Some new light might also be shed by such an approach on the vexed problem of empathy. The packers are totally estranged. In different ways, but with equal force, so are the workers: they are the nearest equivalent to a valid chorus that one can find on the modern stage. Obviously, one does not as readily empathise with an Aeschylean chorus as with individuals. However, the situation is much more complicated for Mauler and Joan. For Mauler, I hold a detailed dramaturgic analysis would prove that the play demands one should oscillate all the time (often within his single speeches[17]) between empathy and distance, in order to achieve a total distance toward him at the end. The empathy is never full (for his 'lofty' soul is also suspect); it should always remain in the service of the distanciation. At the play's end, it should be possible for the spectator to feel he has seen through Mauler, and can now hold him at arm's length.

Joan, I believe, has to be empathised with.[18] The spectator – who will as a rule be neither a big businessman nor a proletarian industrial worker – is supposed to sympathise with her and go through the learning process with her. Her final stifling will then drive home the lesson, in her own words and through her supreme cognitions, just as in the case of Galileo. It follows that the empathy vs. estrangement situation in this play is far more subtle than one would expect from reading some Brechtological glosses (including some of Brecht's earlier exaggerations). Brecht uses both empathy and estrangement in very subtle and effective dosages, differing from figure to figure and scene to scene. Perhaps what Brecht, in the heat of battle, sometimes said elliptically we should today translate approximately as follows: 'I don't want only empathy, I don't want uncritical empathy; but for some stage figures I want total distanciation, for some a balancing between empathy and distance, and for some –

those I agree with, such as Kattrin, or Grusha, or Shen Te, or Joan – I want as nearly an empathy as doesn't matter.' The play is written so that the spectator may learn from it: since Joan is his privileged representative inside the play, the most economical and pleasant way to do so is to empathise with her. That does not mean, as I have argued earlier, swallowing uncritically all she does and says, but it does mean following her general tragic curve of development; if she has led the spectator into some foolish identifications, she is going to tell him so by the end.

All such counterpoints are implicit in the basic dualistic yet subtly mediated vision of *Saint Joan*. The arrested moment of equipoise, the Limbo between Heaven and Hell, the middle and yet decisive social classes that will determine the outcome of the huge social battle, the oscillating fortunes, the precarious view from atop the barricades – all these are variants of the same basic paradigm. Finally, this play too is a seesaw between a failing society and another still unable to be born. Like Joan, Brecht, in a homologous social and ideological position, fashioned a seesaw parable. Unlike Joan, he saw from the beginning that the world stage and the stage world have to be radically altered. To present such a grim and yet vital many-layered structure, an axiologically empty but sensually supreme present (i.e. anti-utopian) world demanded an almost total refashioning of the traditional dramaturgic cosmology and anthropology. *Saint Joan of the Slaughterhouses* can (together with but more neglected than *Man Is Man* and *Mahagonny*) stand as an impressive stage in such a refashioning, in some ways as vital in its very imperfections as any other play of our century. In it, Brecht shows how the stage can talk in iambics and yet about political economics which are salvation or damnation. While working on what was eventually to become *Saint Joan*, he is quoted as remarking, in a crucial insight: 'If one sees that our present-day world does not fit into drama, then drama simply does not fit into the world.'[19] In this play, the world is again shown on the stage, so that the stage can again be analogous to and fit into the world. *Welttheater* and *Theater in der Welt*, it reposes on a basis that leaves us a final image – that of the (still quite unsolved) problem and yet absolute necessity of fitting the dispossessed producers of all the values into the world stage:

Da bleiben, wie immer so auch heut
Der steinige Boden und die armen Leut. (755)

[Today, as always, there remain
The poor people and the stony plain.]

Notes

1 Both 'stockyards' and 'slaughterhouses' are valid translations of different aspects of 'Schlachthöfe', but for my purposes I prefer the latter. This chapter was written as the result of an experimental drama project at McGill University, culminating in a production of *Saint Joan of the Slaughterhouses* in March 1973; cf. the performance programme *Saint Joan of the Slaughterhouses*, ed. D. Suvin, and a collection of the collaborators' articles and discussions in *A Production Notebook to 'Saint Joan of the Slaughterhouses'*, ed. M. Bristol and D. Suvin (both Montreal: McGill University, 1973). I have learned very much from my students who were also the cast of the performance, and from my colleague Michael Bristol, the director.

I have avoided notes except where absolutely necessary, but I am very conscious how much I owe to the secondary literature on the play up to 1973, which I believe I read in its totality in the languages I know. I should like to mention my debt to the general approaches to Brecht by Roland Barthes, Ernst Bloch, Bernard Dort, Reinhold Grimm, Hans Mayer and John Willett, and specifically on this play to the pioneering approaches of Ernst Schumacher, Käthe Rülicke-Weiler, Hans Egon Holthusen, Giorgio Strehler (interview in *Cahiers Théâtre Louvain* No. 12/13 [1971]), and Manfred Wekwerth and the Berliner Ensemble staff (for notes assembled in *Heilige Johanna – Schauspielermaterial,* dittoes); all these works except for the last two can be found in Professor Grimm's bibliography, *Bertolt Brecht* (Stuttgart, 1971). I have also used with great profit Gisela E. Bahr's *Die heilige Johanna der Schlachthöfe – Bühnenfassung, Fragmente, Varianten* (Frankfurt, 1971), and Patty Lee Parmalee's *Brecht's America* (Columbus OH, 1981).

2 Since the translation by Frank Jones, *Saint Joan of the Stockyards* (Bloomington IN, 1971) was usable neither for the stage nor for philological purposes, a new translation of Brecht's play was made at McGill University by Richard H. Howe. It was then revised for the stage by some cast members and myself, and later re-edited by Mr Howe. I am using this translation, but the responsibility for the final formulations is mine. As the translation is not published, the numbers in parentheses refer to the pages of Bertolt Brecht, *Gesammelte Werke, II* (Frankfurt, 1973).

3 See the insightful essay of Käthe Rülicke, 'Die heilige Johanna der Schlachthöfe: Notizen zum Bau der Fabel', *Sinn und Form*, 11 (1959), 429–44; also Peter Demetz, 'Vorwort', in *Die heilige Johanna* (München-Wien, 1964) pp. 25–6; and Bernard F. Dukore, *Drama and Revolution* (New York, 1971), pp. 308–11.

4 Bernard Dort, *Lecture de Brecht* (Paris, 1967), p. 104 (transl. D.S.).

5 Friedrich Engels, *The Origin of the Family, Private Property and the State*, transl. in Karl Marx–Frederick Engels, *Selected Works* (London, 1968), p. 455.

6 Cf. 'Kleines Organon für das Theater', *GW* XVI:696; English transl. in *Brecht on Theatre*, ed. John Willett (London, 1965), p. 202.

7 The crucial informations are communicated by way of letters. Of the letters from New York to Mauler we learn only at the moment of their delivery. Of the letters from strike headquarters to a key group of strikers we learn at the moment when they are sent out. The supposedly crucial one never arrives because of Joan's defection in face of hunger, cold and violence. This is a form at least as old as *Romeo and Juliet* and, of course, Schiller (Brecht's source), and Brecht uses it sometimes heretically and sometimes nonchalantly – he is interested more in the signified than in the signifier. (However, in a contemporary performance, the director would do well to use if not Telsat, then at least a post-Graham Bell form of means of communication.)

8 See Gramsci's prison notebooks, especially those published as *Il Materialismo storico e la filosofia di Benedetto Croce* (Torino, 1948), and *Note sul Machiavelli, sulla politica e sullo Stato moderno* (Torino, 1949), with explicit discussion of the relations between structure and superstructure. This was, of course, unknown to Brecht at the time, but he knew well some similar heresies within socialism, e.g. Korsch's. At any rate, if Joan lacks determination, the Communists in *Saint Joan* lack her superb understanding of the salvational character of political economy.

9 A significant comparison could be made between Joan, arrested in a stasis between two incompatible value-systems (between Imperialism and Leninism), and the Fool in *King Lear* (between 'degree' patriarchy and commercial Individualism). They both see the world as a see-saw: 'Whichever end of the see-saw anyone chooses, the Fool's job is to be counterweight' (Danby, see Bibliography to chapter 1, p. 103); Joan is more ambitious – she wants to be pivot.

10 See his 'Dialog zu Bert Brechts *Mann ist Mann*', *GW* XVII: 978–80, which seems to me an explicative document of the first order.

11 Cf. e.g., Georges Gurvitch, *The Spectrum of Social Time*, (Dordrecht, 1964).

12 I suspect that the opposition between the *apparatchik* named Paul and a religious genius with salvational pretensions goes back to Shaw's prefatory disquisitions on Christianity to *Major Barbara* and *Androcles and the Lion.*

13 I owe this most appropriate association to a discussion with Raymond Williams, reproduced in *A Production Notebook to 'St Joan...'*, pp. 184–98.

14 *GW* XVII: 1018.

15 See also the passage referred to in note 4, above.

16 Ernst Schumacher, *Die dramatischen Versuche Bertolt Brechts 1918–1933* (Berlin, 1955), pp. 443–74, seems in his pioneering discussion of the play to see Mauler as a conscious hypocrite; so clearly does I.M. Fradkin, *Bertol't Brekht* (Moskva, 1965), p. 102; and reports from the Dresden première indicate the director there did so too (cf. the bibliography in Bahr (ed.), *op. city.*, pp. 236–7). On the other side one could mention Adorno – usually unreliable when Brecht is discussed – who seems also to identify Mauler simply with a real-life *raffgierig* [rapacious] capitalist in his highly tendentious and simplified mention of this play, *Noten zur Literatur*, III (Frankfurt, 1965), pp. 118–19. If one turns to the genesis of the play as explored by Grimm, Parmalee and others, it becomes clear that in the literature Brecht read (Norris, Myers, Tarbell, Steffens, Dos Passos, London, Shaw, Bouck White, etc.) there are two psychological types of capitalists. The overwhelming majority of them (Rockefeller, Carnegie, etc.) believe deeply in the morality of their actions. A few, such as the Pierpont Morgan who gave Mauler his first name, are true cynics. Mauler changes from type 1 to type 2 within the play, roughly in scene X.

17 I have analysed briefly Mauler's opening speech to that effect in my essay *'Saint Joan of the Slaughterhouses*: Assumptions, Exchanges, Seesaws, and Lessons of a Drama Module', *A Production Notebook to 'St Joan'...*, pp. 227–50. Mauler's business soul begins to dominate when Cridle asks 'How much?'.

18 Brecht successively put slightly different emphases on such empathy. To begin with, he used to stress the non-Aristotelian nature of the play, but later he explicitly (though unwillingly) conceded that one should 'at times' [*mitunter*] or even 'largely' [*weitgehend*] empathise into Joan in the sense of my argument; see Brecht, *GW* XVII: 1019–21, XV: 314, and Bahr (ed.), *op. cit.*, p. 171.

19 Elisabeth Hauptmann, 'Notizen über Brechts Arbeit 1926', *Sinn und Form Zweites Sonderheft Bertolt Brecht* (1957), p. 243.

6

Brecht's Caucasian Chalk Circle and Marxist Figuralism: Open Dramaturgy as Open History

> Let us not forget for one instant the point which we occupy in space and in duration, and let us extend our view to the coming centuries, the furthest regions, and the peoples yet to be born.
>
> (Denis Diderot)

> Die Weltgeschichte ist das Weltgericht. [The history of the world is its last Judgement.]
>
> (Friedrich Schiller)

> Now doth the peerless poet perform both: for whatsoever the philosopher saith should be done, he giveth a perfect picture of it in some one by whom he presupposeth it was done; so as he coupleth the general notion with the particular example. A perfect picture I say, for he yieldeth to the powers of the mind an image of that whereof the philosopher bestoweth but a wordish description...
>
> (Philip Sidney)

It has been sufficiently noted by criticism of Brecht[1] how his deep-seated concern for the historical fate of people informed and shaped his dramaturgy. I have argued in the previous essays that his plays evince a strong tension between the implied 'look backward' from the historical vantage-point of an anticipated friendly, classless humanity and his intimate understanding of the bloody history of the twentieth century with its class and national warfare; I have argued that Brecht's basic stance is a utopian blend of intellectual and plebeian alienation from the inhuman contradictions of our times. From such a point of view he effects his whole system of 'estrangements' [*Verfremdungen*]. From its heights he judges the world that forces a truly good person to develop a tough competitive alter ego that will protect the tender and friendly ego (*The Good Woman of Setzuan*), the world that uses the humour and shrewdness of a mother only for the petty pursuits of a,'hyena of the battlefields' trying – and failing – to nourish her own family by co-operating with the warmongers (*Mother Courage and Her Children*), the world that forces a passion for reason into officially approved channels of an exploitative science (*The Life of Galileo*). That is why all major plays by Brecht contain an explicit or implicit judgement scene: the basic stance of the author is thus thematised and brought clearly into the open.

However, even among Brecht's major plays, *The Caucasian Chalk Circle* has, I contend, a privileged position. It shares the concern for history as man-made destiny, the tension and the utopian 'look backward', with his other plays. But it was written in 1944, at the brightest and most open moment of history in the mid-twentieth century – the moment of victory over Nazism. Only in *The Caucasian Chalk Circle* and in *The Mother*, his play of the early 1930s, written during the decisive battle of the German Left against Hitler's rise to power, is an approximation to Brecht's utopian standpoint concretised on the stage at any length, and brought into explicit and victorious collision with inhuman history.

The Caucasian Chalk Circle is thus a glaring exception among Brecht's plays that realistically could not but be plays of stark defeat. However, it also poses complex exegetic problems. These do not seem to have been dealt with fully by Brechtian criticism, and yet they are basic to an understanding of how his open dramaturgy relates and is complementary to his vision of an open history. I propose, therefore, to examine first the basic motifs which constitute the play into a meaningful unity, and then Brecht's philosophy of history which makes sense of such a composition, and is therefore not a body extrinsic to literary analysis but central to it. This should enable a final discussion of the relationship between Brecht's dramaturgy and historiosophy to be based on the evidence of the play itself; it should also enable reaching toward some general conclusions about the import of the systematic Brechtian blending of historiosophy and aesthetics into a significant creative method.

1. At first glance, *The Caucasian Chalk Circle* has an

unusually complicated fable, consisting of three stories distributed across two levels, plus a number of epico-lyrical interventions by the Singer and his accompanying Musicians as well as several 'songs' by some other characters. We can distinguish the opening 'kolkhoz story', the 'Grusha story', and the 'Azdak story', the latter two coming together in the 'chalk circle judgement'. The kolkhoz story is located at the end of the second World War, it is chronologically nearer to the audience (in fact, it coincides with the year the play was written), and it acts as a frame to the 'chalk-circle' nucleus which is located in the depths of the middle ages.

The centre toward which the play converges is indicated by its title: it is the legendary decision about the future of a Noble Child, placed between a false and a true mother. However, in a subversion of dominant societal ideologies – such as the one affirmed in the biblical story of Solomon's sword judgement in an analogous dispute – the theme of motherhood in the Grusha story is used to demystify the alleged primacy of the 'call of the blood', of the biological motherhood represented by the rapacious upper-class bitch Natella, in favour of the 'social motherhood' of the dumb servant Grusha, who at a time of political upheaval saved the Noble Child left at the mercy of killers by its biological mother. Yet if this were the whole import of the play, it is scarcely explainable why it would be necessary to supplement this plebeian fairy-tale with the whole history of the judge who hands down the wise chalk-circle judgement. Still less is it clear why this whole nucleus must be performed as a play-within-the-play presented for and by the kolkhoz litigants over the use of a valley. And in fact, the Individualist theatre has often treated the Grusha story as a sentimental fable, supplemented in a pseudo-Shakespearean way by the comic relief of a hammy Azdak; logically, the kolkhoz story was then seen as a piece of 'socialist-realist' propaganda on the virtues of Soviet society and performed with great embarrassment or completely dropped (often on the characteristic but false assumption that Brecht tacked it onto the play later). I am arguing here that such a sundering procedure is false, since it violates the basic presumption of unity and economy in a significant play.

In order to show the unity of the play, it is necessary to analyse more closely the themes of the various 'stories' and see whether they have a common set of references or topic. To go back to the Grusha story, even a first attempt at formulating its theme was impossible without entering into the universe of societal relationships in that story. That universe is, from the beginning, clearly identified as a world of topsy-turvy human relations passing for normal and indeed hallowed, where basic human values are polar opposites to the official ones:

> In olden times, in a bloody time
> There ruled in a Caucasian city –
> Men called it the City of the Damned –
> A Governor.
> His name was Georgi Abashwili.
> He was rich as Croesus
> He had a beautiful wife
> He had a healthy baby.
> No other governor in Grusinia
> Had so many horses in his stable
> So many beggars on his doorstep
> So many soldiers in his service
> So many petitioners in his courtyard. (27 – *GW* V:2008)

This world is a world of war, of class oppression of the poor and powerless by the rich and powerful, and of internecine Hobbesian warfare of each against each in the upper class, engendering a system in which the lower class also has to choose between kindness and survival (for example – the peasant selling milk to Grusha, or her brother). Grusha saves the infant because she is, as Brecht notes, an exceptional 'sucker' (*GW* XVII:1206), that is, she responds to the norms of human kindness even when they threaten her with death in the unnatural class society. Obviously, behind the old legend the basic Brechtian questioning of what is 'normal', of the alienating effect of social power-relations on human potentialities, insidiously re-emerges. Appearances deceive, reality is fraught with murderous contradictions, and any peaceful moment is only an interlude:

> The city lies still
> But why are there armed men?
> The Governor's palace is at peace
> But why is it a fortress?

And the Governor returned to his palace
And the fortress was a trap.
. . .

And noon was no longer the hour to eat:
Noon was the hour to die. (33 – *GW* V:2013)

When Grusha succumbs to the terrible temptation of
goodness and helps a helpless human being, though she is
helpless herself, she has to flee through the Northern
Mountains, encountering in that epic anabasis all kinds of
trials and surmounting them by means of a slowly developing sense of motherhood. To the killings of the princes and
the egotistic insensitivity of Natella she opposes a principle
which is an important as the all-pervading destructiveness of
the upper classes: the principle of *productivity* or *creativity*. If it
were not sufficiently clear from the language and style of the
play, its use of stylised scenery, the Berliner Ensemble masks
for the upper-class characters, etc., even this first approach to
the fable might be sufficient to show that Grusha's actions,
putting as they do into question the norm (e.g. of 'true'
motherhood), are super-individual. As other major figures of
Brecht's, she is both a precisely personalised character and
allegorical in a sense yet to be explored, but more akin to the
Shakespearean synthesis of allegory and realism than to the
Individualist eighteenth to twentieth-century drama. Thus, a
child in Brecht's plays usually carries his basic motif of
posteri, the future generations whose forebears we are. The
tug-or-war between the biological upper-class mother and
the plebeian 'social mother' over the Noble Child is an
exemplum, standing for a decision which social orientation
shall prevail as the parent of posterity, future ages (see the
song 'Had he golden shoes', 125 – *GW* V:2102). Grusha's social
maternity is in terms of an Individualist-derived characterol-
ogy and ethics earned by her labours and dangers, but it is
also the sign of a potential coming into existence of a new set
of human relations, a new normality, which is attained by
standing the topsy-turvy universe of the chalk-circle nucleus
on its head (i.e. by subverting it).

Thus, the maternity motif is here – as different from other
plays by Brecht such as *The Good Woman of Setzuan* –
explicitly collocated within the theme of a reasonable and

humanised *ultimate goal (telos) of history*:[2] a history envisaged as a system of human actions and interactions. The goal toward which class history is moving is, in fact, the main theme of the whole play. Therefore, developing the Azdak story at some length is not only autonomously enjoyable but also essential in order to bring out its theme of an advent of Justice as a *temporary* reversal of historically 'normal' (i.e. alienated) power and jurisprudence. As an intercalary, short-lived exception at the time of a power-vacuum, Azdak can rid the chalk-circle judgement of a non-cognitively fantastic or fairy-tale character. Placed into the Saturnalian tradition of the Oriental and European Lord of Misrule, 'Roi pour rire', whose interregnum momentarily replaces and cancels out the class world and its inhuman laws, the Azdak story validates the outcome of the Grusha story (and by that token itself too) as more than escapism – as an incident, exemplary by its very exceptionalness, and thus in a roundabout but logically unassailable way reintegrated into a theory which sees history as the development of humanity through class conflicts. The combination of Grusha and Azdak, plebeian emotion and plebeian intelligence, revolt against old laws and power over the enforcing of new laws, is necessary for a cognitively credible outcome of the chalk-circle test as an interaction of human wills, where the destiny of people is other people.

The parallels between the Grusha and Azdak stories, which are supposed to happen simultaneously, but are developed successively on the stage, show up their similarities and differences. Both derive their function from an initial impulsive, 'abnormal' humanist action (the saving of the child and of the Grand Duke). This lands them first into trouble, so that they try to backslide into their old ways, but finally educates them into true motherhood and judgeship respectively. As opposed to the upper class, both Grusha and Azdak show by such acts that they are in harmony with nature, outer or inner. Grusha extends her awakened maternal feeling to the wind:

> Grusha: (*turning to the Child.*) You mustn't be afraid of the
>   wind. He's a poor thing too. He has to push the clouds
>   along and he gets quite cold doing it. (*Snow starts*

falling.) And the snow isn't so bad either, Michael. It covers the little fir trees so they won't die in winter. (61 – *GW* V:2044)

Azdak, on the other hand, is an Epicurean, in the double sense of hedonist and of a radical intellectual for whom his own sensual nature, perceptions, and concepts are the only genuinely human touchstone remaining in the desensualised, calculated, brutal world around him. Both Grusha as the herald of a new Nature and Azdak as the herald of a new Wisdom could fail only by selfishness or cowardice, and they both grow by having assumed responsibilities contrary to such temptations of conforming. Without Azdak, Grusha would have been simply a somewhat more violent and expressive Kattrin from *Mother Courage and Her Children*, barely beginning to speak, and reverting to mutism at times of complex stresses involving both emotion and rationality – a frustrated and barren Mother of the New. Without Grusha, Azdak would be only a Saturnalian Falstaff, Schweik or Groucho Marx supplying anarchist entertainment but having no significant, historical 'bearing on our problem' (as the peasant woman in the kolkhoz scene defines the compositional method of the play), a freak without insertion into historical processes. As it is, Azdak can be remembered by the people as an anti-judge whose term was 'a brief golden age/Almost an age of justice (128 – *GW* V:2015). Azdak's anabasis is a flight *toward power* (the Ironshirts) used in a new way, complementary to Grusha's flight *from power* used in the old way. During it, Azdak has grown from a disaffected bohemian, first to somebody reducing the old justice to its absurd conclusions by anarchist parody, and finally to the allegorical herald of a new justice, of the new and coming golden age which will 'transform justice/Into passion' (Brecht's *Address to Danish Worker-Actors*, *GW* IX:766).

The hypothesis that this is a play thematically centred on a theory which sees history as a conflict of social alienations with strivings toward de-alienation, can also account for the unusual kolkhoz story and framework. Its new wisdom of peaceful resolution of the dispute over the valley finds a common denominator with the subversive old wisdom of Azdak's decision in the concluding verses:

That what there is shall go to those who are good for it:
Children to the motherly, that they prosper,
Carriages to good drivers, that they be driven well,
And the valley to the waterers, that it yield fruit.

This also makes of the central action of *Caucasian Chalk Circle*
a performance for an exemplary audience, poetically validat-
ing its settling of conflicts of interest without the violence of
each against each by inserting it into a historical and
philosophical sequence. As Aristotle knew, poetry is more
philosophical than historiography.

2. Brecht's philosophy of history, and the compositional
method in this play, is *Marxist figuralism*.

In his essay 'Figura', Erich Auerbach has outlined the
medieval figural interpretation of history. A *figura* was a real
historical person or event of the Old Testament reaching
fulfilment in another real historical person or event of the
New Testament – say, Moses and Jesus. Neither figure nor
fulfilment were spiritualist moral allegories; the allegorical
aspect in this process was the *intellectus spiritualis* which
recognised figure in fulfilment. Augustine refined this to the
point where things and people could 'prefigure' abstract
fulfilments, e.g. Noah's Ark prefigured the Christian
Church, or the pair Hagar – Sarah prefigured the opposition
Old Testament *vs.* New Testament, also *civitas terrena*
(terrestrial Jerusalem) *vs. civitas Dei* (heavenly Jerusalem).
Brecht does the same when the boy Michael prefigures the
future, so that his redemption from class bondage of his
'terrene', biological mother is *figurally* connected with the
fate of the valley redeemed from private property and its
concomitant warfare-type settlement of disputes.

In Auerbach's definition, 'figural interpretation establishes
a connection between two events or persons, the first of
which signifies not only itself but also the second, while the
second encompasses and fulfils the first. The two poles of the
figure are separate in time, but both, being real events or
figures, are within time, within the stream of historical life'.[3]
This is an allegorical approach which retains and encourages
the historicity of events but inserts them within a formal
process participating both of historiographic facticity and of
utopian expectation. Auerbach observes that 'figural inter-

pretation is a product of late cultures, far more indirect, complex, and charged with history than the symbol or the myth'; on the other hand, complementary to the interpretation of venerable, indeed legendary matter, it is 'youthful and new-born as a purposive, creative, concrete interpretation of universal history' (*A* 57). These observations seem to me to apply with full force to Brecht's theory of history in *The Caucasian Chalk Circle*. Just as the Christian figural interpretation absorbed characters from the Old Testament as well as from lay authors (*teste David cum Sibylla* [witness David and Sibylla], as the *Dies irae* has it) down to the Grail legends, so Brecht's Marxist figuralism absorbed configurations from the New Testament and the old folk legends, generally recognised as the two principal sources of his tradition. It is not difficult to find in the Grusha story the archetype of the hierogamic Holy Family, blasphemously complete with a virgin mother (*figlia del tuo figlio* [daughter of your son], Dante, *Paradiso*, 33), an exalted child, an official father (or two) who does not know how he came by the child, a flight from soldiers sent to massacre the child, etc. In the same way, Azdak's decision is a forerunner of a subversive final judgement. If Michael has overtones of the Christ Child, Azdak finally assumes overtones of Christ as the messianic fulfiller of Moses' leading his people out of bondage: he is beaten and stripped, he tours the country with the sacrament of a new Law:

> And he broke the rules to save them.
> Broken law like bread he gave them,
> Brought them to shore upon his crooked back.
>   (107–*GW* V:2086)

As for the folk legends, the use of the Chinese chalk-circle story, the Egyptian Song of the Chaos, the Judgement of Solomon, and the legend-imbued location on Caucasus may be sufficient testimonials.

No doubt, differences between the medieval Christian and the Marxist figuralism are no less pronounced, and homologous with the differences in the main import of these two major systematic non-Individualistic philosophies of our civilisation. Christian figuralism aims at a super-temporal, theistic resolution, where horizontal temporal prefiguration is possible only because all times refer vertically to divine providence, in whose eyes past and future are simultaneous. Marxism takes from secularised (rationalist and Hegelian) historiography a real pluri-temporality; the orientation toward earthly historicity that began with the Gothic and Renaissance ages grows into the axiological sovereignty of earthly, human reality in all its sensory and historically differentiated multiplicity. Following Feuerbach, Marxism stood the God–Man relation on its head: God is an emanation made in the image of man. Therefore, instead of an incarnation of the Word (*Logos*), a Marxist dramatist will start from a verbalisation and rationalisation of the flesh, from a canonisation of ethically exemplary human relations where the sensual and the visionary are not sundered. Grusha and Azdak behave thus: Grusha's motivation for picking up the child is dumb in terms of Individualist experience (each for himself and the devil take the hindmost), but it affirms a radical humanist *sapientia* as touchstone for the whole play:

> *Older Woman (amiably):* Grusha, you're a good soul, but you're not very bright, and you know it. I tell you, if he had the plague he couldn't be more dangerous.
> *Grusha (stubbornly):* He hasn't got the plague. He looks at me. He's human! (44–GWV: 2023)

Parallel to Grusha, Azadak can unite the dramaturgic function of a figure of new Justice with the character of a comically sensual, anarchistic parodist of old justice. In short, radical religious prefiguration is in Brecht replaced by radical humanist prefiguration, whose historiography is taken from the *Communist Manifesto* with its succeeding stages of class society identified as the human 'prehistory' which should lead to a classless and warless brotherhood of all people on Earth. The specific ideational characteristic of *The Caucasian Chalk Circle* is the encounter of this historiography with radical Marxist and anarchist anthropology in the tradition of young Marx and Rimbaud (forgotten by much official Marxism).

The Marxist theory of history can be envisaged as a dialectical synthesis fusing the useful aspects of the feudal and bourgeois historiosophies. As in the medieval Christian theory of history, the Marxist one has a privileged point of convergence in the future which is the saving *telos* of human history (thesis); but as in the rationalist-liberal theory of history (antithesis), this point is to be reached by a chain of development based exclusively on human interactions (synthesis). The anticipated Golden Age or Terrestrial Paradise is prefigured by a series of more or less short-lived revolutionary and utopian endeavours and visions throughout history, from the equality of tribal society (the 'primitive communism' of Marxist historiography) through lower-class revolts (such as the one of Spartacus, Wat Tyler or the German Anabaptists) and through artistic, scientific, religious or philosophical prefigurations, to revolutions such as the Bolshevik one. The sequence in this play, the Persian weavers' revolt – Azdak's judgeship – co-operative socialism of Soviet kolkhozes, is an obvious example of such prefigurational, humanist salvation history.

However, this is not to be taken to mean that the kolkhoz scene is the final privileged point of convergence, a static utopia of perfection. Beside Brecht's reservations on the development within the Soviet Union, the usual static confrontation of two (only sometimes three) points in Christian history (figure and one or two fulfilments) is here replaced by a dynamic development along an infinite curve of succeeding prefigurations hopefully ever closer to fulfilment. On this asymptotic curve, the chalk-circle point and the kolkhoz point serve merely as dramatically powerful examples and determinants. The 'chalk-circle', inner part of the play has to be much longer than the kolkhoz frame because it focuses on the human potentialities of Grusha and Azdak as opposed to powerful societal alienations in the barbaric class system; their success can then be transferred *a fortiori* to the more rational kolkhoz situation. But the quote of Mayakovsky characterising the kolkhoz situation says: 'The home of the Soviet people shall also be the home of Reason', prefiguring a further future (the German original 'soll auch sein' is formally an imperative, but also with future-bearing function: 23 – *GW* V:2005). Then too, and more obviously, as in the inner play there is still war in the kolkhoz story (although it is a just one, as opposed to the unjust one about which Azdak sings the 'Song of Injustice in Persia'). Also, the

frame story itself is a dispute about stewardship of possessions which recalls the fierce ownership battle around the
Noble Child, the inheritor of the Abashwili estates (although
the battle is now fought with statistics and not with swords).
The social differentiation between the direct producers (the
peasants and the artist) on one hand and, on the other, a
centralised State apparatus, represented by a delegate from the
nearby town, still exists – and Brecht was very aware of its
degenerative potentialities. In fact, the type of decision
reached by the kolkhoz villagers without a court judgement
and by mutual agreement, which acts as a fulfilment of the
unorthodox Azdak judging, would be illegal in the Soviet
Union of 1944 as of today (though not of 1920), as the Soviet
critics of Brecht have clearly stated. Another pointer is the
deliberate onomastic mixture: Grusha is a Russian name with
Dostoyevskian (or anti-Dostoyevskian) echoes of the humble
being exalted, Azdak an Iranian one with radical and
salvational echoes.[4] Also, the mixture or indeed mix-up of
mostly Grusinian place names with Russian and Azerbaidjani
ones makes out of the kolkhoz situation a very stylised reality
indeed (in 'real life' the Nazi army came only to the border of
the Grusinian Republic, and never to Azerbaidjan). The
kolkhoz in the play is thus more of a model-like fulfilment of
the legendary Azdakian golden age than a 'socialist-realist'
reflection of 1944 Transcaucasia. This too is of a piece with
the figural method; as Auerbach noted, there is always a
certain contradiction between figure and history. History
(*historia* or *littera*) 'is the literal sense or the event related;
figura is the same literal meaning or event in reference to the
fulfilment cloaked in it, and this fulfilment itself is *veritas*' (*A*
47). The human relationships in the Grusinian kolkhozes are
thus not to be taken either literally or as a final truth, but as a
'middle term' (*A* 47) between their historical literality and a
dynamic fulfilment: they are themselves another, more
advanced figure.

  In the same way, the figural parallels of the disputed valley
to young Michael are clear: the fruit-growers have a better
right to it partly because they fought for it against the Nazis,
just as Grusha did against the Ironshirts and other vicissi-
tudes, but mainly because they propose to use it more
productively. The question which Azdak decides in the

chalk-circle judgement is not at all who should 'possess'
Michael, and by implication 'own' the future. As his
questions and the final verse show, the decision hinges on
who will be better *for the child*. Not the child to his mother,
but the child 'to the motherly', the maternal ones, says the
singer in the quoted conclusion – a stylistic device taken over
by Brecht from the Luther-Bible style which substitutes the
nominalised adjectival quality for a static, fixed substantive.
The child and the valley area are not objects to be allocated to
subject-possessors; they are entities, subjects in their own
right, and the users have only rights of stewardship over
them in the name of human productivity. The formal
analogies to the medieval theory of property and just dealing
in the name of divine justice are clear. Such analogies are not
syllogistic proofs, since a prefigurational parallel is never
complete: a certain tension between *figura* and fulfilment is
immanent to this approach. Yet, like the fruit-growers,
Grusha too had to earn her right to motherhood, and indeed
Parts II and III of the Grusha story show the birth of Grusha
as a 'motherly one'. Her nascent capacities for feeling are
criminal in the chaotic world around her:

> She sat too long, too long she saw
> The soft breathing, the small clenched fists,
> Till toward the morning the seduction was complete.
> . . .
> As if it was stolen goods she picked it up.
> As if she was a thief she crept away. (46 – *GW* V: 2025)

Yet such feelings grow into a justification of Grusha's right
to be the noble child's parent – hers is the true nobility, and
the blood-and-water baptism of Michael and changing of his
clothes are initiation rites for Mother Grusha:

> *Corporal:* Fine linen!
> *(Grusha dashes at him to pull him away. He throws her off and again
> bends over the crib. Again looking round in despair, she sees a log of
> wood, seizes it, and hits the Corporal over the head from behind. The
> Corporal Collapses. She quickly picks up the Child and rushes off.)*
> *Singer:*   And in her flight from the Ironshirts
>   After twenty-two days of journeying
>   At the foot of the Janga-Tau Glacier
>   Grusha Vachnadze decided to adopt the child.

Chorus: The helpless girl adopted the helpless child.
(Grusha squats over a half-frozen stream to get the Child water in the hollow of her hand.)
Grusha: Since no one else will take you, son,
I must take you.
Since no one else will take you, son,
You must take me.
O black day in a lean, lean year,
The trip was long, the milk was dear,
My legs are tired, my feet are sore;
But I wouldn't be without you any more.
I'll throw your silken shirt away,
And wrap you in rags and tatters,
I'll wash you, son, and christen you in glacier water.
We'll see it through together.
(She has taken off the child's fine linen and wrapped it in a rag.)
(57–8 – GW V: 2040–1)

The *telos* of Marxist figuralism is indeed, notwithstanding dogmatic obfuscations, not to be found in any particular, arrested point. Though in its dynamic theory of historical equilibrium the direction of humanity is always clear, each point reached should also be the starting point for new contradictions and resolutions: Judgement Day is also Genesis. It might seem curious that Brecht at some moments insisted that the inner play in *Caucasian Chalk Circle* is not a parable (though its story is told in order to clarify the kolkhozes' decision about the valley), but another (unde-fined) kind of exemplary narration, to whose 'practicability and also genesis' the kolkhoz story 'assigns a historical localisation' (*GW* XVII:1205). In fact, this is an aesthetic correlative to a salvational perspective in which history has no end, so that the kolkhoz story is simply a *presently possible* society in which Azdak's exceptional drawing of a chalk circle has become the normative or dominant use of pencils instead of pistols.

3. The curve of prefiguration leads thus not only from the chalk-circle nucleus to the kolkhoz frame, but also from the Singer's final verses to the temporal point of the audience – 1954, 1983, or any time at which the prefiguration of a golden age has not been fulfilled although it is felt as absolutely necessary. The play is fully relevant only for such an audience, and it becomes clear why for an audience with a different attitude it must seem a chaotic mixture of fairy-tale, clowning and propaganda. It is no accident that the first prefiguration of such a fulfilment was written by Brecht in 1944, at the most promising moment of modern history, the moment of the victory of the antifascist coalition, and that he placed at least the frame story into the year in which he wrote it (an extraordinary exception rarely paralleled in modern dramaturgy). Drama and history touched in a privileged moment, an epiphany, lending its effulgence to both. History is here shown as open-ended though clearly not value-free: there is a fixed provisional goal, but it will be reached only if the spectators learn what it means to become parents of the New, of the future (as Grusha and Simon learned), and if they realise that the victory of the golden age of justice depends on the ability of later Grushas to act, and later Azdaks to be in the arbiter's seat. Whether the historical horizon of a just, classless humanity will be reached depends on a further powerful conjunction of subversive emotion and subversive reason. For this change of the times ('thou hope of the people', 35 – *GW* V:2015), the play is a dyamic *exemplum*. Fittingly, its structure as an open drama exemplifies its message of an open history.

The open structure of the play is communicated through a number of devices. I have already touched on some effects of the play-within-the-play form which results in two audiences. We watch the kolkhoz both act out the chalk-circle story and function as its audience, in a prefiguration of the participatory or doing-your-own-thing theatre, of politics as theatre rather than theatre as politics; and we see the kolkhoz members obtaining insights which justify their decision about the valley as a step in the necessary humanisation of humanity. By watching this, we as the 'outer' audience gain not only the 'moral of the story' but also the reasons why and ways how it is moral. We see, as Brecht wrote in his *Address to Danish Worker-Actors* that 'only he who knows that the fate of man is man/Can see his fellow man keenly with accuracy' (*GW* IX:764); and we see this cognition presented as delight.

One could embark upon a discussion of songs, and many

other devices in the play (crucially perhaps, the series of Azdak's complex court cases), but I want finally to consider here only the Singer-narrator. He seems to me to be much more than a formal device, in fact a semiotic model which not only signifies but is significant in its own right as showing Brecht's dramaturgy and theatre aesthetics in action. As with almost all major modern dramatists (and indeed artists in general), the theatre's reflection about life is at the same time a reflection about itself and its own role in life. The play, and its performance, is a seduction to goodness in the exemplary type of Grusha, and to justice in that of Azdak. It seduces through a method uniting in its allegorising the corporeal and spiritual (in)sight, *eros* and *agape*; it warns against the difficulties on the road to goodness and justice presented in Grusha's archetypal flight and Azdak's tempestuous ups and downs, the small-scale land-locked *Odyssey* and *Iliad* of this stage narration.

Parallel to this, the Singer personifies the right type of dramaturgy and theatre for an audience interested in the delightful didactics of history; the chalk-circle nucleus which he narrates and his approach to its narration and performance are supposed to represent the proper message and the proper style of a plebeian, liberating theatre. The Singer is the only stage figure participating in both the kolkhoz frame (as character) and the chalk-circle nucleus (as narrator and commentator). He mediates between the stage and the audience (both the stage audience and the 'real' one); he prevents the kolkhoz audience (and us) from forgetting that it is (that we are) seeing the exemplary reality of a performance and not illusionistic slices of life. Like a novel narrator (or an oral storyteller), he manipulates time and space rhythm at his will, he knows the motives and thoughts of all characters. His comments suggest to the audience the most economical attitude proper to the play and its unified understanding. The comments have a family likeness to those of a Greek chorus, or of Hamlet in the Mousetrap play-within-a-play, they unite epic coolness and lyrical emotion, such as in 'O blindness of the great':

O blindness of the great!
They go their way like gods,

Great over bent backs,
Sure of hired fists,
Trusting in the power
Which has lasted so long. But long is not forever.
O change from age to age!
Thou hope of the people! (35 – *GW* V:2015)

Compared to Bob Dylan's 'The times they are a-changing'
this singer-narrator (*cantastorie*) is obviously better trained in
philosophy and sociology, but he is turned much in the same
direction. His arsenal of devices ranges from narrative
interjections to the equivalent of operatic arias such as the one
just quoted, and encompasses the stichomythic questions and
answers he exchanges with his attendants and the gnomic
fixations of pantomimic events such as Grusha's seduction by
the Child. With Grusha and Azdak, the Singer is the third,
and perhaps central *dramatis persona* of this rich tapestry in
time and space: he too, beside being Arkadi Cheidze, is the
New Theatre – a male plebeian Thalia, an open, liberating
dramaturgy which has assimilated manifold devices of
written and oral literature, spectacle and cinema, in order to
present us with a useful and delightful lesson about our
existence.

The basic tension between utopia and history, humanity
and class alienation, results here in a vision of open history
transmitted through open dramaturgic structures. I have
discussed above how history can be open yet meaningful in a
mature Marxist figuralism. The dramaturgy is open in a
double sense. First of all, it openly shows its artificial nature,
from the fact that it is an art form consisting of scenic signs of
reality and not reproducing it, right to the particular
techniques used – beginning with the fact that a particular
kind of people (actors) portray 'iconic' relationships between
other people (*dramatis personae*). Further, its structure is open
toward the spectators' reality, in which such dramaturgy
finds its culmination and resolution. It becomes a significant
unity only by its effect on the spectators' reality, whose
change it wants to help along by aesthetic exemplarity. Based
on a similarly grand sweep of historical and philosophical
horizons as the medieval drama, the Brechtian one differs
from it mainly in the imaginary ideal onlooker for whom it is

written. In the middle ages, that ideal onlooker was he to whom all unfamiliar events were familiar because he saw their eternal essence through surface differences: i.e. God. For *The Caucasian Chalk Circle,* the ideal onlooker is one to whom all familiar events are unfamiliar because she looks for the unrealised potentialities in each historical stage of Man's humanisation: i.e. a prefigured Man with the ethics of a blessed classless Future. This ideal onlooker is both demanded and shaped by Brecht's play. Showing us an open dramaturgy correlative to open history, the play itself contributes to such opening.

Notes

[1] See Reinhold Grimm's bibliographical handbook *Bertolt Brecht,* 3d edn (Stuttgart: Metzler, 1971). A long select bibliography, which I contributed to, Erika Munk (ed.), *Brecht* (New York: Bantam, 1972) indicates perhaps how conscious I am of trying to stand on the shoulders of other viewers of Brecht's opus, beginning with his own. Yet to total drowning in a sea of footnotes I have preferred the *terra firma* of concentrating on the text and the implicit performance, trusting that my use of insights by Brecht himself (*GW* XVII:1197−210) and say, Eric Bentley, Ernst Bloch, Hans Mayer, Reinhold Grimm, Hans J. Bunge, Bernard Dort or Albrecht Schöne is readily apparent.

This chapter was first presented as a lecture at Toronto University in 1970, and then as a paper in the Forum 'Perspectives of Marxist Scholarship' on the margins of the 1972 MLA meeting. I am grateful to my colleagues Don Bouchard and Yehudy Lindeman from McGill University and David Stratman from Colby College for suggestions how to improve it. All quotations from *The Caucasian Chalk Circle* are from Eric Bentley's translation (New York: Grove, 1967), and will be indicated by page number in parenthesis – to which is added the volume: page of Brecht's *Gesammelte Werke* (*GW*). See also the general approach in chapters 3 and 4 of this book; while chapter 5 examines a crucial phase of Brecht's arriving at such a stance.

[2] Georg Lukács's definition in *History and Class Consciousness* supplies a Marxist approach pertinent to this discussion. 'The ultimate goal (*Endziel*) is rather that relation *to the totality* (to the whole of society seen as a process) through which every aspect of the struggle acquires its revolutionary significance. This relation

dwells within every moment in its simple and sober ordinariness, but it only *becomes real by becoming conscious,* and... raises the moment of daily struggle to *reality* out of *mere factuality.' Geschichte und Klassenbewusstsein* (Berlin, 1923), pp. 36–7 (transl. D.S.; cf. also the translation by Rodney Livingstone, London, 1971.) This opposition between factuality and an ontologically and axiologically more significant 'reality' seems analogous to the medieval opposition between *historia* and *figura,* just as the 'ultimate aim' is analogous to the fulfilment which is the only real truth or *veritas*; see my further discussion and Auerbach's discussions in the work cited in note 3. An argument parallel to Lukács's, but better known to Brecht, is in Karl Korsch, *Marxismus und Philosophie* (Leipzig, 1923; Frankfurt, 1966).

3 Erich Auerbach, 'Figura,' in *Scenes from the Drama of European Literature* (New York, n.d.), p. 53; further quoted as *A* with page number in parenthesis.

4 Mazdak was a Communist Zoroastrian heresiarch and leader of a plebeian revolt in sixth century Iran. See Firdusi's epic *Shahnamè*; also A.E. Christensen, *Le Règne du roi Kawādh I et le communisme Mazdakite* (Copenhagen, 1925); N. Pigulevskaia, *Goroda Irana v rannem srednevekov'e* (Moskva-Leningrad, 1956); and, on Mazdak's later influence, Ziia Buniatov, *Azerbaidzhan v VII–IX vv.* (Baku, 1965); and Dzhamal Mustafaev, 'Priroda sotsial'nykh utopii stran Blizhnego Vostoka', *Voprosy filosofii,* no. 8 (1968), 115–24.

7

Brecht's Coriolan,[1] *or Leninism as Utopian Horizon: The City, The Hero, The City That Does not Need a Hero*

1. There are two main oppositions in Brecht's *Coriolan* – the latest, and in some ways the most intriguing, version of that ancient historiographic and dramaturgic legend. The first and basic opposition in the play is that between *war and peace*; war or peace prevail either horizontally, between the ethnic units, the city-states of Rome and the Volsci; or vertically, between the two Roman classes – the direct producers, little people or plebeians, and the rich power-wielders and political-military leaders or patricians. The second and central opposition or conflict is that between *Caius Marcius* (later called Coriolan) *and his city-state of Rome*. The class conflict between patricians and plebeians within the Roman state is evident in their spatial opposition within the public places of Rome right from the first scene, but is retracted in their final co-operation. The ethnic conflict between the states of Rome and the Volsci is evident in the battle scenes, but is retracted both in the meeting of two plebeians from the two states on the highway (IV.i) and – after overcoming Coriolan's militarism – in the final scene when the Roman Senate passes the plebeian tributes' motion to return the confiscated Volscian land. The conflict between Coriolan and the Roman plebeians widens in the second half of the play into his conflict with the whole Roman nation, evident in the scenes in the Volscian camp, and ends only with his death. The two conflicts – first, the wars of classes and nations, and second, the war of the great individual against his society – are intertwined and influence each other intimately within the dialectics of the play. However, for purposes of initial analysis, they could be considered separately. For reasons explained later, I shall call the wars of the classes and nations the *democratic* or *Leninist* conflict, and the war of the great individual against society the *Individualistic* or *Shakespearean* conflict; and it is my thesis that the peculiar strengths as well as problems of Brecht's play arise out of the fact that these two conflicts are not wholly compatible, and yet that their shock is mutually very illuminating. My analysis will first consider what Brecht could use not only from the Shakespeare play he was 'adapting', but also from the whole historical legend about the 'great man' Coriolanus, and continue with Brecht's modifications in the era of High Stalinism.

The legend begins with Titus Livius. Now Livy was a staunch partisan of the official Roman state party-line in historiography which, in a not too original fashion, ascribed a special virtue to the behaviour of Roman warriors and statesmen that ethically and almost cosmologically guaranteed their victories. What that virtue of *pietas* was exactly like is almost less important than the fact that it was correlative to winning (i.e. an ideological sublimation of the old sayings that might is right and the end justifies the means) and the ensuing central textual presupposition that here we see the victors writing their history. True, as Brecht liked to point out not only about Antiquity but also about the Renaissance, those were bloody and barbarous times, times of 'human sacrifices' (*GW* XVI:677). But there are sacrifices and sacrifices, and there is quite a difference between, for one example, the official Elizabethan and the no less official French Classicist heroic virtues or, for another, between the official Roman and the no less official Hellenic ones. The latter difference is cognate to *Coriolan* – a play rich in Homeric echoes – as well to the Coriolanus legend, suspected from Cicero's times of Hellenic contaminations, and deserves therefore some explanation.

The Hellenic ethnic epics, being products of small rising and falling states rather than of an imperial power, were not primarily concerned with proper winning but with properly noble living and dying. In the *Iliad*, the wrath of Achilles and indeed the defeat of Hector are more important than the victory of Agamemnon and Menelaus. What is more, Homer followed this up with the *Odyssey*, the theme of which is not so much life's battles as life's marvellous voyage toward oneself. Though significant works of literature cannot be ranked like football teams (first, second, semi-finalists, etc.), if I had to choose one single epic to my desert island, I would certainly take the *Odyssey*. It is not only a beautiful *voyage extraordinaire* with monsters, pretty girls and other thrills, but it is also concerned with what I would at that point have recognised to be the deepest wisdom of them all – that the proper voyage is to return home; and I believe that most modern critics would agree with my choice. However, I suspect that an exiled Roman general or dictator (say, Coriolanus) would have chosen to take with him a scroll containing the *Iliad*, thinking of himself as a combination of Achilles and Agamemnon. Indeed, Coriolanus can be thought of as an exasperated and inferior Achilles, the great warrior but sulking mental adolescent turning traitor, who is none the less superior to Agamemnon in that he does not want carnage at any price, and who expiates that superiority by being killed before instead of, Agamemnon-like, after his victory. The proof that I am right in my speculation on the official Roman reading habits is, I would maintain, the official national epic of the Romans, Virgil's *Aeneid* (mainly a smug redoing of the *Iliad*, in which the fact that the hero Aeneas will found Latium and the clan of the Julii – i.e the Roman principate of Virgil's time – makes him divinely right in all his wars and other rather dubious enterprises, such as the betrayal of Dido): for such is official Roman piety, that the end justifies the means in him who is invariably called the 'pious Aeneas'. Now Livy – Virgil's contemporary and ideological ally – pursues the same idea: the purpose (*telos*) and main thesis of his work is that such 'piety' rules Roman history, *res populi romani*, and makes Rome great. Therefore, he is interested in Coriolanus only in so far as that little episode demonstrates that proper education in Roman *pietas* will overawe even a wayward warrior who was exiled for politico-economical clashes with the plebeians and took up arms against the Urbs, the City: when it comes to the crunch, his inner-directedness will out, and the majestic flow of Roman destiny – evident in the struggles between patricians and plebeians as well as between Rome and its neighbours, and in the imperial outcome of those struggles – will roll on undisturbed. What Coriolanus does later is irrelevant, and Livy says that some rumours have him killed and some living to a ripe old age.

On the contrary, Plutarch – who was after all a Boeotian and not a Roman, although a citizen of the Roman Empire – is centrally interested not in Coriolanus's siege of Rome but in an individual split between the good and the bad, who is compared disparagingly and yet with a wealth of biographical details to another great political exile, Alcibiades. In fact, Plutarch is interested in history only as a gossipy backdrop to the individual trajectories of great men, who are as it were supra-historical, abstracted from history into pseudo-eternal idealised regions of moralising about freedom, patiotism, heroism and similar. He is not interested in *the statesman* but in *the man*, and his subject-matter is not Livy's epically dynamic p cess of a political organism developing but an ahistorically organised series of static contrasts between great individuals, always opposed to their backgrounds in the manner of a Renaissance portrait, with the subject in the first plane and the florid landscape as backdrop.

Now Shakespeare's Renaissance dramaturgy was, in spite of his agreement with Plutarch in this play, not simply Individualistic, but rather a very contradictory passage from medieval collectivism to bourgeois Individualism, from orthodox Christianity to atomistic humanism. His major plays therefore often transcend Individualism, and I have argued this extensively in chapter 1. Yet Shakespeare comes closest to Individualism, and indeed becomes its legitimate co-founder in dramaturgy, in two domains: the sexual (e.g. *Othello*) and the openly political or monarchist (e.g. *Coriolanus*). The collectivism turns here into Menenius's cynical fakery, a background against which Coriolanus's frenzied invectives against the citizens are at least sincere. For the purposes of comparison with Brecht, Shakespeare's play can therefore, I believe, be analysed on the basis of his undoubted and overriding affinity for Plutarch's dramatically simplified clashes between the great individual and the backdrop of petty bickering around him. Shakespeare's Coriolanus is practically the whole play; furthermore, he is the noblest Roman of them all, a hero not only with and in spite of a tragic flaw of pride and anger, but practically because of it. In

Plutarch, these flaws were explained as stemming from a deficient upbringing – an explanation contrary but also complementary to Livy's triumph of *pietas romana* in the final instance. In Shakespeare the flaws as well as the virtues stem from the mysterious, 'not to be questioned further, depths of a great man's individuality whose essence has nothing whatsoever to do with the formative influences of his environment – although the individuality can after all be *shown* only by the interaction with this environment turned into backdrop. The dramaturgic *raison d'être* of the whole scenic microcosm (Rome, Corioli, Antium, the battlefields and highways joining them, the patricians and plebeians inhabiting them in strife and co-operation) is to allow the hero to manifest himself. Logically, many a Shakespearean tragic hero will manifest himself most clearly when he is practically or literally alone on the stage, when the microcosm has been emptied of other necessary but cumbersome figures: in the great monologues, in the internal emigration or external exiles of Hamlet, Macbeth, Lear – and of Coriolanus. As Brecht noted in 1928, characterising with an anthropologist's harshness the empathy with suffering specific to Individualist dramaturgy, beginning with Shakespeare and ending with, say, Hauptmann:

Shakespeare drives through four acts the great loner, a Lear, an Othello, a Macbeth, away from all his human ties of family and state and onto the heath, into total isolation, where he has to show greatness in his downfall. . . . It is passion which keeps this machinery going, and the purpose of the machinery is the great individual experience. Coming ages will call this drama a drama for cannibals and will say that man was at the beginning devoured pleasurably, as Richard the Third, and at the end devoured compassionately, as Waggoner Henschel, but that he was always devoured. (*GW* XV:149)

Clearly, a dramatist who, like Brecht, concluded from modern urban and mass society that to define the dramaturgic microcosm exclusively through its central figure of the great individual was by now not only ethically dubious but, worse still, unbelievable, could not accept Shakespeare's way. Brecht thought of Shakespeare's plays as anticipating '300 years in which the individual developed into the capitalist, and [as] being superseded not by what follows on capitalism but by capitalism itself.' To the objection that it is shallow to define Shakespeare's tragedy as dealing with the decline of great feudal men and concepts, Brecht replied: 'But how could there be anything more complex, fascinating and important than the decline of great ruling classes?' (*GW* XVI:587–8). From that vantage-point, Brecht strove to fashion a dialectical synthesis out of Livy's thesis that only social piety matters, and Shakespeare's antithesis that only the individual law inside a great person's breast matters. Brecht's attempt at synthesis presents a new type of social piety being formed, in collision with a character of genuinely great potentialities which become destructive when he uses them for class warfare against the plebeians and for national treason. As in the whole Coriolanus legend, the Hero and the City clash; as in Livy and contrary to Shakespeare, the City is right; as in Shakespeare and contrary to Livy, it is a pity that the Hero's qualities had not been used for better purposes. But above all – and contrary to the politics of the whole Coriolanus legend – it is a new, imaginary, wish-dream, or utopian City that is right in *Coriolan*, a City of popular unity and popular democracy guaranteed by the armed militia of the plebeians who have coalesced with the patriotic patricians. And contrary to the Individualistic psychology of the whole Coriolanus legend, the hero cannot be envisaged as either Livy's episodic maverick or Plutarch's great man; for these absolute and static, either/or terms are not believable or realistic any more. Any Brechtian character is both/and: Coriolan is *both* a supreme leader in the vital business of war, *and* a supreme menace to civil peace. The tragedy for Brecht is a radically new type of tragedy, quite different from Greek or Elizabethan dramaturgy. First of all, it is a bipolar or double one: 'the tragedy of the people that has a hero against it' (*GW* XVI:877) *and* the tragedy of the great personality who believes he is irreplaceable (*GW* XVI:886). Secondly, the civic pole of this double-headed situation turns out not to be a tragedy because of the self-help of the Roman people; whereas the individual pole turns out to be a tragedy only because the great man is blind to the Antaean necessity to be in touch with the people, because he is simply an anachronism and his greatness an over-specialisation, a professional disease. Brechtian tragedy is frontally opposed to theories of an unchangeable Fate (be that Fate called the Gods, or Society, or History, or even Political Economy), and it flows from the hero's blindness to changed necessities of social existence. Mother Courage does not see that little people need a long spoon to sup with the demon of war, nor does Galileo see that scientists need the contact with the practical life and ethics of the little people if they are not to become a race of inventive dwarves sellable to the highest bidder – who will again turn out to be the demon of war and destruction. Coriolan's tragedy is quite paralled: he does not see the necessity and/or the possibility of metamorphosis from antediluvian warrior – monster into a leader at a time of civic and international peace.

This complex of political motives, dealing with the ostensibly great leader *vs.* the people, with pathetic personal heroism *vs.* the workings of mass or statistical forces centred on economics, with the nature of true victory and defeat, had fascinated Brecht from his very youngest days. Subsequently, the experiences of the Germans in the first World War, the October Revolution in the Russian Empire, the various brief European revolts after it, the exacerbated class struggles in the Weimar Republic, the internal struggles in the Soviet Union, the rise of the Nazis and the second World War, the Cold War between East and West and the formation of the two German states corresponding to the two power blocs in Europe, Stalinism and the harsh last years of Stalin – all of these were fundamental factors in the existence of Brecht's generation, and thus in his life and work too. The cannibalistic violence of war and civil war determining the most intimate reactions of people is perhaps his most persistent *leitmotif,* from *The Bible* and *Man is Man* to *The Caucasian Chalk Circle, Antigone* and *Days of the Commune.* In particular, his first major encounter with Shakespeare's *Coriolanus,* which made of him a perennial advocate of the unorthodox view (shared by T.S. Eliot) that it was 'one of Shakespeare's grandest plays' (*GW* XV: 181), was a performance in Berlin by one of his favourite directors, to whom he felt so much akin that he later took him into the Berliner Ensemble, Erich Engel. Brecht allotted to Engel's 1925 staging no less than a 'decisive importance' in the development of epic theatre (*GW*

XV: 133–4). Along with the formal stage devices, what must have appealed to Brecht is that the Coriolanus story was played as a parallel or analogue to that same unsuccessful Spartacist revolt which he had skirted in his early play *Drums in the Night.* According to contemporaries, one saw on Engel's stage the German paramilitary right-wingers, the Steel Helmets, fighting with grey proletarians with flour-powdered miserable faces in a *décor* more reminiscent of the working quarters of 1919 Berlin than of consular Rome.[2] From that point of view, Coriolanus's figure stands – as in Eliot's poem from the same years – for a would-be fascist dictator, and the plebeians for the failed communist revolutionaries of Central Europe's interwar years.

A direct line leads from such a Coriolanus both to Brecht's parody of Hitler as Chicago gangster in *Arturo Ui* and (somewhat less grotesquely) to the falsely great Romans of Brecht's exile years, the famous politician Caesar in the novel *The Business of Mr Julius Caesar* and the famous general Lucullus in the radio play *The Trial of Lucullus.* But in comparison to all these completely negated upper-class leaders, victors of destructive and therefore empty victories over their own people as much as over other peoples, Brecht's Coriolan – shaped six to nine years after the end of the second World War, when both reflection and new problems had intervened – is seen as a more complex figure. An anti-social one, to be sure, and therefore, finally, rightly rejected; yet at the same time one with some genuine qualities of leadership and even of Shakespearean integrity. Indeed, pride, anger and a disgust at electoral politicking were incipient virtues rather than sins in Brecht's materialistic anthropology (see e.g. his *The Seven Deadly Sins of the Petty Bourgeois*). The dramaturgic investigations into Coriolan as character and type are focused on this very fact of genuinely exceptional faculties being turned to destructive purposes. As a note of Brecht's – a capital document for understanding his play – puts it:

In Plutarch as in Shakespeare, *Coriolanus* is the tragedy of a great and irreplaceable man. Even if Coriolanus goes too far in his demands, this is only the excess of an in itself grand attitude, which then becomes the reason for his tragic fall.

In the adaptation, a *tragedy of the individual* shifts into a *tragedy of the belief in irreplaceability.* It turns out that the belief in irreplaceability does destroy the individual, but not necessarily the people. True, a great number of persons can be put into a tragic position – but then they have to liberate themselves from the individual who has risen up against them.

Our tendency: the individual blackmails society by means of his irreplaceability.

That is a tragedy for the society. It loses 1. the individual; 2. it must expend vast means to defend itself. But most of all it is a tragedy for the individual, who has wrongly thought of himself as irreplaceable.

The apparent irreplaceability of the individual is a gigantic theme for a long time to come, leading from Antiquity to our period. The solution has to be a positive one for society, i.e. it is not necessary for it to let itself be blackmailed by the individual. The problem can in principle be solved, society can defend itself. In *Coriolan:* the way out for the *plebs* is self-defence.[3]

To recapitulate: the theme in hand is structured around two closely intertwined basic conflicts – the wars of the classes and nations, and the war of the great individual against society. Both conflicts are clearly delineated in the historical legend of Coriolanus; though Shakespeare was interested in both, it was the second or Individualistic one which was not only quite central but also the only tragically worthy conflict for him. Such a reduction of an originally bipolar situation could not satisfy a playwright such as Brecht, marked by the great mass social convulsions of our times, and he therefore, very ambitiously, proposed to do full justice to both these poles and types of conflicts in a new way, by presenting a new view of the Hero as well as of the City. Brecht's Hero is a dialectical contradiction between his genuinely great potentialities of leadership and his petty, obtuse wrong-headedness in channelling them against the good of a new society. Brecht's City (of which more below) is in a dialectical process of transcending the class oppositions into a popular democracy, opposed to the Hero as justice to privilege and as creativity to destruction. (These two oppositions are manifested by the Popular-Front Senate deciding at the end of the play to restore the lands to the Volscians and to construct the aqueduct; the Senate disallows mourning for Coriolan in order to continue with such business.)

Yet, even if it were agreed that all this has been demonstrated, some questions, I think, would remain. It is very curious that Brecht, choosing to adapt a play which shows his unquestionably deepest lifelong aversion, a warlike and slaughterhouse world, retained (say, in comparison to Livy) a relatively great role and even a dialectical respect for the destructive warrior-hero. How is it to be understood that, at the height of his playwriting career, he seemingly returned to focusing on the passion of a 'living embodiment of war' (II. i) – on one of those great lone leaders whose 'running amuck', as he liked to say, makes 'life and not death obscene' (*GW* XVI: 677) – instead of focusing on the little people? One has only to imagine a play centred on the generals of the Thirty Years' War instead of on Mother Courage and her children, or on the Grand Duke and the Caucasian princes instead of on Grusha and Azdak, in order to see the force of such questions. In brief, how come that Brecht found some elements in the Shakespearean 'drama for cannibals,' for psychic parasites who delight in other people's downfall on the stage (*GW* XVI: 666), useful?

At one point of his famous discussion of how to adapt the first scene, Brecht almost blithely justifies war as a normal economic necessity for a class society such as ancient Rome (*GW* XVI: 881). In capitalist terms, just as (to quote a chairman of General Motors) the business of America is business, the business of Rome was war. Virgil put it into his usual memorable imperialist form in the *Aeneid:* 'Remember, O Roman, that it is your business to bring down the proud and spare the subjected' (the proud ones being those who refuse to become subjected to Rome). In Marx's terms, as quoted from him by one of Brecht's closest collaborators in the *Coriolan* adaptation, at that stage of development of the productive forces 'war is the great overall task, the required communal work'.[4] This quote may have been – and the argument certainly was – known to Brecht, but its use is quite uncharacteristic for him, as can be seen if we compare his passionate position against war not only in his plays with a more 'modern' localisation but also in his *Antigone* play, whose story happens at a time of even greater primitivism and tribal barbarism than that of the Roman Republic. Thus, Coriolan, an incarnation of the passion for warfare just as Galileo was of the passion for science, becomes, also like

Galileo, a dialectical tragic hero. True, in these Brechtian dialectics we are not supposed only to feel with but also against such a tragic hero, and we are finally led to distance ourselves from him (*GW* XVII: 1252–3); even so, Coriolan is vastly superior to Arturo Ui or Lucullus. Where Ui is a hyena and Lucullus a peacock, Coriolan is a tiger, dangerous and to be disposed of, but undeniably fascinating. As Tynan noted, the animus of the Brechtian play and production is not against Coriolan himself but against 'the social role in which he is cast'.[5] What, then, is Coriolan's 'social role'?

2. The answer has to be approached through a considera-tion of the other pole of this play, the *plebeian democracy* of Rome – the citizens and the tribunes. For, as Brecht also noted during the adaptation: 'As far as the delight in the hero and the tragedy is concerned, we must go beyond the simple empathy into the hero Marcius in order to arrive at a richer delight; parallel to the tragedy of Coriolan, we must at least be capable to "experience" also the tragedy of Rome, especially of the *plebs*' (*GW* XVII: 1252). Indeed, if Brecht kept much from Shakespeare's Coriolanus pole, he decisively stood on its head – or stood back on its feet – Shakespeare's view of the 'citizens' or plebeians. The great Brechtian constellation of an at least balanced dramaturgic presentation of the rulers and the ruled, the social heights and depths, decisively enriches and widens the scope of the play from an Individualistic tragedy to a collective education for the spectators. As a Shakespearean scholar has remarked *à propos* of the first scene: 'One is forced to believe, not only by political passages in *Coriolanus* but by such passages in Shakespeare's work generally, that the reason why Shakespeare does not provide these opponents of Menenius and Coriolanus with an effective argument in favour of democracy is simply that he does not think any can be offered'.[6] Brecht supplies the missing arguments, not so much by any long speeches put into the citizens' mouths as by their behaviour and actions – especially by that of their most resolute or vanguard group led by the two tribunes. Where Coriolan begins as supremely good at war, the citizens begin as unwilling to fight, and are for that reviled by him:

> Anyone who trusts you
> Finds hares when he wants lions, geese when he looks
> For foxes. You hate the great because they are great. (I. i)

But Coriolan could not have been more wrong, for Brecht. After the plebeians get a political and economical share in the common wealth of the commonwealth, they turn out to be not only foxes, slyly easing Coriolan out of his consulship, but also lions, prepared finally to defend the walls of a city 'worth defending/Perhaps for the first time since it was founded' (V. iii). Thus, in a dialectical paradox, the plebeians are shown as being or becoming the only ones to possess the quality of the lion-cum-fox which Machiavelli – that best student of Livy before Brecht – claimed for his Prince: the plebeians grow into a lower-class version of Plato's collective Guardians of the *Politeia* or *res publica*. The citizens' share in the power of Rome amounts to a new founding of it upon the basis of social justice, which is at least as important as Romulus's drawing of the city walls in the blood of his brother Remus. Coriolan's fratricidal city of false betters, the fathers or well-born called *patritii*, up in arms against false inferiors, the offspring-begetters called *proletarii*, turns in this utopian vision of Brecht's into a fraternal city of land distribution and irrigation – i.e. of justice and creativity.

A famous poem of Brecht's, 'Questions of a Worker-Reader,' questions the usual history without the people:

> Who built seven-gated Thebes?
> The books give names of kings.
> Was it kings who hauled the lumps of rock?
> And the oft-destroyed Babylon –
> Who built it so oft up? In which of the houses
> Of gold-glittering Lima lived those who built them?
> On the evening the Chinese Wall was finished,
> Where did the masons go? Great Rome
> Is full of arcs of triumph. Who reared them up? Over whom
> Did the Caesars triumph?
>
> (adapted from H.R. Hays' transl.)

A history of the emperors and generals is, however, exactly Coriolan's view of history. His view of the world is even bloodier and bleaker: it is the Hobbesian view of man being wolf (or literally being a cannibal) to man. Here is what he shouts at the Citizens in the first scene, both in Shakespeare and in Brecht: 'You curse the senate who with the help of the gods/Maintain some little order. If they didn't/You'd *feed upon each other*' (emphasis added). Therefore, when Coriolan sees the (to him) totally unnatural sight of the masons arming to 'defend their walls' (V. iii), of hares turning lions, he is shattered. It is when he realises that even plebeians can be a new type of (a collective) lion or tiger that, stripped of his irreplaceability, he collapses in the meeting with his mother. This is one of the crucial scenes in Brecht's play, for here the dramaturgy is openly informed by a basically different motivation for this collapse: for Shakespeare's Individualist psychology, a Freudian mother-fixation of Coriolanus's, Brecht substitutes collective psychology, an Adlerian King-of-the-Beasts or King-of-the-Castle fixation.

However, this scene – and the whole play – will, of course, work only for an audience that accepts the plebeians as invested with the strong affective charge of Brecht's Marxian utopianism, which is in this play not too dissimilar from the contemporary concepts of Ernst Bloch. Indeed, the Roman plebeians and their tribunes are the radically democratic, Leninist and, if you wish, Jeffersonian or Painean, pole of his play. They are the rabble-in-arms, as in the American and Russian Revolutions, and their success is a Brechtian wish-dream and counter-project to the failed plebeian revolutions in Germany after both World Wars. *Coriolan* is, therefore, richly but at times puzzlingly, not only a rewriting of Shakespeare and ancient Roman history, but also a rewriting of the Leninist theme of state and revolution and modern German-cum-Russian history.

The main object of Lenin's writings in the summer of 1917 was to draw conclusions from the various French revolutions and the two Russian revolutions of 1905 and February 1917 as to the proper relation of revolution and state. In the situation of acute civil conflict (the nearest presentation of which in drama might be the opening of *Coriolanus*), an irreplaceable plank in his programme of gaining power was the arming of plebeian masses. Even his vocabulary can be found in Brecht's reworked play. Thus, Lenin's first major article on this theme is called 'On Dual Sovereignty'; at the height of the confrontation with the plebeians, Coriolan calls out:

That's dual sovereignty [*Das ist die Doppelherrschaft*],
...where greatness, power and wisdom
Can't move a step without the yes or no
Of the unreasoning mob. (II. iii)

Lenin's article defines the new type of power and state, on the model of the Paris Commune of 1871, as built on three pillars: first, the source of power is not Parliament but the direct initiative of popular masses from below; second, the army and police are abolished and replaced by 'direct arming of the whole people'; third, the bureaucracy or administrators are either abolished or put under special control with the possibility of instant recall by the people (L.9–11). In a second article, 'The Tasks of the Proletariat in Our Revolution,' Lenin devotes a chapter to 'dual sovereignty'. He finds that the main characteristic of the Russian situation between February and October 1917 is the existence of two governments: the main or executive one of the upper class, and the supplementary or 'controlling' one of the Petrograd Soviet or Council of Workers' and Soldier's Deputies. The first government controls the state institutions, the second a great majority of the people, the armed workers and the soldiers. He also notes that one of the principal signs of each revolution is the sudden growth in the number of people actively participating in political life and the structure of the state. Finally, in his book *The State and Revolution* Lenin sums up all his conclusions from the nineteenth-century revolutions, culminating in the Paris Commune, and of the Russian revolutions, culminating at that very moment, as the necesity of breaking up the bureaucracy and the standing army, which is replaced with the people in arms. He defines the essence of the whole matter of state and revolution as: 'Is the oppressed class armed?' and democracy as 'a state organisation that recognises the subjection of the minority to the majority.'[7]

In the 1950s Brecht was fresh from studying this whole theme while writing his play *Days of the Commune*, itself stimulated by his returning to a divided post-war Germany, where the question of revolutionary power and of competing armies and state authorities was a most crucial one. Immediately after his work on *Coriolan* he supervised an adaptation of Farquhar's *Recruiting Officer* which associated its sympathetic lower-class characters with the idea of

'Franklin, Jefferson and Washington', of the Declaration of Independence by a 'rabble-in-arms', a militia of the oppressed. The position of Brecht's *Coriolan* between these Paris Commune and American Revolution plays characterises its political locus too. For, heretically, Brecht does not follow Lenin's warning that 'double sovereignty' can only last a very brief time.[8] Instead, he fuses Livy's thesis (echoing even in Plutarch) that just such a civic co-operation between the upper and lower classes made for a strong Rome, with the post-1930s' Marxist practice of a Popular Front of all patriots – ideally from both upper and lower classes – against militarism, right-wing dictatorship, and Fascist aggression. This political practice led to the establishment of broad wartime coalitions in countries such as France or Italy and of 'people's democracies' after the war, from China to Yugoslavia – and to East Germany. Whatever some of these Popular Fronts and Democracies may or may not have turned into later on, under the impact of the Cold War and Stalinism, it is evident that Brecht had a great sympathy for their original warm impulse. The famous, and in the play's original demagogic context evidently false, parable about the belly and the members as 'incorporate friends' (I. i) is taken seriously and literally by his plebeians. Where Menenius tries to convince them, against the evidence of their hunger, that when the Senate-belly is full the citizen-members are also full, the tribunes demand – and enforce – a real distribution of the corn and olives among all members of the body politic. Quite logically in terms of the above parable, the citizen members will not work or fight if they cannot eat. However, when evidence for the 'incorporation' is obtained, when their delegates control the bureaucracy and the professional warlord is exiled, so that life, liberty, and the pursuit of happiness are open to them – then they are ready to enrol into a Jeffersonian or Leninist militia organised by electoral districts not too dissimilar from a Soviet. In this 'democratic Rome... with the tribunes of the people' (*GW* XVI: 880–1) hare turns lion, or as Brutus the tribune says after the people's readiness has devastated Coriolan:

> The stone has moved. The people takes
> Up arms, and the old earth shakes.
> (V. v. Adapted from R. Manheim's transl.)

Such telescoping and foreshortening as well as distancing or estranging of urgent current historical issues into or between the lines of Shakespeare's play can, I would submit, also explain the contradictory nature of Brecht's Coriolan, so much more than simply a fascist-type general. In the famous discussion-essay on the first scene of this play, mentioned above, all the East Berlin discussants in 1952–3 agree that for them the play comes to life only when it is centred on Coriolan's belief that he is irreplaceable. Thereupon, a pupil asks Brecht whether that feeling stems from the fact that 'we find the same kind of thing here and feel the tragedy of the conflicts that result from it?' Brecht's answer, simply and starkly: is 'Undoubtedly' (*GW* XVI: 886–87). Now, in that era of High Stalinism, the great leader running berserk and believing himself to be indispensable could not fail to be associated with Generalissimo Joseph Stalin (and possibly the lesser Stalins that Stalinism bred). Stalin was emphatically an individual who blackmailed his society 'by means of his irreplaceability' as leader and organiser; this is why Brecht's long note quoted earlier discreetly alludes to the fact that such 'apparent irreplaceability' is a gigantic theme in 'our period' too.[9] Stalin was officially proclaimed a strategist of genius, victor both in the Civil War and the second World War, both times in the city to which he was eponymous as Coriolan to Corioli – the city of Stalingrad. Furthermore, Trotsky perspicaciously compared his (and our) age to the bloody Italian Renaissance and Stalin to a *condottiere* (much like Coriolanus). But even apart from such direct parallels, Coriolan's expertise and usefulness in war is mainly a parable for Stalin's expertise and usefulness in organising social productivity in the USSR, which Brecht always valued highly. (See *Me-Ti, GW* XII. I believe that this evaluation was rather too cheerful, though Brecht can be largely – not wholly – excused by the fact that the full story of Stalin's immense anti-plebeian outrages was not yet documented at the time.) Stalin's main failing was, to Brecht's mind, that his political capacities were not on the level of his organisational ones, so that he turned into a 'workers' and peasants' emperor' rather than remaining the tribune of a Leninist popular democracy (*GW* XII: 538–41). Analogously, all of Coriolan's wisdom is in warfare and none in politics. Furthermore, the precariousness of Stalin's political basis made it necessary for him, as

Brecht noted, to be adulated as the greatest rather than the most useful one (*GW* XII: 467, 491, 536). Much the same is said of Coriolan in the final explicit judgement on him, passed by Aufidius in words which are Brecht's addition to the legend:

> He could not exchange
> The saddle for the seat of government
> Or war for peace. His deeds are great
> But he dwarfs them by extolling them. Our merit
> Depends upon the use our epoch makes of us.
>
> (IV. iv)

Coriolan, like Stalin, did not allow the epoch of the *plebs* to make full – or indeed any – use of him.

The confrontation of the two tribunes and Coriolan is therefore, on one level of this complex dramatic parable, also a confrontation between the pristine revolutionary impulse (in German terms, echoing the Spartacist tribunes Luxemburg and Liebknecht) and – as Brecht hoped – the resurgent democratic Leninism of the plebeian masses with the once – but now no longer – useful bloody stage of Stalinism. (It speaks for Brecht's perspicacity that the arming of the workers and the lifting of military threat is exactly what happened when Gomulka faced Stalin's successor Khrushchev in Warsaw in 1956; whereas it is exactly what Dubček failed to do when faced with Khrushchev's successor in 1968 – he relied instead on a Volumnian pleading.) This very important constellation of forces is, I believe, the reason why Brecht returned in this play to the theme of the greatly talented *condottiere* or leader abusing his talents against a possible utopian step forward in history. Such a hero is no longer necessary to the self-governing City.

3. In conclusion, then, this play signifies an evolving and in fact radically changing world of modern politics based on popular power *vs.* either upper-class usurpation or Individualist King-of-the-Castle heroism. The direct participation of citizens in state affairs is identified with peace, unity and creativity, and the oligarchic or monarchic irreplaceability with war, dissension and destruction. The great but berserker – yet also berserker but great – Hero is tragic because he becomes useless and indeed dangerous to his City. The City of popular unity can avoid tragedy and dispense with the Hero by becoming a directly self-managing state, where – as the dramaturgy shows in the play's balance of private and public scenes – all the quondam places of privilege have become as non-antagonistic as any family or private house. Or better, the distinction between harmonious privacy (usually shown as an upper-class one) and disharmonious public life of class strife is fading, parallel to the fading of ethnic usurpation through warfare.

Further, Brecht's version of the Coriolanus legend, though it has remained in a first draft stage, must be acknowledged as one of considerable originality. An anecdote relates that when Piscator staged Schiller's *Robbers* in the 1920s and gave to Karl Moor, the leader of a bandit or guerilla group, the mask of the leader of the Red Army, Trotsky, he (Piscator) said: 'I wanted the audience to notice that 150 years are not a mere trifle.' His friend, Brecht, wanted us to notice that the 2000 years since Livy or even the 350 years since Shakespeare are no mere trifle: history and the views on history evolve, and we cannot think of plebeians today as of Shakespeare's 'rats,' 'dissentious rogues,' 'curs,' 'quarter'd slaves,' 'fragments,' etc. (all of these lofty expressions from his first scene only). If '[the] plain fact is that [Shakespeare] is on the side of the patricians whenever they are to be taken as representing a theory of government, and that he gives them an advantage even in the first scene of the play', then the plain fact is that Brecht is on the opposite side: his is a plebeian theory of government. Quite formalistically, one can point to this as the most original twist to the Coriolanus legend in 2000 years. But more than formal matters are at issue: let us call them ethical and dramaturgic ones. Just as the Elizabethan monarchist playwright, so the Leninist plebeian one, though living in even bloodier times, 'shows a singular detachment in his ability to find human faults on both sides and a singular breadth of sympathy in his ability to find human virtues on both sides.'[10] On the one hand, the plebeians can fall under the spell of national victories and foolishly choose Coriolan for ruler – as the Soviets chose Stalin; the tribunes can foolishly refuse to believe the news of Coriolan's rising against them, as Stalin refused to believe the news of Hitler's aggression (and as Ulbricht will refuse to believe in the workers' revolt of June 1953). On the other hand, I have argued how many virtues the Leninist playwright finds in the great leader Coriolan – almost, though not quite, as many as the monarchist playwright. But ultimately, no doubt, Brecht is plumping here for the second term of his permanent dilemma between the society's need for heroes and danger from them, most succinctly expressed in his *Galileo* as the famous replies:

Andrea: Unhappy the land that breeds no hero.
Galileo: No, Andrea: Unhappy the land that needs a hero.
                                                    (transl. C. Laughton)

Thus, Brecht is, of course, a playwright supremely interested in the interaction of the Hero and the City (Livy's *Urbs* or Aristotle's *polis*), and he can therefore be with Aristotle defined as a civic or political playwright. Even so, he is after all more playwright delighting in a good villain than politician eliminating his opponent: on condition that the villain be finally defeated at the hands of the self-helping, self-governing, self-managing City which needs him no more.

The 'raw material' of Shakespeare's beautiful barbaric play in its contradictory richness was indispensable to Brecht; he 'merely' tried to reconduce it from Individualistic tragedy into bipolar dialectics. He is reported as saying that 'He inclined to displacing contemporary problems into the past, as Shakespeare had done. The reason is simple: problems could be distanced, thereby more easily understood as well as presented in an unaccustomed, interest-rousing form.'[11] In that perspective, Shakespeare is no more just raw material but an example of 'great historical theatre' which is neither parodied nor simply reversed but 'reintegrated into a dialectics of society.'[12] Obversely, as Brecht was fond of saying, only sacrileges sanctify (*GW* XV: 335). Whether we agree with him or not, *Coriolan* has 'left an indelible mark on Shakespeare's.'[13] I do not believe that anybody can perform *Coriolanus* henceforth without defining him or herself in relation to *Coriolan*.

This is itself as much as theatre can do to theatre. But Brecht had even larger ambitions: he wanted theatre to do

something to the spectators, so that they would do
something to reality. In his poem 'Address to the Danish
Worker-Actors' he wrote:

> You actors of our time,
> The time of change
> And the time of the great taking over
> Of all nature to master it
> Not forgetting human nature, . . .
> Give us the world of men as it is,
> Made by men and changeable.
> . . .
> You with the intentness of your studies
> And the elation of your knowledge
> Can make the experience of struggle
> The property of all
> And transform justice
> Into a passion.
>
> (*GW* IX: 761 and 766, transl. J. Berger and A. Bostock)

Brecht's play *Coriolan* is an attempt to transform justice into a
passion.

Notes

[1] In order to avoid confusion, I shall call Brecht's protagonist and
play Coriolan (as in German), while Shakespeare's protagonist
and play, as well as the protagonist of the historical legend, will
be called Coriolanus.

This essay was written as the result of an experimental drama
project at McGill University, culminating in a production of
Brecht's adaptation, re-adapted with new text supplied by
myself, George Szanto and the students in my dramaturgy class
who were also the cast of the performance; cf. the performance
programme *Brecht's 'Koriolane'*, ed. D. Suvin (Montreal: McGill
University, 1976). As in previous essays, I have avoided notes
except where absolutely necessary, though the project involved
a great deal of research into Roman history, Shakespeare and
Brecht (including a review of the whole secondary literature on
this play of his to 1975). Beside the general approaches to Brecht
and his earlier plays mentioned in the notes to the preceding
chapters, I have particularly profited by the works of Dieck-
mann, Dort, Kuczynski, McCann, Mayer, Rülicke, Strehler,

Tenschert, Tynan, Weigel, Wekwerth and Witzmann listed in
Grimm's bibliography, p. 86. To them should be added at least:
Ernst Bloch, 'Die Fabel des Menenius Agrippa', in *Vom Hasard
zur Katastrophe* (Frankfurt, 1972); Heike Marten Brunkhorst,
Shakespeares 'Coriolanus' in deutscher Bearbeitung (Berlin, 1974);
Ruby Cohn, *Modern Shakespeare Offshoots* (Princeton, 1976);
Ladislaus Löb and Laurence Lerner, 'Views of Roman History:
Coriolanus and *Coriolan*', *Comparative Literature, 29* (1977),
35–53; Werner Mittenzwei, *Brechts Verhältnis zur Tradition*
(Berlin DDR, 1973); R.B. Parker, 'Dramaturgy in Shakespeare
and Brecht', *Univ. of Toronto Quarterly, 32* (1963), 22–46;
Arrigo Subiotto, *Bertolt Brecht's Adaptations for the Berliner
Ensemble* (London, 1975); and Rodney T.K. Symington,
'Coriolanus', in *Antike Tradition im Werk Bertolt Brechts* (Berlin,
1964). Cf. also the notes in the *BBA* (Bertolt-Brecht-Archiv,
Berlin DDR), Signatur 650 and 672, also 93, 173, 238, 670, 673,
1647, 1769, 1823; and the drafts of scenes noted in Hertha
Ramthun (ed.), *Bertolt-Brecht-Archiv: Bestandsverzeichnis des liter-
arischen Nachlasses* (Berlin DDR, 1969), I: 238–45. As in previous
chapters, Brecht is cited by *GW* volume: page. It must be
mentioned that the eventual Berliner Ensemble production in
1964 largely forsook Brecht's horizon and changes, so that a
different essay would be needed to deal with this further,
post-Brecht version.

2 Cf. the accounts of Jacobsohn and of Wiegler, quoted in Peter
Gebhardt, 'Brechts *Coriolan*-Bearbeitung', *Jahrbuch der deutschen
Shakespeare-Gesellschaft (West) 1972* (Heidelberg, 1972), p. 113.

3 This quotation from Brecht does not seem to have been
published either in *GW* or in its supplement, the *Arbeitsjournal*
(Frankfurt, 1974). The part I translate here is quoted in full in
Henning Rischbieter, *Brecht II* (Velber, 1966), p. 75, and in part
by Brecht's then assistant Manfred Wekwerth, *Notate* (Frankfurt, 1967), p. 130–1, who identifies it as a note in Brecht's
working diary from July 1952, as well as by Subiotto, *op. cit.*, p.
166, who found it in *BBA*, Signatur 650. At any rate, Brecht
uses extremely similar formulations in, e.g., *GW* XVII: 1252–3
and the *Arbeitsjournal* II, pp. 572–3 (entry of 20 May 1951). In
fact, based on these sources as well as on the famous discussion
of the first scene in *Coriolanus* (*GW* XVI: 869–88), the *BBA*
material, and Brecht's general approach to Shakespeare (cf. also
GW XV: 127, 149, 181, 332–6, and *GW* XVI: 586–93, 666–7,
809), it is clear Brecht intended throughout two basic changes in
his adaptation. One was replacing the attitude of 'wounded
pride' in the protagonist by the newly relevant attitude of 'belief

in his irreplaceability'; the other was a radical change in the
attitude of (and thus also toward) the plebeians – see *Arbeitsjournal*, loc. cit.

4 Karl Marx, *Grundrisse* (Berlin, 1953), p. 391, quoted in Käthe
Rülicke-Weiler, *Die Dramaturgie Brechts* (Berlin DDR, 1966), p.
149; the writer was, together with Wekwerth, one of Brecht's
assistants in the 1950s.

5 Kenneth Tynan, *Tynan Right and Left* (New York, 1968), p. 161.
On rulers as members of the animal kingdom, see Brecht's
pertinent 'Die Ballade vom Wasserrad', *GW* III: 1007–8 ['Ballad
of the Waterwheel']:

> Ah, we've had so many masters,
> Swine or eagle, lean or fat one:
> Some were tigers, some hyenas,
> Still we fed this one and that one ....
> (transl. H.R. Hays)

Subiotto, *op. cit.*, p. 184, draws a pertinent parallel to Schiller's
insight in the preface to *The Robbers:* 'If I wish to warn against
the tiger, I may not omit his blindingly beautiful spotted skin, in
order that the tiger should not be absent from the tiger [*damit
man nicht den Tyger beym Tyger vermisse*].'

6 Willard Farnham, *Shakespeare's Tragic Frontier* (Berkeley, 1963),
pp. 228–9. From the large critical literature on Shakespeare's
play, I have further found most useful: A.C. Bradley, *A
Miscellany* (London, 1929); Kenneth Burke, *Language as Symbolic
Action* (Berkeley, 1966); R.W. Chambers, *Shakespeare's Hand in
the Play of Sir Thomas More* (Cambridge, 1923); William Hazlitt,
Characters of Shakespear's Plays (London, 1812); Herman Heuer,
'From Plutarch to Shakespeare', *Shakespeare Survey, 10* (London,
1957), pp. 50–9; Clifford Chalmers Huffman, *'Coriolanus' in
Context* (Bucknell PA., 1971), L.C. Knights, *Some Shakespearean
Themes* (London, 1959); Millar MacLure, 'Shakespeare and the
Lonely Dragon', *Univ. of Toronto Quarterly, 24* (1955), 109–20;
J. Palmer, *Political Characters of Shakespeare* (London, 1945); E.C.
Pettet, *'Coriolanus* and the Midlands Insurrection of 1607'
Shakespeare Survey, 3 (London, 1950), pp. 34–42; J.E. Phillips,
The State in Shakespeare's Greek and Roman Plays (New York,
1940); and A.P. Rositer, *Angel With Horns* (London, 1961). For
the overall relation of Brecht and Shakespeare the basic special
studies are those of Dort and Parker (see note 1), but see also the
book-length parallel in Karen Hermassi, *Polity and Theatre in
Historical Perspective* (London, 1977), which includes Aeschylus;

and the brief but stimulating mention in George Szanto, *Theater and Propaganda* (Austin, 1978), pp. 194–5, within a general juxtaposition of Beckett and the Wakefield Mystery Cycle.

7 V.I. Lenin, *Gosudarstvo i revoliutsiia*, in *Izbrannye proizvedeniia v dvukh tomakh* (Moscow, 1946), II: 176, 180, transl. D.S. (cf. in English, *The State and the Revolution* (Peking, 1973), pp. 89, 97). The two earlier named articles are 'O dvoevlastii,' ibid., pp. 5–11, and 'Zadachi proletariata v nashei revoliutsii', pp. 12–36.

8 Ibid., p. 15.

9 Cf. on the central Brechtian innovation of the protagonist's 'irreplaceability', note 3. The debate on Brecht's relation to Stalinism, which was complex, has so far been a rather unenlightening, often materially wrong axe grinding. I shall here identify only the main passages in *GW* to be taken into account for a balanced judgement: the *Me-Ti* parables, in particular XII: 422, 467, 491, 523, 535–40, 554; the notes on politics, in particular XX: 60–5, 98–121, 325–6; the *Arbeitsjournal;* and correspondence or reports, e.g. Walter Benjamin's diary note in *Understanding Brecht* (London, 1973), pp. 117–18. For a first comment, taking into account the very relevant influence of Rosa Luxemburg and Karl Korsch on Brecht, cf. Heinz Brüggeman, *Literarische Technik und soziale Revolution* (Reinbek, 1973), pp. 104–9.

Practically all the comments of people connected with the Berliner Ensemble hint more or less openly at the parallel Coriolan–Stalin. The clearest is perhaps Wekwerth's note from 1964 on the adaptation's use of the 'personality cult... an observation of events from our times', *op. cit.*, p. 124.

10 Both quotations in this paragraph are from Farnham, p. 227.

11 Ernst Schumacher, 'Er wird bleiben', in Hubert Witt (ed.), *Erinnerungen an Brecht* (Leipzig, 1964), p. 332.

12 Bernard Dort, 'Brecht devant Shakespeare', *R. d'histoire du théâtre*, 17 (1965), p. 83.

13 Tynan, *op. cit.*, p. 162.

Marching Thru' The BB Mountain Range

The pleasure of dazzling peach and sweet plum is quick
And simple, the pleasure of the great pine stretching tall
Deep and complex. Blossom-time is beautiful but soon gone
Petals revert to brown earth and fade in, the pine grows
Needles all the time, eventually cones, goes on branching
Slow and sure like sexual congress on the morning
Of the fifth night.
I love the textual melody of old Bert for he memorably
Mingles the deep and quick rhythms grasping the palpably present
Things and relations of our unrepeatable but alternative worlds
How they are and also could be, altered. From his youth he was
Wholly a passion for the just gesture, a serious jester exiled by
The scary witless theatre of power. With him went always
The little scroll of the Skeptic, the cloth cap of finest material
And plebeian cut
And the nodding model donkey who had to understand too. Shifting
Clockwise he ran hoops around the fascists in three world
Theatres of deadly power, his own Pale Mother, imperial
Muscovy like the banks of the Styx, on to the Dream Factory where
Lies are sold extricably mixed with truth, always typing
Without caps for the once and future Berlin workers of the world
Stories of wily
Swabian peasants, a classical Chinese-style poet, public
Intellectual impatient of dominant hierarchies if domineering
Himself: a high range we can however not only lift eyes
Toward and see but also tread upon, going up.
                                        Yet by now
Mountain grave has grown a marble monument, and we must remember
How he said progressing is better than being progressive
And leave to go
Further thru' wild grass, following the present star of pleasure,
The breeze playful in our hair, nevertheless bearing along
As we traverse new rocky passes, seedlings planted
On BB Mountain Range; many of them still growing, tight
Blind scale-work cones, as with passion and regret we move
Pleasurably on.

8

Beckett's Purgatory of the Individual, or the Three Laws of Thermodynamics

(NOTES FOR AN INCAMINATION TOWARD A PRELIMINOUS EXAGMINATION ROUND HIS TEMPORIZING DEDRAMATURGIFICATION)

A critic of modern dramaturgy with a bent for Brecht and Chekhov, for the Berliner Ensemble and Théâtre National Populaire, Strehler and Planchon in the 1950s and 1960s; for Marx and Bloch – one, in other words, who enjoys the dramaturgy and theatre fully when they participate, by means of their specific, exemplary sensual presentness, in the great liberating effort of our century – has one outstanding difficulty to come to terms with, if he or she is to be sincere to his trade and even to her or his (*ex hypothesi*) encompassing horizons: Samuel Beckett. If the chief measure of a major dramatist is a happy union of relevance and consistency of dramaturgic vision, there is little doubt that in our cultural circle – middle and western Europe, based on the Mediterranean, with the massive wings of the Soviet Union and North America – the two major dramatists since the second World War are Brecht and Beckett. Yet it is rare for a critic devoted to Beckett seriously and knowledgeably to face Brecht. I can think of only one such comprehensive effort – Martin Esslin's – and that one, to my mind, is finally unconvincing. Conversely, however, I can think of no critic of the Brechtian bent who has attempted a comprehensive study of Beckett. This chapter cannot, of course, pretend to such comprehensiveness, but it may suggest a need for it and lines of further exploration. In the process, I would claim for it at least one merit: that of shunning the prevailing tendency to accept or reject Beckett on purely ideological grounds, because of the closed existential horizons of his works. There are many instances of uncritical acceptance of Beckett's works. As for uncritical rejection, I will quote only one example from Werner Hecht, a prominent theatre historian and theoretician from the Berliner Ensemble, in an article whose ironic title translates as 'Brecht "and" Beckett – An Absurd Comparison': 'Yet, for people who want to change the world to make it habitable, Beckett's theatre is uninteresting, lacking in matter and wit, simply: very old wine in not even quite new bottles.'[1] The best way to avoid aprioristic refusals, as well as fashionable adulations, seems to lie in trying, first, to consider Beckett's dramatic vision of world and man fully, in its internal consistency. From there, one should place it in its genetic and anthropological perspective in order, finally, to arrive at some conclusion about its external relevance.

1. Beckett's world[2] is, first of all, a closed one, of the cosmological family to which a Ptolemaic world also belongs, yet differing from that world by being dolorously and morbidly (some sicknesses induce a special awareness for certain relationships) conscious of the theoretical possibility, and perhaps need, for a transcendental vertical opening. Such a possibility is shown on the stage in *Act Without Words 1,* and it provides one of the poles of tension in *Waiting for Godot.* This does not mean that such an opening implies (or that Godot is to be equated with) a Christian, Buddhist, or any other kind of god. The closeness and distance between God and Godot is exactly indicated by their names. Godot is a kind of (small, impotent) god, being for Didi and Gogo absent from that place where God used to be present for Christians. Yet in his vanishing elusiveness Godot is at the same time a pseudo-god, a surrogate of doubtful existentiality; in fact, as biologists would have it, he is functionally analogous to God, as gills are to lungs. The existence of the closed world, however, is not in doubt, and its constantly renewed implicit comparison with more open alternatives is a fundamental device by means of which the encapsulated Beckettian world is felt as unnaturally small, oppressively claustrophobic:

Hamlet: Denmark's a prison.
Rosencrantz: Then is the world one.

Hamlet: A goodly one; in which there are many confines,
            wards and dungeons, Denmark being one of the
            worst.

                                          (*Hamlet*, II. ii)

As compared to Hamlet's scope, Beckett's world has shrunk,
it is not even a 'goodly' prison, yet it manages to include
quite a few 'confines, wards and dungeons', strikingly
visualised in the celebrated jars of *Endgame* and *Play*, or the
canned voice-confines of *Krapp's Last Tape* and *Cascando*.

One cannot but interpolate here that such a world excludes
most empirical perceptions and values, that it intersects with
the empirical 'only in the most desolate instances or at certain
almost unbearable moments.'[3] Again, by the strange Beckettian twilight dialectics, this is and is not a living world. It is a
life-in-death or death-in-life fauna and flora, almost like the
world of a Lovecraft fantasy or a surreal limbo. With its lack
of movement and activity – and the cyclical repetitiveness
that I shall discuss further on – it is clearly a hopeless version
of Dante's Purgatory (more particularly, as Beckett's interest
in the figure of Belacqua proves, of the lowest 'leap' of the
Antepurgatorio, where the negligent await the end of their
punishment): an inverted Purgatory, with life over but not
finished.

Terra Beckettiana is an aimless island universe, not only
desolate but constantly running down. The objects, colours,
energies are all in a state of degradation, visible as the
cumulative fatigue of Gogo and Didi and the physical
deterioration of Pozzo and Lucky (in which context I feel that
the flowering tree is no more than an ironically ambiguous
pitfall), the running out of food and drugs in *Endgame*, the
growth of the heap entombing Winnie – as a general 'cascando' rhythm both of the whole and within the particular
instances. This universe tends asymptotically to an absolute
zero of energy, the famous *Wärmetod* – an end of the universe
in absolute lack of light, movement and warmth – with
which the *fin-de-siècle* physicists (Boltzmann, etc.) used to
scarify a tired *fin-de-siècle* Europe.[4] Professor Kenner has
wittily noted that the main characteristics of the Beckettian
cosmos—a closed system and the degradation of its energy –
are in fact the two laws of thermodynamics. There remained
unnoted, however, the third law of thermodynamics

(Nernst's theorem: absolute zero can only be approached asymptotically, i.e. getting ever closer to it without ever reaching it) which is just as characteristic of Beckett's rhythm and vision, and which should be accorded as important a place in any conclusion about him.

In such a world, where senselessness has radically blurred any clear aims, gestural and verbal action becomes purposeless and formal. It moves in a peculiar repetitive shuttle:

> *Estragon:* Funny, the more you eat the worse it gets.
> *Vladimir:* With me it's just the opposite.
> *Estragon:* In other words?
> *Vladimir:* I get used to the muck as I go along.
> *Estragon:* *(after prolonger reflection).* Is that the opposite ...?

Such a vicious circle, repeated at length, turns exertion into stasis, human existence into an inconsequential nightmare, the passage of time into an effect of timelessness. It subjects the reader or onlooker to disillusion at the end of each illusory period of achievement. The interchangeable nature of these periods, of the whole 'going along', creates an indeterminate time both temporal and timeless, correlative to the nondescript, purgatorial quality of the space. Time, whose measure is movement and change, has almost come to a stop. But not quite; there is still some rudimentary activity and consequence: "Ma vie ... est finie et elle dure à la fois, mais par quel temps exprimer cela?' (*Molloy*).[5]

A time characterised by arrested development in a vague world is a time of infantile characters,[6] whose inability to transcend a religious framework is counterbalanced by their consciousness of the absurdity of such a situation. This sliding between two epistemological levels constitutes the saving Beckettian dry black humour, which has probably been the decisive *aesthetic* factor in establishing his dramatic vision. Beckett's savage wit – at times Swiftian – leads to playing existential games, emulating and parodying empirical reality and trying arbitrarily to establish some structure in the near-vacuum of his world. Any work of his may be regarded as one extended game involving a limit-situation of human consciousness – a 'limit' translated into time (at the point of death, or perhaps of a ritual birth) and space (a limbo, or the beach of *Embers* and *Cascando*). Such an

Einsteinian time/space system is dominated by 'the mirthless laugh ... the saluting of the highest joke' (*Watt*): the game is played as a mirthless laugh both at the unseen powers which have sardonically foreordained such a world and at the world itself.

For a game, there must be two or more players: in this bleak system, a pair (present or implied) is the favourite number. Two people not only throw cues and responses to each other, they also play out a certain gamut of relationships towards objects and each other, engaging in music-hall cross-talk (as do Gogo and Didi), or demonstrating a power relationship (as do Pozzo and Lucky). Beckett's nature – including human nature – is 'a composite of perceiver and perceived'.[7] In his pair of figures each is the other's perceiver and perceived, the speaker and the listener necessary for communication in a closed world. Their sardonic game is played within each play by a 'comic gamut' of estranging, impudent devices, carried out by clowning. As an acute French critic observed, 'Floating between frank grossness and poignant poetry, his plays have the charm of a circus, the fascination of thought. They are illustrated philosophy (like the circus): an image of man is placed in the ring'.[8] The clown is a comedian consciously focusing his and the audience's awareness on his impotence, an epistemological rather than psychological stage figure. He is usually childishly gullible before objects, yet constantly, if with little success, reaching out toward understanding and refusing to submit to the entropy of order. Beckett's clowns are dehumanised because apparently deprived of history: yet history has shaped the presuppositions of their purgatorial environment. It is no longer only a background (as it would have been, say, in Ibsen) but has pervaded them so completely that they can no longer enter into any real collision with it: not even with their 'inner environment', as was possible for Pirandello's Eve and Lina, or Brecht's Shen Te and Shui Ta. The pseudo-escape from history has only delivered them more completely and helplessly into its hands. Even their language has become functionally transparent, just bricks for the building of scenic situations which show exhaustively that there is nothing to show. The grim and pedantic sticking to banalities is offset only by bawdiness and by a certain melancholy which seems to settle over the forlorn quest for sense. They are clownish victims, existing because of a 'hypothetical imperative', oscillating between attempts at a ludicrous gentility and *Lumpenproletarian* obscenity and violence, arrested between apathy and a hope of Nirvana. Here Nirvana is a consummation devoutly to be wished for, and blasphemously disbelieved in.

2. Why is Beckett's painfully consistent world such as it is? As Brecht would put it, what events behind it are the key to its events? An answer is necessary before judging Beckett's world-view. Has the author, as many apologists claim, in his nightmares and fears just happened to hit upon some archetypal horrors of the self, presumably identical in – and relevant for – a Vietnamese peasant, a Yugoslav worker, a French intellectual, and an American businessman (or at least, as the more cautious acknowledge, the last two)? No doubt, any valid artistic vision is a product of the 'inner evironment' of its author; depersonalised writing, ads or slogans, can only use clichés, scraps of once valid visions. But to argue on the basis of this tautological commonplace (as Beckett too seems to do in the case of Proust) that the inner reality of any valid writer is beyond history because the writer himself (or his critic) rejects history, means to forget not only the great maxim which D.H. Lawrence formulated as 'Never trust the teller; trust the tale', but most human and critical experience too. The sardonic fate of Beckettian figures, caught in the viscous substance of arrested history because of their refusal to intervene into history, should be an appropriate warning.

   Many students of Beckett have noted that his work is a radically foreshortened recapitulation of a certain cognitive and artistic tradition, almost a boiling down of a segment of intellectual history. A few have gone as far as to identify that segment, mostly at its source: 'all Beckett's work paradoxically insists upon and rebels against the Cartesian definition of man as "a thing that thinks", ... the Cartesian cleavage between the world *in re* and the world *in intellectu* ...'[9], but sometimes at its silting-up point: 'Beckett's *Comédie* is Feydeau seen from beyond the grave',[10] or as a comprehensive *Götterdämmerung* (here said *à propos* of his prose but applicable to all his work): '[behind Beckett's novel trilogy lie] acres of fictional moralising, reams of gnomic self-praise, and bundles of romances chronicling the acquisition and dispersal of portable property, from *Robinson Crusoe* to *The Spoils of Poynton*.'[11] If Beckett's work is, as the above further concludes, a 'compendious abstract' of a certain epoch 'in most general terms', these general terms should be accorded much greater, perhaps central, attention by any critic believing that (as the biologists would put it) the 'inner environment' is genetically shaped too – in the case of the human animal much more by social than by biological heredity. As argued in the first part of this book, that epoch's 'most general term' and stylistically decisive category is Individualism, i.e. a vision, feeling, or cognition of human relations with the world of things and other people from the standpoint of the Individual as the irreducible, atomic touchstone and measure. Individualism is a world-view arrived at in Italy at the time of Petrarch and Machiavelli, a century later in France and the Netherlands, and another century later in England. There it eventually found a most striking literary exemplification in the archetypical figure of Robinson Crusoe on his island, justly felt so relevant to Beckett's pairs of Robinsons and their latterday island worlds.[12]

The centuries of Individualism between Bacon or Descartes and Proust or Beckett are, of course, the time of the definitive victory of money economy over natural economy. This *Instauratio Magna* led to many and great triumphs of man over nature, but the price paid for it was stiff, probably exorbitant. The price of the new enterprising 'Faustian'[13] spirit may be summed up as *desensualisation* and *reification*. Desensualisation of man's relation to material reality is a direct result of all commodities being reduced to the tyrannical common denominator of money. All phenomena appear then as subject to quantitative measurement; all values, including God, can be treated as entries in an individual profit and loss *conto corrente*. The *en gros* sale of indulgences which enraged the sturdy sensitivity of Martin Luther was only the logical end-result of a system where posthumous legacies were supposed to atone for their own usurous sources. The dominant middle-class feeling treats

God increasingly as the owner of a huge and many-sided commercial firm, larger than but not differing in principle from those of Bardi and Peruzzi, the Medicis or the Fuggers. All of the middle class being God's children, he is according-ly each one's potential senior partner.

Estragon:	What exactly did we ask him to do for us? (...)
Vladimir:	Oh ... nothing very definite.
Estragon:	A kind of prayer.
Vladimir:	Precisely.
Estragon:	A vague supplication.
Vladimir:	Exactly.
Estragon:	And what did he reply?
Vladimir:	That he'd see.
Estragon:	That he couldn't promise anything.
Vladimir:	That he'd have to think it over.
Estragon:	In the quiet of his home.
Vladimir:	Consult his family.
Estragon:	His friends.
Vladimir:	His agents.
Estragon:	His correspondents.
Vladimir:	His books.
Estragon:	His bank account.
Vladimir:	Before taking a decision.
Estragon:	It's the normal thing.
Estragon:	Is it not?
Vladimir:	I think it is.
Estragon:	I think so too. (*Silence.*)

In the balance sheet of individual life, the new 'double-entry' bookkeeping (*ragioneria*, systematised by Fra Pacioli in the fifteenth century) severs money invested from its natural-economy function of acquiring objects necessary for life: in the new system money acts autotelically, existing purely for quantitative self-propagation, which gave canonic Christian writers a good deal of trouble right up to the time of Ben Jonson.[14] All the qualities of objects become thus irrelevant for commerce, which has the great convenience of sweeping away the limitations imposed by human nature and personal needs (one can eat, wear out, etc., only so many objects in a given time). The sensual data of cloth or cloves, flour or colour, surrender pride of place to the rational information about the amount of capital invested and profit earned, which can be only larger or smaller; quantity is money's only quality. Success in Individualist life manifests itself as the size of the profit. The ideal entrepreneur of a money economy measures values against a phantom scale of ciphers overriding the terrene, sensual reality and isolating the measurer from that reality: *quod non est in libris, non est in mundo*. The ideal capitalist should, thus, live privately in one and socially in another world: he moves into the familiar field of a growing split between ambition and enjoyment, body and reason, feeling and thought, the immanent and the transcendental. In the somewhat obscure terminology of T.S. Eliot (who has, however, the merit of having been the first modern Anglo-American critic to draw attention to this group of facts) – his sensibility dissociates.[15]

The profit principle and the ideology of Rationalism meet on the grounds of belief in omnipotent quantity – in the number. The very term *ratio* (*ragione, raison*) slides from the classical, Ciceronian sense of 'reason, relation, manner, calculation, account' into the sense of an entry (*conto*) in ledgers, and finally into that of a commercial establishment or concern. Rationalism means, quite literally, the ideology ('-ism') of business ('ratio'). It is not by chance that Individualism acquired a Rationalist philosophy, a Cartesian image of movement, and a Newtonian cosmography. Double-entry bookkeeping had introduced into daily economic life account entries functioning as objects; once set into motion, such financial and numerical bodies move in calculable, mechanically determined grooves. Figures in art tend to acquire analogous fundamental characteristics: their setting into motion is increasingly (compare, say, Shakespeare and Ibsen) determined by calculation of profit or loss, whereas all other hypothetical motivations leave them inert. Finally, Beckett's figures find themselves in a permanent 'Buridan's ass'-type of tension between an ideal norm of rest (Nirvana, thermodynamic death) and motions caused by flickers of the 'hypothetical imperative', each motion meriting detailed description and deliberation as an aberration from the norm. Rationalism, analytic mathematics and mechanics are most intimately interwoven: in none of them is there a place for *qualities*, for fertile deviations from fixed positive laws. Fertility and vitality, divorced from the unique

and the particular, become vested in institutionalised generalisations; just as the 'legal person' of the enterprise grows
distinct and separate from the sensual person of the entrepreneur, whom double-entry bookkeeping sees as a third
party merely administering lent capital. *A fortiori*, other
people too are interesting only rationally, as buyers or sellers
of determined amounts of commodities (including their
labour power) measurable in money and in time. Time,
sluggish or non-existent in the feudal natural economy,
becomes equivalent to finances and their ever swifter
turnover. In the fourteenth century, amounts of time begin
to be exactly measured and laments heard over its rapid flow,
all of which ascends with commerce from Italy northward to
England. St Antoninus, from the financial emporium of
Florence, admits then the subversive novelty of time being a
'res pretiosissima et irrecuperabilis',[16] a direct first progenitor of
the American slogan: 'Time is money.' Together with an
unbounded mechanical space organised around individual
nuclei of force, an arithmetic time, neutral yet increasingly
problematical, completes the Cartesian dimensions of an
analytical Individualist cosmography, where Man becomes
to Man merely an object of attraction or repulsion in time.

Desensualised calculation encroaches upon fundamental
human relationships of producer to product, man to woman,
parent to child. The brief interlude of a harmonious
Renaissance whole of autonomous personalities – still visible
in Boccaccio, Rabelais, or some of Shakespeare's comedies and
romances – draws to an abrupt close. Man can no longer
attempt to realise himself within such a flexible whole, whose
'clearly limited several members were bound into a harmony
in which each tone as such sounded with perfect clearness',[17]
but only as a severed individual ruling 'at the expense' of
nature and other exploited individuals – women, children,
workers, economically weaker citizens, poorer peoples. In
such a context, intimate contacts of one individual with
another grow increasingly intolerable. Drama shows this
very clearly: Shakespeare's socially unmotivated but full-
blown figures can touch, clash and harmonise; Diderot and
Lessing present only a pragmatic social morality of cooperation between individuals of a young and still oppositional
class. Following this downward trajectory, Individualism

arrives by way of the anti-social Romantic revolt (early Schiller, Hugo) to wholly egotist moral Robinsons (realist drama). Finally, as the only connection possible between the desert islands of individual psyches, there remain psychotic conflicts – a connection, *sit venia verbis*, by ground-to-ground missiles across the seas of incommunicability (from natural-ists through psychoanalysts to psychopathologists, say, Hauptmann–O'Neill–Williams).

Beckett has, after all this, understandably preferred to leave his figures without any bounds to speak of – except the scenically functional ones. When the rule is that Man is wolf to Man, then a ruthless defence of the self and denial of human solidarity becomes a realistic alternative. (Shaw played on this, sometimes questionably, from *Mrs Warren's Profession* to *Major Barbara*.) In throwing out the baby of 'Man to Man', Beckett's *dramatis personae* may get rid of the dirty bath of wolfishness.

Reification, the subordination of man to objects or things, is the second main aspect of the price exacted by Individualism. Within desensualised relationships *things* in their quantitative-ness take pride of place. The arithmetic equivalents of things, *bodies*, and of their quantitative relations, *forces*, constitute the backbone of the clear and impoverished world-image of Rationalism. Here the ideal of plenty is no longer a stimulus for sensual enjoyment, a glorious and beautiful means as it was for Boccaccio, Alberti, Leonardo or Rabelais. No longer controlled by generic human values, quantitative abundance turns into an end in itself, running riot. Production divided from the producer is objectified. This process goes on until in the ideal-typic case of bourgeois Individualist society 'the capital is independent and personal, while the active indi-vidual is dependent and impersonal.'[18] Man, the producer and creator, is depersonalised on all fronts: economically (the capital), physically (one operation in the work process, soon mechanised), organisationally (the factory and its equiva-lents), legally (the company, increasingly anonymous in ownership and management), cognitively (specialisation, later institutionalisation), politically (the growing apparatus of states and parties), and so forth. The dehumanised Leviathans of economics, society, state, correspond to reified people. The lay deity of things, commodities, possessions, dominates in such a world over a degraded personality. Beckett will try to escape this domination by rejecting things, while retaining and insisting on the degraded figures: *results without causes* make up the Beckettian world.

If Beckett's world can thus be most usefully understood as a balance sheet which 'takes stock ... and reduces to essential terms the three centuries, during which those ambitious processes of which Descartes is the symbol ... accomplished the dehumanisation of man',[19] the question posed at the beginning of this section assumes the following shape: what kind of reduction does this world represent? To put it baldly, is it a laudatory or condemnatory balance in its judgement on the great Individualist tradition? The shying away from any unique individual experience and its replacement by reiterated, pseudo-allegorical events whose superimposition creates an apparently timeless experience – indeed, the whole savage degradation of world and man (a main theme of Beckett's opus), which can be identified as a *reductio ad absurdum* of Individualist relationships to their logical and historical end-result – all such pointers leave little doubt of the implied sardonic comment. Lucky's speech, or any number of shorter examples, can be cited in proof:

Pozzo:	He used to dance the farandole, the fling, the brawl, the jig, the fandango, and even the hornpipe. He capered. For joy. Now that's the best he can do. Do you know what he calls it?
Estragon:	The Scapegoat's Agony.
Vladimir:	The Hard Stool.
Pozzo:	The Net. He thinks he's entangled in a net.
Vladimir:	(*squirming like an aesthete*). There's something about it ...

Few people would, I imagine, dissent from a comment such as: 'The theatre of Beckett is a testament where the ruin of a civilization is written.'[20]

The stance or *Gestus* of a sardonic judgement on the history of Individualism, its import, thought, and art, explains why Beckett accompanies his bleak abstraction of its relationships with harking back, in some aspects, to pre-Individualist forms and modes. For all its Newtonian inner relations, this closed universe has a distinct affinity with the Ptolemaic world. A kind of infantile nostalgia for sweeping the board clear and returning to supposedly less complex and compromised relations seems implied in many facets of Beckett's universe. Their subsidiary status indicates, I think, that the author is aware of the impossibility of devolution. History may come to a stop, but it cannot run backwards. Beckett's arrested Individualist, and individual, Purgatory is godless because Individualist – frozen because Beckett is unable to believe in Individualism any longer. His own unhappy Rationalist consciousness is continually faced with a paradox insoluble from within the Individualist frame: 'I speak of an art turning from [the plane of the feasible] in disgust, weary of its puny exploits, weary of pretending to be able, of being able, of doing a little better the same old thing, of going a little further along a dreary road.' The Beckett of *Three Dialogues* prefers to that art an 'expression' in which the consciousness that 'there is nothing to express' joins hands with an equally strong consciousness of 'the obligation to express'.[21] The Self, final atom of the Individualist world, has broken up, leaving a void; yet the Individualist tradition of self-questioning goes undaunted on, tragicomically enclosing the void.

3. It is now perhaps possible to approach some conclusions about the relevance of Beckett's vision to people in today's historical situation. Most conclusions affirming that relevance rely on two groups of arguments. The *first* claims that Beckett's figures stand for millions of workers and other people deprived of mastery over the result of their actions, or uneasily and anxiously aware of the senseless and even suicidal nature of these results, for whom action amounts to pseudo-activity. Furthermore, the full representativeness of Beckett's *dramatis personae* is seen in that they not only do nothing but at the same time keep wanting to go on: 'What Beckett presents is not nihilism, but the inability of man to be a nihilist even in a situation of utter hopelessness.' As a proof of this, we are offered the tone or mode of sad farce informing his work, which reflects the 'sadness of all human fate', creating human solidarity and compassion which 'may make this fate a little less unbearable.'[22] This claim consists, then, of two assumptions: (1) about the deeply gloomy present-day status of man; (2) about the wittily cognitive and comfortingly humanist nature of Beckett's comment on it. Beckett himself emphatically supports the first assumption, and there is no doubt that it constitutes the focus of his world view. In the few interviews he has given, he explicitly attributed to any conscious person today the consciousness of his ignorance and impotence, in a world which is a 'mess'.[23] I see no reason for rejecting the first assumption – supported by many aspects of the Seventy Years' War (so far) and other reifying processes of this century, and very much akin to Marx's boiling shame and Brecht's frozen indignation at the world and men around them – provided one does not intolerantly claim that facet of human affairs as an exhaustive and timeless picture of 'all human fate' ever or today. It is also true that the persistence of Beckett's figures, in spite of the void in which they find themselves and which is found in them, implies that their situation still contains at least some sense. 'I persist, therefore I am' could be their slogan (literally true on the stage). In a way, they are obviously not complete nihilists: ideal-typic nihilists can hardly be shown in any kind of scenic performance, including Happenings. Any gestic or verbal action, with however little sense, implies some rudimentary orientation towards values. But Beckett's basic formal device is *a hesitating balance*, without any clear leaning to either side. (I would myself venture the hypothesis that this balance is a quite interesting expression of the present arrested balance in European and world history – and I do not mean the pragmatic balance between the great powers.) To say that Beckett' figures show the inability of man to be a nihilist is to see clearly one side of the balance; but the correspondingly prominent other side shows at the same time the inability of man to be anything but a nihilist. The cognitive and humanist – although not the witty – aspect of Beckett's standpoint remains thus to be proved. Even a superficial glance at, say, *Waiting for Godot*, its two-act structure, two pairs of figures, balancing situations, etc. points to this balancing-act. In some dialogues, even the central 'indifferent' pointer of the balance is clearly seen: '*Vladimir:* Now ... (*Joyous.*) There you are again ... (*Indifferently*). There we are again ... (*Gloomy.*) There I am again.'

Another approach, still within the first group of arguments, purports to prove the humanism of Beckett by his integrity in facing the void of the *condition humaine* without yielding to temptations of facile consolation.[24] Again, one has to recognise that in his best works Beckett does take up such a stance, which is far more dignified and realistic than any shallow optimism peddled by organisation men of the *status quo*. The religious oleograph, the pseudo-idyll of a prosperous labour/capital embrace, or the buxom milkmaid/smiling tractor driver pastoral are all of them unworthy escapes from a complex reality. Yet this approach too seems to go begging the main question, which is: can the human situation be wholly equated with a hopeless anguish? If this is not answered in the affirmative, then no posture before an only partly understood situation can be accepted as intellectually satisfactory, much less as a tragic revelation. This argument covers also the – in part undoubtedly valid[25] – third approach of this group, which claims that a clearly described internal reality of some people, or any person, is relevant for all, and that even showing the absurdity of existence in a world without certainties is a first step towards mastering reality. Since the Bomb – to name only a most visible element – all men are more than ever members of each other's internal, even psychotic realities; but mastering our common reality depends, again, on our mature identification of the world as a process, not as an arrested Faustian anti-wish or curse – *'Verweile doch, du bist so – ungewiss!'* [O Time, arrest your flight, you are so – uncertain].

The approaches of this first group have a common denominator in supposing Beckett to be more or less mirroring an existing state of reification, void, absurdity. The *second* group – a much fainter voice among West European and American critics – finds: 'He destroys in order to construct a city which never rises; but the space is cleared.'[26] A destroyer of the Terrene City clearing the ground for the Heavenly City, which could be implied *a contrario* to what he feels as horrible and therefore destroys – this view of an anti-bourgeois St Sam the Baptist is undoubtedly attractive to any sympathetic criticism with religious overtones, from Christian to some passing for Marxian. What is more, up to a point it can be quite plausible. Beckett did clear quite a lot of ground. For

example, after *Waiting for Godot*, writing dramas as do Eliot
or Williams, Camus or later Ionesco is no doubt still possible,
but it can no longer be regarded as a significant artistic
pursuit. In a wider context, his merciless devaluing of all
Individualist values, his presentation of depersonalised agents
and spaces certainly has a latent element of deadpan social
satire. Brecht was probably going to use this element in his
first go at an adaptation of *Waiting for Godot*, where the
figures and their dialogues were to have been socially
anchored (Estragon being a worker, Vladimir an intellectual,
Pozzo a large landowner, etc.)[27] Quite coherent performances of Beckett as a realistic awful warning can be given by
emphasising this aspect: I have seen *Endgame* convincingly
performed with the fundamental directing idea of an atomic
shelter after global destruction, i.e. as prophetic, anti-utopian
science fiction (in the Zagreb Drama Theatre, season
1958–9).

   This side of, and apology for, Beckett can best be clarified
by a comparison with the first great anti-Individualist writer,
Swift. Both of them write as inhabitants of some cursed
islands, of wholly black regions from which there is no way
out. Both respond to this dystopian Rationalist world by
pushing Rationalist propositions to their absurd extreme in a
cold and savage anguish. Yet the parallel breaks down at a
decisive point: Swift's sarcasm demonstrates implicitly (and
sometimes explicitly, see, e.g. the Lindalino or Roman
Senate episodes in *Gulliver's Travels*) the necessity of a radical
transvaluation of all values to reverse the tide of Individualist
beastliness. Beckett's clowning spurns any such possibility.
He demonstrates a valueless, dehumanized world; but, in an
almost as dehumanized way, he lacks values in the name of
which to resent such a world. His destructiveness has thus
the effect of abolishing all horizons behind which a new City
of the Sun may rise. Finding themselves in a destroyed
world, his figures harbour a pathological fear of any
'potential procreator'.[28]

   In the final balance, then, all presentations of Beckett as the
cognitive mirror of a desensualised and reified humanity, or
as the symbolic destroyer of such a humanity clearing the
ground for a new City, fail in my view to prove a full relevance
of the mirroring or the open-ended character of the

destroying. Let us not forget that Beckett deals in peripheral, exasperated situations of man and his consciousness. The gamut of his clowning devices has turned the poverty of his means – story, figures, environment, language – into an out-standing case of making a virtue out of one's limitations; yet the limitations remain. Epistemologically, they centre in the aprioristic conviction that Man exists, and has to endure, not only in an unchanging but in an absolutely unchangeable world: what might fairly be called a 'Platonic Gothic' parable. Beckett's avowed remoteness from the 'Apollonian' in art and his insistence that the 'mess' of our world cannot be explained or understood[29] are aspects of that conviction. If his key word 'Perhaps' does not prevent attempts at action and understanding, it does not encourage them either; in times of most dire need for them, as ours is, this may make quite a difference. On the other hand, whole reaches of profound and most relevant human experience – from the joy of harmonious achievement, through the tragedy made possible by ideals, to the keenest intellectual pleasure in a critical understanding of the rich and pulsating dialectics of life, of people in society – are simply outside Beckett's waveband. The logic: Didi and Gogo are sadly hopeless; they are men; therefore all men are sadly hopeless – has the fundamental flaw of not distinguishing between the particular and the general, thus falling under the rule of categorical syllogistics *ex propositionibus mere particularibus nihil sequitur.* (This last, I hasten to add, is meant for apologetic Beckettians more than for the artist who largely operates by another kind of logic.)

Yet the lack of a central and all-embracing relevance should not, despite apologists who simply overlook such fundamental facts, make us forget what relevance can be found in Beckett's work: for where and when it is relevant, it is supremely so. I suggested earlier that it was relevant in random and closed situations of human existence: in war, camps, prisons, sickness, old age, grim helplessness of all kinds. As children of this century, however, we have seen that it is often very difficult to tell the centre from the periphery. The threat of grim helplessness hangs continually over all of us collectively, and unduly often over many of us personally. Beckett's stoic compassion is clearly relevant to situations which their protagonists are unable to change, as long as they are unable to change them. Of course, in the worst dehumanizing hells of Nazism, Stalinism or, say, Southern racism, even in concentration camps, the flame of human revolt has never quite died (third law of thermodynamics!): Farinata and Ulysses have had a progeny as well as Belacqua. Beckett's work lacks the vivifying tension between Belacqua and Ulysses, the revolt of life. Yet its tragically sterile, ahistorical hatred of Individualist sham and dehumanisation remains a historical and aesthetic fact – as does its uncritical fascination with the death of energy.

The uses of Beckett in a non-Individualist tradition remain therefore manifold, from transmutation into social criticism, through deeper understanding of some new black facets of global human (and particular socialist) experiences, up to formal, material delight in this sleek 'dying gladiator' in the stockyards of our age. I do not think it is by chance that Brecht, who wrote plays on the saints of these stockyards (Joan and Simone, Vlassova and Grusha), was trying to find and reclaim what he could use from the waiters for Godot. On the contrary, I think such uses would clearly have been, and still are, based on the fact that alienation of man has been up to now persistent in the brief history of socialist societies, even shaping some new varieties of crass institutionalization. While this does not speak against the great experiment in changing Man and the world, it certainly speaks for an intelligent and judicious inclusion of Beckett's gloomy opus and vision within its larger horizons, as a possible dead-end to be kept in mind, understood and avoided. Also, and above all, to be performed, with the pleasure of beholding which arises from the possibilities of understanding – yes, and of learning – latent within it, as within any genuine work of art.

With all these preliminaries over, one could begin to enter into a true inside dialogue with Beckett's dramaturgy and with his plays.

Notes

[1] Werner Hecht, 'Brecht "und" Beckett', *Theater der Zeit,* 14, (1966), p. 30. See also the similar, if politer, view of the Russian

critic Surkov, quoted in Pierre Mélèse, *Samuel Beckett* (Paris, 1966), p. 159. Even Lukács has at times taken up similar simplified positions. But cf. the significant parallel between Brecht and Beckett in Hans Mayer, 'Brecht's *Drums,* a Dog, and Beckett's *Godot,*' in Siegfried Mews and Herbert Knust (eds), *Essays on Brecht* (Chapel Hill NC, 1974), pp. 71–78 (original in *Theater heute*, no. 6 [1972]: 25–27).

2 This first task of identifying Beckett's *Weltanschauung* seems to have been very skilfully accomplished by American, French and some other West Europen exegetes. I can only refer here to such critics as Anders, Coe, Cohn, Fletcher and Spurling, Kenner, Mueller and Jacobsen and Webb to whom this chapter is indebted, although I do not share many of their presuppositions and conclusions. I hope not to be misrepresenting a certain *consensus doctorum* if I condense such analyses in a survey from my own vantage-point.

3 Josephine Jacobsen and William R. Mueller, *The Testament of Samuel Beckett* (New York, 1964), p. 161.

4 Cf. for some among a host of examples, Camille Flammarion's novel *La Fin du Monde*, or H.G. Wells' *The Time Machine.*

5 S. Günther Anders, 'Being Without Time,' in *Samuel Beckett: A Collection of Critical Essays,* ed. Martin Esslin (Englewood Cliffs N.J, 1965).

6 This has been well noted by Beckett's director Roger Blin, quoted in Mélèse, *op. cit.,* p. 149; it could also be called psychotic: see Jacobsen-Mueller, *op. cit.,* pp. 70–1.

7 Cf. 'Three Dialogues – by Samuel Beckett and Georges Duthuit', *Samuel Beckett: A Collection of Critical Essays,* p. 17.

8 Madeleine Chapsal, in *L'Express*, 8 February 1957, in Mélèse, *op. cit.,* p. 163.

9 Ruby Cohn, 'Philosophical Fragments in the Works of Samuel Becket', in *Samuel Beckett: A Collection of Critical Essays,* p. 170.

10 G. Sandier, in Mélèse, *op. cit.,* p. 169.

11 Hugh Kenner, *Samuel Beckett* (New York, 1961), p. 63.

12 Cf. Kenner; and Anders, *op. cit.,* p. 147.

13 Cf. Oswald Spengler, *Der Untergang des Abendlandes I* (Munich, 1920); and the more substantial works of Marx, Sombart, Simmel, Lukács 1971 and Hauser in the bibliography to chapter 1.

14 Cf. the works of Weber, von Martin and Tawney, in the bibliography to chapter 1 (where this argument is more fully developed), and an early application in L.C. Knights, *Drama and Society in the Age of Jonson* (London, 1962).

15 T.S. Eliot, 'The Metaphysical Poets', in *Selected Essays* (London, 1961).

[16] Alfred von Martin, *Soziologie der Renaissance* (Stuttgart, 1932), p. 119.

[17] Heinrich Wölfflin, *Kunstgeschichtliche Grundbegriffe* (Munich, 1927), p. 169.

[18] Karl Marx and Friedrich Engels, *The Communist Manifesto*, Chapter 2.

[19] Kenner, *op. cit.*, p. 132.

[20] P. Marcabru, in Mélèse, *op. cit.*, p. 165.

[21] 'Three Dialogues', *op. cit.*, p. 17.

[22] Anders, *op. cit.*, pp. 144, 151; the argument summarised here runs through most of his essay.

[23] As reported by I. Shenker in the *New York Times*, and Tom Driver in *Columbia University Forum*, both in Mélèse, *op. cit.*, pp. 137–40.

[24] Cf. Martin Esslin, 'Introduction' in *Samuel Beckett; A Collection of Critical Essays,* p. 14.

[25] The million spectators of *Waiting for Godot* in its first five years cannot be dismissed out of hand; nor the fact that the Belgrade troupe Atelje 212 performed it on and off for ten years.

[26] Jacobsen and Mueller, *op. cit.*, p. 163.

[27] Main fragments of this adaptation have been quoted in Hecht; but see also a report on a later and different plan of adapting in K. Rülicke-Weiler, *Die Dramaturgie Brechts* (Berlin DDR. 1966), pp. 154–6.

[28] *Endgame.* The French text, suppressed in English, is much more explicit; e.g. see the trilingual edn *Dramatische Dichtungen in drei Sprachen* I (Frankfurt, 1963), p. 304: '*Clov:* ... Quelqu'un. C'est quelqu'un! *Hamm:* Eh bien, va l'exterminer ... (*Vibrant.*) Fais ton devoir!'

[29] Cf. the interviews with Shenker and Driver. Adorno has observed that in *Waiting for Godot* (as well as in *Endgame*) there is a dramaturgic episode shaped by Hegel's master–servant motif, one of the central contradictions of our epoch: Theodor W. Adorno, *Aesthetische Theorie* (Frankfurt, 1981), pp. 370–1. But another way of getting at the anti-Apollonian one-sidedness of *Beckett's* dramaturgy would be to reverse Adorno's powerful vindication by stressing that Pozzo and Lucky are a *dismissed episode.*

9

Reflections on Happenings

The great difference lies in man's knowing what he is; only then is he truly that.

(Hegel *Lectures on the History of Philosophy*)

1. Taxonomy With Examples

The phenomena loosely associated with the term Happenings can be differentiated into at least four different types: Events, Aleatoric scenes, Happenings proper, and Action Theatre (but see the reservation about the latter below, which reduces the number of types to three).

Events (or Pieces)
An Event is a scene containing a single activity, either brief or repetitively drawn out; it is close to a children's game or an adult gag. An Event can range from an exercise in perception (Cage's *Silent Piece* or *4'33"*) to the enactment of a basic metaphor which allegorises the participants. A good example of the latter is Allan Kaprow's *Overtime* (outline quoted from Schechner[1] 150):

Sundown. (flashlights) 200 straight feet of snow-fence erected in woods. Groundline drawn with powdered chalk. Posted with red flare and marked number 1.
Fence moved next 200 feet, maintaining direction. Groundline drawn. Flare and marker number 2.
Fence moved next 200 feet. Groundline. Flare. Marker 3. (portable radios, food deliveries.)
Process repeated every 200 feet for a mile. Lighted flares maintained along entire line throughout night. Fence removed.
Line and markers remaining. Flares out. Sunup.

Any interpretation of this Event would have to start from

Kaprow's 'grounding' of the age-old metaphor of the wild dark wood, omnipresent in art from the times of *Gilgamesh* through the *selva oscura* of Dante's *Inferno* to our days. Its menace in the wintery season is being turned into a humanly-mapped grid, a surveyed and tamed space complete with the basic necessities of food, light and communication. The enactment thus 'de-charges' the metaphor and, by collective labour which unites man and nature, translates it from a horror into a domesticated piece of environment. Its non-urban character is due to Kaprow's personal propensity for the bucolic – most authors of Happenings work in an urban environment where metaphors are less easily identifiable in terms of the cultural tradition, though no less present or powerful.

'Events' are related to music and dance – primarily modern – since they deal with a rhythmic use of a *delimited time duration*. In *Overtime* this is the sundown to sunup interval; its title is, I take it, a pun on this 'overtime' work which is also dominant or victorious 'over' a structured time (as well as space). Cage's 'Pieces' indicate this relationship still more clearly, being largely unconcerned with space. Space (say, a concert hall) is for Cage a neutral constant and not a dynamic variable, which is the aesthetic characteristic of music as the purest time art. In so far as an Event is homologous to a basic 'compartment' within Happenings proper, which ideally also enacts one basic metaphor, this Cage strain or orientation is significant for all Happenings.

Aleatoric Scenes

The provenance of aleatoric or chance scenes, such as Jackson Mac Low's *Marrying Maiden*,[2] is clearly musical. They have a more complex structure, based on a combination of authorial choice (Mac Low chose the text, the *I Ching*, and a list of 500 adverbs indicating the manner of speaking fragments from it) and chance from aleatoric music (in this case the order, duration, tempo, volume, and inflection of the verbal material). As Dick Higgins has pointed out, Cagean aleatoric technique in reality only places the decisions at one remove from the composer, allowing the material to be determined by the system the artist-composer determined: 'And the real innovation lies in the emphasis on the creation of a system'

(Higgins 55–7). Though permutations exist, any performance will still be a performance of Jackson Mac Low's
Marrying Maiden (i.e. within a *field of possibilities* which,
although much larger than that of a univocal script, is in
principle a closed field just as that of *Hamlet*). Conversely,
any theatre or concert performance is always one variation on
an underlying score, libretto, or text.

Unless the aleatoric technique is used simply to modulate
unit-Events (a rather primitive limit-case), its meaning lies
basically in its commitment to a quantified view of the world
as an assemblage of neutral molecular units, which obey the
law of large numbers (the only way to escape utter boredom
in permutations). I would imagine that aleatorics, as an
exclusive principle of structuring, work only with fairly
general texts, which have low message significance and high
entropy – texts of a general incantatory nature such as the *I
Ching*, applicable to everything vaguely because (and therefore) applicable to no precise interpersonal situation at all,
like a soothsayer's prediction, or a horoscope. Aleatorics
would also seem to work dramaturgically only with fairly
neutral or abstract *dramatis personae*, who are neither Individualist characters nor allegorical in any clearly defined
system.

Happenings Proper

Three examples are necessary to indicate the main outlines of
this type.

(1) In Kaprow's *Eat* (see TDR 30) there is a field of
possibilities – physical materials and gestures – connected
with the topic or theme of food and the ritual situation of a
communal meal-feast (the author calls it 'a quasi-eucharistic
ritual'). Its enacting depends on participants interacting with
a rehearsed troupe. This Happening is situated halfway
between a religious Mass and the cold buffet at a modern
Individualist party, and its rehearsed actors halfway between
acolytes and choice-triggering hosts at the party. The
participating audience is supposed to be reawakened to a
sense of communion, and to a sense of the miraculousness of
food. Yet it remains unclear what type of communion is
desired and why food is miraculous: the only value-system
implied is the lowest common denominator of a biological

solidarity of human beings.[3] Compared to the real complexity of human relations this approach may be a convenient jumping-off point, but little more. Let us take for the moment a grisly real-life happening, such as the My Lai massacre: it is surely true to say that the massacred Vietnamese were human beings, and that this – as against a comparably gratuitous killing of 200 or 300 apes or boars – is the basis for our feeling of outrage. But the deeper, significant, operative truth about My Lai is not simply that both Vietnamese peasants and American soldiers are biologically human: it is that the latter are killers and the former are their victims, at which point a political, economical, and ideological analysis of the reasons for that situation would have to set in. To stop at the first-level approach is simply liberal sentimentality. Analogously, Kaprow's refusal to make further distinctions which could adequately deal with civilisational complexities is simply a Rousseauist persuasion that a return to supposed fundamentals outside civilisation will illumine present-day life. Pseudo-biological values substituted for historical ones: a Eucharist without a Real Presence, a dumb Symposium. (Here I am singling out authors only in so far as their talents clarify the tendencies of a whole group: it is a representative, and therefore ideal figure I am calling 'Kaprow' or 'Oldenburg,' etc. for convenience's sake.)

Indeed, one whole aspect of Happenings reposes on what I have called the Rousseauist approach: it either escapes into nature (*Eat*'s cave being in this respect prototypic, indeed a touch of genius) or it tries to convert the urban American environment into a new naivety without physically changing it. This second wing is more original and sets itself a more difficult goal. Yet it too approaches its new environment in a very old way, by a yoga-type process of re-education from within. It supposes, or wants to achieve, a 'dérèglement systématique de tous les sens' (as Rimbaud and the Surrealists would have it) which would make out of the jungle of cities a wonder, and out of city-dwellers swains of a paradoxically urbanised pastoral – 'peasants of Paris', as Aragon once formulated it. Circuitously, we are back at a debased Rousseauism: Rousseau at least wanted *the whole society* to devolve back into natural nobility. A tempting way to account for the debasement would be to note that the Happenings are sociologically a product of the same class Rousseau hailed from – the petty-bourgeois artistic intelligentsia – but that this class has in the meantime been forced from the public into the private sphere.

All these observations are, of course, not exorcisms, but merely attempts at understanding and judging. For a more certain judgement, however, we need far more sociological data. In the meantime we must make do with basically impressionistic hypotheses. It seems that nobody writing about Happenings has escaped such a proceeding.

(2) Claes Oldenburg's *Fotodeath* (TDR 30) is a developed urban Happening with a conventional division between actors and spectators. It can be compared to a *Commedia dell'arte canovaccio* (scenario) without speech and the *lazzi* tradition, or to a multi-focus mime without plot. It consists of three sets of five Events (scenes) each, forming a spectrum of situations from a crowded urban environment. The unit-Events are contiguous in space (as medieval Mysteries), but the space is not coordinated along the axis of a firm value-system (e.g. from Heaven upstage left, to Hell upstage right). Oldenburg himself, quite lucidly, calls his Happenings events in an associational pseudo-plot and confesses to a preference for 'a structure which is an object in itself', such as snapshots or circus (in Kirby(ed.), 201–2). Correlatively, Oldenburg's events have no temporal focus either (e.g. the medieval vertical vanishing-point of god's timeless glance), they are performed simultaneously on a neutral, geometrically-divided stage. This results in a multi-focus stage, with all five events of the same set contiguous and simultaneous. They are coordinated like a family of parallel, coexisting time/space systems in a roughly synchronic cross-cut, i.e. Like Einsteinian co-variant island universes each of which is autonomous but all of which are deduced from the same basic formula by varying some parameter(s) in it.

Each of Oldenburg's three sets of five Events has a common theme, and each set seems to possess what I call a 'pilot-scene' explicating more clearly than the other scenes the common denominator of the set (see the script in TDR 30, 87–93). The theme of the first set is the futile enacting of roles in a topsy-turvy world – by implication our world: (1)

man posing before mirrors, (2) girl in jingoist poses, (3) man wrestling with a soft laundry-bag, (4) transvestite confusion of sexes, and (5) pilot-scene explicitly showing a family's unsuccessful posing for a photograph in front of landscape samples. There are marked similarities to allegorising painters from fourteenth-century Italy to sixteenth-century Flanders, say to Breughel's *Wedding* or *Proverbs*. The theme of the second set is futile search for partnership: (1) narcissistic woman, (2) bygone times of a naive adolescent friendship, (3) man leaving invalid woman for a party, (4a) two drunks unsuccessfully helping each other up, and (4b) man picking up spilled cans but not the fallen partner. The third set tops the futility of social posing and the breakdown of human friendliness with a final bogging down of all situations in a mechanical, reified denial of vitality as in a nightmare of arrested or viscous time. It features: (1) a mechanical majorette, (2) a wounded man (a soldier in the performance) unable to sit down – like Clov in *Endgame,* (3) the pilot-scene of the USA as a collage of objects in a viscid paste, (4) dinner with a dead woman, and (5) men degraded to movers of a huge assemblage of black boxes.[4] In the whole Happening (itself only one part of a tripartite Piece called *Circus*) there is a clear progression through the three sets from singular through dual (the woman in the second set 1 is also dual, faced with her own mirror-image, while the family in the first set 5 constitutes only one unit) to general, and from futility to death. This was effected by a series of brief snapshot situations (an idea developed in a more formalistic way by the Living Theatre's 'snapshots' scene in *Mysteries and Smaller Pieces*), amounting to a kind of foreshortened, aerial survey of the American anthropological situation. The title of *Fotodeath* indicates the diagnosis.

(3) In Dick Higgins' *The Tart, or Miss America* (TDR 30) words acquire greater importance. There is an abundant use of chance techniques, but the material manipulated is, first of all, a set of socially typical cliché phrases, written by the author, and combined with bodily actions, optic or acoustic effects, and some scenery (this Happening was performed in a boxing ring – an old dream of Brecht's). Secondly, the words and gestures are performed by 'stock urban characters' (Higgins, TDR 30, 133), by typical agents or *dramatis personae*

akin to what Diderot called *conditions*. Their number is changeable, and the same stock character can be acted simultaneously by several actors, but at the very least a central triangle is always present consisting of The Tart, The Young Man and Mr Miller, a subtopian Babbitt – Everyman; further typical *dramatis personae* might include a Prophet, a Steelworker, a Drinking·Man, *et sim*. Each performer had thirty-six different non-verbal situations in which he was assigned at random one sentence, one action, and one special (optic, acoustic, or kinetic) effect. Permutative collage-scenes resulted, quasi-simultaneous actions supplemented by the activity of a Special Performer, a coordinator responsible for cueing and flow, who had a collection of Americana ('the relevance to be determined by the social intent of the performance' Higgins, ibid., 135) which he produced at random. There are only thirty-six lines in the whole play, and they were always explicitly quoted as said by one of the 'roles', regardless of which role or *persona* actually pronounced them. (I particularly liked sentence 13: 'The steelworkers say no. No, say the steelworkers. (No. No.)') Higgins was clearly aiming at an estrangement effect of the Brechtian type, which would prevent the audience empathising with the *persona*: 'I wrote *The Tart* to express a sociological concept [about women]…my hope was that the audiences would sympathise with the performers (not the characters) in their social contexts and that the lines would be more tragic than funny' (ibid., 132).

This type of Happening explicates the specific allegorical quality of *dramatis personae*, and begins to utilise the unequalled suggestiveness of language. A similar approach is found in the first scene of *Mysteries* by the Living Theatre (a performance which is in a way an anthology of different types and uses of Happenings). It featured a pantomime of militarism developed from a scene of *The Brig* and joined to fugal chanting of a poem by Jackson Mac Low consisting exclusively of the words found on the US $1 note. ('One dollar – In God we trust. – Douglas C. Dillon.' – if memory serves). It ends with the gradual formation of a drilling platoon and a final incomprehensible harangue of the commander, saluted with a roar of 'Yes, Sir!' Its effect is a powerful, foreshortened glimpse of the military-industrial complex operating in the flesh of people. Not much is needed to transform this type of Happening into Action Theatre – it would suffice to allegorise the performance space and thus conjure up the vague outline of a story. This explains why Higgins claims *The Tart* is not a Happening. However, I would assume his boxing ring had not quite become an imaginary universe of its own suggesting an autonomous story or diegesis. Therefore, one would have to consider *The Tart* as a very advanced form of Happenings, while scene 1 of *Mysteries* trembles on the brink of Action Theatre because of its inclusion of the *Brig* scene.

Action Theatre
When Happenings' techniques are elevated into a staged performance 'matrixed' in space and plot – such as in Kenneth Brown's *The Brig* as performed by the Living Theatre – one gets a play using repetitive and permutative techniques and a minimum of verbal information, yet clearly nearer to drama than to Happenings. Except in terms of mutual influence and coexistence there seem to be no valid reasons for aesthetically grouping Action Theatre with the Happenings.

Comment
This brief taxonomical survey indicates the existence of a *typological series* of ascending complexity. The series starts out from single non-verbal activities (Events) and longer aleatoric activities where text is treated mainly as sound (or indeed noise) and the allegorising of participants is vague and very general. Kaprow seems to be the master of this approach, and he is out of his element as soon as he leaves it for what I have called Happenings proper (e.g. in *Eat* or *Courtyard*.) It should be remembered that the Kaprow performance which gave a name to this genre was called *18 Happenings in 6 Parts,* (i.e. that, characteristically, he thinks of Happenings in terms of what is usually, and in this chapter too, called an Event. The culmination of this typological series – from which I am excluding its overspill into dramatic theatre, the Action Theatre – are Happenings proper, which range from a non-verbal symbolic field of activities with the nuclear performing troupe used as seeders only, through

mime with typified *personae* who demand well-rehearsed actors and contain a clear compositional progression, to aleatoric use of a purposefully composed text with rehearsed acting of social stock characters or types akin to those in modern allegorising plays (expressionist, surrealist, Brechtian, absurdist, etc. – the conception of *The Tart* seems rather akin to a play such as Pirandello's *To Clothe the Naked*).

Thus, there seems to be little reason to treat Happenings with less scholarly attention than, say, *Gorboduc* or the plays of Noel Coward. Their significance can be looked at from two aspects which are blended in any particular Happening in very different proportions. It can be thought of as an exercise in unclogging the perceptiveness of participants, in which case it is properly speaking pre-theatrical or propedeutical; or it can be thought of as the use of a meaningful semiotic structure with some kind of role-playing and an organised rhythm – even if the figures and the organisation of events are difficult to recognise because they are of an unfamiliar type.

Many Happenings were simply Events or Aleatoric Scenes. Often they seem to have been akin to unclear and under-rehearsed mimic psychodramas. This is, however, not the fault of this form or genre as such, but of the societal and ideological situation in which they were performed. This situation also accounts for the frequent indifference or hostility of the performances toward the audience. Though this is sociologically very significant (see section 4), it seems aesthetically more important to note that Happenings can assign to the audience the same ontological status as to the performing troupe: both can provide events for the performance by action and provoked reaction; both can be, and often are, treated as objects.

2. Aesthetic Location and an Attempt at Definition

Location
'Are Happenings theatre or not?' The answer is an exercise in semantics. If we define theatre as implying the performance of an action organised in a plot, which is the dominant trend

since the fifteenth-century Aristotelians, then they obviously are not. If we define it much more broadly, as Cage does, as a performance which engages simultaneously the two public senses of eye and ear (see TDR 30), then they are. In the absence of any convincing definition of theatre, it might be more useful to start by identifying Happenings as a form of *spectacle* – a wider aesthetic category embracing dramatic theatre, mime, ballet and opera as well as the non-plotted genres such as pageants, fair shows, jugglers and circus, and the intermediary genres of music-hall and cabaret, vaude-ville, burlesque, etc. The common earmark of spectacles is the presence of *actions by human performers*; according to the immediacy or reality of that presence, theatrical spectacles are further differentiated from films, television, etc. The non-plotted genres are sociologically, as a rule, lower-class forms.

In the 1920s, the Russian Formalists held a theory that literary and artistic genres evolve not in a straight but in a zig-zag line.[5] The pioneering work of Viktor Shklovsky held that in each artistic period there are several schools in any one art; they exist simultaneously, with one school the most orthodox at any given time, and others coexisting with it, uncanonised and spurned by official aesthetics. In the early nineteenth century in Russia, for example, the courtly tradition in literature existed simultaneously with 'low' vaudeville verse and adventure novel prose which were creating new forms on a despised, 'subliterary' level. Such creativity in the societal depths brings forth a 'junior line' which grows up to replace the old: 'Chekhov introduces the low farce and *feuilleton* into Russian literature; Dostoyevsky raises to the dignity of a norm the devices of the dime story' (Shklovsky, *Rozanov*). The eighteenth-century western European novel stems from imaginary voyages and trave-logues (Defoe), diaries and manuals of letter-writing (Richardson), etc – *not* in a straight line from the major epic form of the preceding epoch, the verse epic. Pushkin's lyrics come from album verses and folk songs, Blok's from gypsy ballads, Mayakovsky's from comic periodicals. The 'junior line' or 'low' genre (which is as a rule also a 'small' form) is then canonised by an artistic revolution which transforms it into the accepted 'senior line' or 'high' genre (and as a rule into a 'large' form) of the new period.

The Formalists recognised that artistic evolution is never as pure as a critical model, but is contaminated by many inner and outer factors. Nevertheless, they asserted that there is a law in the history of art by which 'the legacy is transmitted not from father to son but from uncle to nephew' (Shklovsky, *Literatura i kinematograf*). The admission of attitudes and genres from popular culture, existing on the periphery of official aesthetics, into the consecrated precincts of official Art, runs parallel to societal changes in which the tastes of the 'upper' classes are supplanted by 'lower' popular tastes. Today, we might add to the Formalists' insights that artistic and societal change are in certain complex ways causally connected. In France in the 1820s, for example, the assumption of devices from eighteenth-century bourgeois sentimental comedy into the ossified *ancien régime* tragedy resulted in the romantic tragedy of de Vigny, Dumas père and Hugo. This was clearly related to the sharp conflict between the lifestyles and world-views of the feudal reaction and those of the young democrats, a conflict representing antagonistic class interests in culture. A history of literature or theatre should seek to explain the rise of any new genre by focusing on the 'lower' artistic levels and forms from which it sprang. 'Each period of creative flowering is preceded by a slow process of accumulating means of renewal in the lower, often unrecognised strata' (Tomashevsky). In spectacle too, the non-plotted genres which I am discussing are, as a rule, sociologically lower-class forms. In our century – just as in Antiquity and in the middle ages – these forms are lifted into the realm of official aesthetics by the pressure of new societal forces and structures of feeling.

Elements for a Definition

As soon as there are human performers – implying a real or imaginary audience – it is inevitable that they adopt implied or explicated, shifting or stable *roles*, or better *stage types*, of some kind, e.g. 'young intellectual Everyman', 'the artist as sufferer (or more rarely 'as celebrator'), or similar. Robert Whitman, for example, wanted 'clean-cut American teenagers' for two girl performers in *Water,* and dressed them accordingly.[6] As Kaplan (95–8) pointed out against Kirby,[7] misunderstandings arise primarily from the fact that these roles are matrixed in an unclear way (usually in very vague allegorical frameworks) so that they do not amount to Individualistic characters. I called them types or Diderotian *conditions*, Higgins called them stock characters, and possibly a still better name may be found: but surely this *different* matrixing should not be taken as representing non-matrixed acting. Whatever their seeming unorthodoxy to our conditioned eyes, these *dramatis personae* are aesthetically nearer to a Shakespearean or Sophoclean character than to a man walking down the street.

Furthermore, and contrary to a widespread prejudice, it is clearly not necessary that Happenings be based on improvisation, or on aleatorics (chance or random effects), or on the absence of a division of labour between troupe and audience; the testimony of *Fotodeath* could be multiplied. Against this, and against the equally unconvincing necessity for an absence of roles, Kirby's identification of Happenings as non-matrixed in regard to *time and space* seems valid, fundamental and never seriously transgressed. A forest/room/street/city or whatever the space of a Happening may be, is a forest/room/street/city or whatever, in the manner of Gertrude Stein, and does not pretend to any other imaginary localisation; the time-duration likewise. Space and time revert to an empirical status identical to the status or epistemological level of the audience's direct experience before and after the performance. Space becomes, in principle at least, the sum of all objects (including people) and the dimension of their displacement; time is not the space of causal sequences but the measure of qualitative change (very slow or – more rarely, alas – very fast). Both space and time are no longer given conventions but problematic materials, whose extent and character, structured through object-relations, largely *are* a Happening. The structuring will necessarily be discrete or compartmentalised, carrying to its ultimate conclusion the tendency of modern theatre toward open composition, or episodic autonomy in Aristotelian parlance (cf. Chekhov, Brecht, Beckett).

It dramaturgic time and space do not pretend to a different epistemological or even ontological status (which is what I take matrixing means), the dramaturgic situations cannot be organised into an imaginary universe which impinges on our universe only at the privileged 'holy circle' of the stage. This imaginary scenic universe with own laws and constellations of forces is constituted by means of a causal story or plot. Borrowing a term from film theoreticians and from aestheticians like Souriau,[8] one can call this universe of the theatrical plot *diegetic* (from the Greek *diegesis* – a story told). The unfolding of a Happening does not give rise to another imaginary but vivid and coherent space/time universe overlapping with our own: *a Happening is non-diegetic.* Paradoxically, any diegetic theatre genre, such as mime, or indeed drama, can thus be envisaged in aesthetics as a limit-case of a non-diegetic genre (such as the Happening) whose time and space had become fixed into a constant. In mathematical notation, if a Happening is a function of time, space, dramaturgic figures, and dramaturgic situation:

(1) $H=f$ (t, s, fig, sit)

then for (2) $t/s = k$ (which is the case in drama),

(3) $Dr=k \cdot f$ (fig, sit)

The constant k is then the time/space relation or form characteristic for each major epoch of drama (and diegetic theatre).

Historically, Happenings have used various materials grouped around the stylised activities of human performers, as dramatic and diegetic theatre also does (dance and mime, music and noises, light and scenery, film, literary texts, etc.). But Happenings have used these materials in new and sometimes startling ways. Persons are treated as objects, enclosed in shrouds or sacks, wrapped in paper or tin-foil, painted or used as surfaces for film projection, etc.; indeed, many Happeners seem uncomfortable with normally clad or normally nude figures. Only the best authors escape this hysterical syndrome, an aspect of the Happenings style which Susan Sontag explains by the experience and pressures of New York painting, preoccupied with urban junk and highly aggressive not only against the audience but above all against their medium and materials – a style based on the artefacts and human relations of the modern American city: 'the brutal disharmony of buildings in size and style, the wild juxtaposition of store signs, the clamorous layout of the modern newspaper' (Sontag 271–2).

A Tentative Definition

A tentative definition might thus read: *Happenings are a genre of theatre spectacle, using various types of semiotic signs and media organised around the action of human performers in a homogeneous and thematically unified way, and a non-diegetic structuring of time and space.*

Happenings are differentiated from dramatic theatre (including opera, ballet, mime) by the absence of a coherent diegetic universe. They are differentiated from fairs, pageants, and other similar non-diegetic spectacle genres by their dramaturgic homogeneity, and from circus (a genre to which they appear to be aesthetically closest) by their more unified themes or semiotic fields.

A definition of drama adapted from Aristotle's *Poetics* (part VI) by updating the language and leaving out the parts specific for the Greek conception of theatre and for tragedy, as well as the dubious, contested and structurally unnecessary reference to catharsis, might be:

Drama is the presentation (*mimesis*)[9] (1) *of a complete action* (2) *which is of a determined magnitude,* (3) *in differentiated and heightened language,* (4) *in the form of events, not of narrative.* Compared to the above definition of Happenings – and leaving aside for the moment the moot factor of language, to which I shall return at the end of this chapter – we note the universal hallmark of spectacle common to both in (4) and the differentiating factor of a predetermined magnitude (i.e. of plot in time) in (2), which latter is a hallmark of diegetic genres only. We are then left with an open question about factor (1) – are Happenings simply 'free form' or are they thematically unified, possessing a complete action (*praxis*) or indeed story (*mythos*). I would argue that there is no such thing as free form in art: a form called free is either inoperative or new. In that sense, I trust even my brief analyses indicate that any successful Happening has a limited thematic field, and that its action, though oscillating, is complete unto itself. Further, I would argue that – as different from plot, which is based on univocal causality – Aristotle's notion of *fable* or *story* could and should be salvaged for any modern theory of theatre and spectacles. Aristotle's definition, taken from the same place and adapted in a similar way, would be: *The story* (mythos) *is the presentation of actions; for by story I mean the arrangement (composition) of incidents.* This is elastic enough to encompass both univocally causal relations of incidents and any number of transformational or associational arrangements of incidents, just as in contemporary poetry and other arts: e.g. isomorphic, isogenetic, isothematic (by formal, provenance or thematic resonances or associations).

Genetics
This is not to deny that, genetically, Happenings evolved through theatricalisation and spectacularisation of music and the plastic arts, and only secondarily from older scenic genres such as dance. Historically, *plastic arts evolved into temporality* through mobiles, collages, and kindred developments: Calder, Duchamp, Gabo, Rauschenberg, Tinguely, and many other experimental artists and groups strove to make an art-form out of the environment. At a later stage, human beings used as objects were brought into the environment,[10] which then immediately tended toward theatre. Traces of that procedure are frequent in painters' Happenings (e.g. Kaprow's *Eat* or Oldenburg's *Washes*) and have infiltrated the style of the whole genre. Simultaneously and complementarily, *concert music evolved into spatiality*, directly from music performing (Cage) or still more easily through scenic *dance* to music (Cunningham, Halprin).

3. Some Historical Analogies – the Masque

Happenings have some curious and instructive analogies with a number of other non-dramatic scenic genres. These analogies need to be discussed with in a proper theory of theatre based on a sociology of spectacle forms. I shall mention a few, centring on the English Masque,[11] in an attempt to bring out salient features of the Happenings' sociological profile.

The Masque
The Masque has been defined as 'an evening entertainment in which the chief performers were masked courtiers, accompanied by torchbearers, all in costumes appropriate to the

device presented: the elements of song and dialogue were developed later, the original nucleus being dances and conversations with spectators selected by the masquers' (Cunliffe, 146). It developed when a variety of medieval folk customs – chiefly the 'mumming', a procession of disguised people, but also the 'king-game', the election of a mock Saturnalian ruler, and the sword dance, a mimic combat – were appropriated by the upper class for an evening entertainment leading up to a banquet. The entertainment absorbed in the sixteenth-century influences from Italy (directly or by way of France), where Renaissance revels had reached unprecedented splendour in theatricalising public living, and translating it to the stage, and in which all the known arts were used to express a world of ideal loveliness. This led to many modifications of the original simple procession with dance, chief of which is the introduction, first, of conversations and set speeches, and, at the apogee of the Jacobean Masque, of elaborate singing and plotted, diegetic dialogue. The nucleus of the Masque is thus non-diegetic, simply a potlatch-type procession-cum-dance organised within a certain field of posibilities (the 'device', e.g. the Green Men or similar) to which costumes, masks and dances were related. Its primal character of a communal fertility rite was modified into aristocratic conventions of conviviality promoting Tudor upper-class unity and, increasingly, the splendour and magical position of the Court itself.

Parallels and Oppositions

Some obvious parallels would thus include the one-shot or two-shot nature of any particular Masque performance, and its division into open-air and 'palace' forms. Further, it was based on a closely knit, numerically small social group which resulted in the use of allegorised themes and figures played by members of the audience (with a few resource persons such as the author and the choreographer). Though disguised as symbolic stage figures for the duration of the performance, they returned into the audience for the final celebratory dance (as is often the case in Action Theatre today, e.g. *Mysteries* and *Dionysus in 69*). The Masque took over from Italian public entertainments a new usage of combining all known types of semiotic signs on the scene. The Happenings, though more hesitant (perhaps because they have not had the evolutionary span of the Masque), and more suspicious of the celebratory media of speaking and singing, have similarly pillaged the new music, the plastic arts, and in some indirect and incomplete ways even drama and poetry. The fascination with theatrical machinery in the Masque has no full parallel in the Happenings, but it has cropped up in some related projects such E.A.T. and Joan Littlewood's plans for an electronic fun-palace – not to mention the electronic and other modern gadgetry often present in Happenings themselves. Most important perhaps, the Masque also attempted to allegorise the audience, and its appeal, as that of any coterie 'myth-play', was 'a curious mixture of the popular and the esoteric; it is popular for its immediate audience, but those outside its circle have to make a conscious effort to appreciate it' (Frye 282). Finally, the Masque 'even at its best was an attempt rather than an achievement, but although it never quite gained an intrinsic and permanent value, it had a deep, fruitful, and lasting influence' (Welsford, 243–4) – not only on poetry but also on theatre, which enriched itself by incorporating many of its elements and ways of using space, music (i.e. time) and actors.

On the other hand, the late, Jonsonian Masque added a danced scene which showed disruptive powers at work against the advocated harmony and which was often more striking than the celebratory scene. The basic aim of this 'anti-masque' was to enact a deadly threat to, or sickness of, the contemporary way of life, identified with the monarchist state, and its final triumphant recovery ending with the symbolic harmony of banquet and dance. The Masque often relied, both in its general form and in its dance patterns, on a quasi-Pythagorean or Neoplatonic numerology claiming to represent an arithmetical, geometrical and musical harmony of spheres which symbolised and guaranteed the harmony of the political microcosm. 'The masque writers were bound to represent both marriage and monarchy, not as faulty human institutions, but as joyful mysteries.... This enforced orthodoxy led, as it was bound to do, to a stiff insincerity, very alien from the true spirit of romance' (Welsford 290–1). As different from the more sophisticated and mediated medieval approach, from which it ultimately derived, the late Masque idealised the values represented by its audience, the ruling social class. Compared to medieval dramaturgy, which was based on an Augustinian theory of salvational history, the Masque therefore had only an intra-class, institutionalised function but no generally valid *telos*. Where the Elizabethan History Play still had the ideologically powerful, though secularised, 'Tudor myth' to inform its structure, which therefore emphasised the deadly threat of civil war with only a perfunctory final communion (e.g. at the end of *Richard III*), the Masque had to fall back on a stock Morality plot and a narrow cast of types, usually from classical mythology. 'The dramatist might depict life as sorrowful or ridiculous or contemptible, but in the masque absurd or malevolent beings appeared only to be put to flight by the entry of the noble joyous and joy-bringing masquers' (Welsford 366).

Reacting against new Individualist myths which celebrated a false civil community, late nineteenth-century drama began again to grope for more mature allegorical forms. Much of modern drama from Jarry on is an anti-masque-like recognition of the 'absurd and malevolent' as the new normality, or indeed, with Wagner's *Ring of the Nibelungs*, Ibsen's *Ghosts* or Strindberg, of the bourgeois reality as a horrifying and haunted space and time. For example, Mallarmé envisaged the future work of dramatic art as a sacramental participation in mystery, presenting the *mise-en-scène* of the State religion.[12]

As opposed to all such attempts at sacramental yea-saying comedies, the nay-saying Happenings want either to escape from capitalist society or to pull it down; they emphasise either the necessity for a non-existing communion or the alienation of a life without it (sides of the same coin, in fact). For the authors of most Happenings there is both a crying need for (and a total absence of) any supra-individualistic social entity in which one could believe sufficiently to celebrate its order. That is why – unlike the Masque or the early French *mascarade* and ballet – the Happenings have steadfastly refused to take their cue and devices from the prevalent dramatic form, even to the point of being somewhat hysterically suspicious of its dominant medium, words, regardless of the uses it might be put to. Again, numerology is very evident in Happenings, but is based on nineteenth-century thermodynamics, implying that humanity and its affairs exist as aggregates in a mechanical, valueless universe subject to the laws of chance and large numbers (that 'Welfare State of the mind' – Kaplan, 96). Though Happenings often revert to ritual attitudes, their ritual is subjective and almost myth-less. The 'anti-masque' stage has completely taken over, and from the point of view of a world of clear and constant values it would not be too difficult to see the world presented in the Happenings as a demonic chaos rampant with secularised monsters of ultimate neo-capitalist alienation.

4. Happenings and Their Times – Cognitive and Nihilist Estrangement

Effect

Most Happenings seem to have been rather unsatisfactory in their own terms – primitive or muddled – often through lack of time and money, but also through lack of clear aims. One has to insist that in Happenings, as in all spectacles, the effect will depend on clarity of gestural and verbal actions, on their social meaningfulness (different fields of possibility or topics are not aesthetically equivalent), on the skill by which a coordinated series of situations is performed, and on the overall consistency of purpose embodied in the selection and the space/time spread of the materials used (i.e. on the authors' point of view). This last point is the more interesting since the audience's possible reactions often have to be included as a margin of co-authorship in the authors' point of view: this is touched upon at the end of this chapter.

Theoretically, however, if and when these demands are met, a Happening should have a specific effect on participants. By getting drawn into a 'real' event (i.e. one not taking place in a special diegetic universe) the participants should experience a shock of poetic cognition directed at the performance's thematic field, and beginning with themselves and their environment. A Happening 'is designed to stir the modern audience from its cozy emotional anesthesia' (Sontag, 275); 'some specific frustrations, caused by cybernated

life, require accordingly cybernated shock and catharsis'
(Nam June Paik, *Manifestos,* 24; 'the highest priority must be
given to the re-education of its audience's perceptions'
(Baxandall, 29). A Happening is, according to Schechner,
'(1) an attempt to bring into celebratory focus the full
message-complexity of a downtown street, and (2) a playing
with modes of perception' (Schechner, 148); it isolates events
or images in order to revitalise them: 'Deadened habits,
routine images, unused sensibilities, and even places (Kaprow's highways and supermarkets) are reinfused with
meaning', he concludes optimistically (Schechner, 154).
Dominant fossilised views of reality should, when juxtaposed to 'unpackaged' events, be revealed 'as grotesque,
inadequate and dangerous':

In a performance by the Once Theatre, bureaucratic dossiers on
young people were monotonously read, while technicians encased
the individuals, upright and nearly nude, in a box one by one
between layers of plastic sheeting. They looked like frozen fish on
ice, bugs in an ice tray, people in an apartment house. – The banal,
aggressive or grotesque may also be aestheticised before one's eyes.
In *Meat Joy* by Carolee Schneemann, the lovers, having undressed
one another, paint the flesh of the other. In Ken Dewey's *Without
and Within* a rough tug-of-war with audience participation is
transformed into a deliberate ritual, then into dancing which ends
with rock-and-roll. Hostility into beauty into joy. (Baxandall,
32–3)

Baxandall's 'Alienation Antidote' Hypothesis

Even if one does not quite share the millenarism of Higgins,
who programmatically states that we are 'approaching the
dawn of a classless society, to which separation into rigid
categories is absolutely irrelevant' (Higgins, 11–13), Happenings at their best may prefigure possible new modes of
human relations and living, construed as fragments or
elements of a new aesthetics (and ethics), 'the outlines of
everyday life for the post-compulsive, post-manipulated
man' (Baxandall, 33). Upon such elements, some left-wing
or radical critics, such as Baxandall and Schechner, have
based their defence of Happenings, claiming for them the
hypothetical status of an *antidote to existing forms of alienation*
(reification, desensualisation) in the mass society of corporate

capitalism. They argue that Happenings use special devices in order to overcome communication and perception barriers in the manipulated consumer society, in an age of television addiction, public-relations credibility-gaps and mass propaganda techniqus marketing everything from pollutants to genocidal imperialist wars, such as that in Vietnam. In such a context, a re-education of audience perception, a de-pollution of senses, is most urgent; mimetic recognition (*anagnorisis*) in Happenings functions as a therapy counteracting the brain-washing effects of contemporary, profit-oriented life, and demystifying the ruling relationships in life and on stage. They envisage Happenings exclaiming with Yvonne Rainer: 'NO to spectacle no to virtuosity no to transformations and magic and make believe no to glamor and transcendency of the star image not to the heroic no to the anti-heroic no to trash imagery no to involvement of performer or spectator no to style no to camp no to seduction of spectator by the wiles of the performer no to eccentricity no to moving or being moved' (TDR 30, 178).

This leads to a fundamental question, upon an answer to which a judgement on Happenings would depend: Are Happenings really all that demystifying, or do they bear in themselves a new mystification? Do they shock for therapeutic or terroristic ends? Do they celebrate a forward-looking defiance of the ruling myth, or a Black Mass of their own? Have they, in Schechner's terms, the cruelty of childish gratification, or of adult perception? This may be a variant on the general question facing critics of the Establishment or State power-machines – namely, how much destruction is necessary for a reconstruction – but the answer has to be found autonomously in each separate instance. Artaud's and Camus' ambiguous plague imagery is clearly unable to help us here. It seems, then, most useful to approach the answer in terms of the other main figure and tradition in modern theatre: Brecht.

Brecht, Happenings and Their Times
Brecht's dramaturgy is the principal example in this century of an assumption of the plebeian spectacle tradition into drama. Logically, its substratum of popular fairs, folks comics, cabaret, burlesque and other spectacle (what I called

in chapter 3 the Azdak–Schweik 'look from underneath' of plebeian demystification) has some affinities with the stance of the Happpenings.[13] He too passed through a phase of writing for a closed and homogeneous group during which his aim, in the 'plays for learning', was to make the participants more active and critical, with the audience secondary or unnecessary. More generally, Brecht felt the routine actions and situations, representing the anthropological commonplaces of our way of life, should be estranged in order to recognise and expose their alienated quality. Happenings estrange basic conventions of spectacle such as entering by an aisle or sitting in front of the performance area, as well as the field of possibilities presented in their performance. They also lift everyday commonplaces – 'the visit to the supermarket, eating TV dinner, TV, the preliminaries of sex' (*Baxandall, 32*) – out of the 'ordinary' aura and into the focus of attentive scrutiny. However, they very rarely – and this is clearly a weakness – focus their attention on political or economic relationships of any kind: Happenings are more than a little socially inbred. None the less, they theatricalise the audience and its relationships: the audience becomes to a certain extent its own spectacle. This may be in a way a logical extension of Brecht's approach; yet the methodology of Brechtian dramaturgy and of Happenings differs considerably, and for good reason.

The comparison is crucial because Brecht too started out (c. 1916–28) as a Villonesque or Rimbaudesque nihilist. The 'storm and stress' in Europe after the first World War, the exemplary experience of the Leninist phase of the Bolshevik Revolution, proved to him that human relations (i.e. people's 'nature') can be changed by intelligent and organised, though painful, intervention into them. After *The Threepenny Opera* he ceased writing for bourgeois audiences, however liberal or dissident they might be, and turned to performances of workers' and schoolchildren choruses (c. 1929–34). At that point, he began functioning as a partisan or guerrilla in the Lukácsian sense of a creator who coordinates his actions with a disciplined revolutionary 'main body,' but proceeds on his own responsibility, autonomous yet not independent. (This epicyclic way of operating makes nonsense out of the division between inner-directed and outer-directed action, which has befuddled so much liberal criticism of Brecht before and after Esslin.) The experiences of his two phases fused the nihilist clean sweep of the artists (the familiar which is systematically rendered incomprehensible to the senses) with Marx's gnoseology and dialectics which used the resulting view of alienation not as an object of subjective empathy but of cognition. Even after the catastrophic Nazi advent of 1933, Brecht never forsook such a synthesis. Indeed, his path through the 'didactic' phase, and in particular the much undervalued impact of his new audiences, made it possible for Brecht to return, in his mature phase, to a new concreteness enriched by an insight into the inner model of empirical existence, the 'events behind the events'.

The Happenings' authors' critical dates were not 1917 and 1933, but 1945–7 and the mid-1950s to the mid-1960s. The first period is the time of their first conscious experiences of social relations, of growing up in an USA which was turning from a contradiction-filled Rooseveltian anti-fascism to the Cold War outside, and the 'witchhunt' repressions and stagnation within. The second period is the breakdown of that stagnation in an inconclusive flurry of shocked recognitions of America's papered-over contradictions. The Happenings were created in this period, and shared in its inconclusiveness. The New York *bohème* lacked available or persuasive foreign models, lacked strong native workers' or socialist movements, and was subjected to new and more pervasive methods of mass persuassion based on the lure of prosperity. Because of these and many other factors, the Happenings' authors did not emerge out of nihilism into the universe of people enmeshed in political economy and a theatre interested in civic responsibility. Instead, they emerged as an isolated little group catering more or less to each other: their lack of interest in audience was formally analogous to, but sociologically poles apart from, Brecht's second phase. Rejecting American capitalism, but disbelieving in the possibility of a humanising social change, Happenings were as a rule more pessimistic than Brecht's plays. Together with much contemporary European drama, they postulated an absurd, meaningless reality: '... there is the traffic jam, the construction job, the bus that gets four flat tires all at once for no readily explainable reason, the train that stops mysteriously in the middle of the tunnel under the East River. To the average persons, these might be minor tragedies; a happening person would exult that the normal, mundane order of things had been suspended or changed vividly.'[14] Faced with such attitudes, one recalls the witty definition of the absurd as 'a dialectical situation seen by a masochist' (Eco, 237).

Cognitive and Nihilist Estrangement

Comparing the just quoted little exemplum of Hansen's to, say, Brecht's stance toward a traffic accident in his essay *The Street Scene*, it becomes evident what Happenings assume: that the techniques of mass persuasion have badly weakened the normative powers of reason, and the only approach left is to subject people to a non-explicit, more primitive and aggressive kind of experience, which will reorientate them by 'direct perception' (the protracted exposure time of Happenings issuing out of this). The premises of such a proceeding are strictly magical: it can be called an infantile celebratory myth of 'social reconstruction through sensory awakening' (Schechner, 155). In other words, the Happenings' authors expanded their magical nihilism into the only other direction available when one rejects the Brechtian horizon of humanity alienated into political economy: into a religious, non-cognitive estrangement. Affecting a ritual and mythical rather than a cognitive approach, Happenings therefore opposed a *nihilist estrangement* to Brecht's cognitive dialectics. Of course, it might sometimes be useful to think of these oppositions as polar possibilities present in each significant Happening, and reduced to the nihilist pole only in the less significant ones. It would then be the task of a sensitive critic to characterise each particular performance on its own merits (certainly *Fotodeath*, for example, is not predominantly absurd or nihilist: it shows absurdity up).[15]

Brecht himself did the spadework in defining a non-cognitive estrangement by pointing to the Asian and generally pre-Individualist theatre techniques. Such estrangement 'from the right,' so to speak, is nihilist rather in a religious than in a political sense, and an unkind way to described the atmosphere of a number of Happenings would be to call them a sort of bohemian Moral Rearmament – a very American form of nativistic movement (Schechner, 155). The most sophisticated nihilist religion is, of course, Zen Buddhism, and a quote from the Zen precept of Gautama Buddha in his fundamental text on contemplation and meditation, *Satti−patthana−sutti*, immediately calls to mind the technique of primitive Happenings:

How does the anachorete carry out the exercise of contemplating the body in the body?−Having gone into a wood, at the foot of a tree... the anachorete sits with feet crossed, holding his body in a vertical position, with fixed attention. He breathes in with full attention, and breathes out with full attention. Drawing in a long breath, he knows: 'I am drawing in a long breath,' drawing in a short breath, he knows: 'I am drawing in a short breath.' Drawing out a long breath, he knows: 'I am drawing out a long breath'; drawing out a short breath, he knows: 'I am drawing out a short breath'; that is the way to exercise. 'I will breathe conscious of my whole body'; that is the way to exercise.

(Cf. Kaprow's *Calling*, TDR 30, 202ff.). Buddhist contemplation paradoxically uses estrangement and a perverted form of cognition to advance toward Nirvana. It is a beatific vision of the discontinuous flux of things, related to a consciousness of the limits of philosophical humanism and of the positive meaning of alienation. As such it is the horizon of all consistent nihilist estrangement. It may be unnecessary to mention how strong an attraction Zen has therefore provided for the social group from which Happenings too have sprung.

Even if one assumes that Happenings are not predominantly a new mystification of the Zen type but a necessary forerunner of cognitive estrangement, there is little doubt that 'a greater art emerges from the dramatisation of historical reason, than from theatre historically condemned to prepare the ground for reason's resurgence' (Baxandall, 35).

5. Some Words at the End, But Not in Conclusion

The Happenings are forcing us to rethink a number of basic spectacle concepts. Their non-diegetic organisation leads us to re-examine the concept of dramaturgic fable or story – i.e.

to think in terms of an integrated effect of non-verbal materials and non-narrative relationships. The very concept of theatre has to be redefined in order to include a number of genres hitherto neglected as too vulgar (from Latin *vulgus* meaning people) for official aesthetics. This can only lead to a more precise definition and delimitation of drama and other canonic genres, and have a quite salutary effect. However, when the impact of Happenings works in the direction of a simple-minded denial of the relevance of drama, story, etc. in our times, the baby is being chucked out, instead of its bath water renewed: sterility ensues. The struggle between cognitive and nihilist attitudes is at its clearest in the theoretical domain, which by nature does not tolerate much vagueness. Nevertheless, such sterility is not a consequence of the rise of Happenings, but of their context. Among other things, Happenings are thus a socio-cultural document. Above all, they show the potentiality of new forms and materials for theatrical communication, and challenge our aesthetics.

Yet the uncertain status of Happenings in theatrical theory and practice is, to a large extent, due to intrinsic problems of their development. As I have tried to point out in this chapter, their point of view or principle of allegorical stylisation is unclear. In the allegorical mode an antecedent situation is juxtaposed to the present fable, the two being connected by a belief, purpose or ideal which provides the point of view. For an allegorical work of art to succeed, its creator must be able to derive his authority both from his personal achievement of a new structure and a new meaning, and from an antecedent ideal which is in some way classical. As a rule that purpose or ideal is absent from Happenings, which are concerned primarily (in a way that is perhaps understandable but none the less crippling) with nay-saying – or with a vague and general yea-saying which is equivalent to an absence (see pp. 231–3).

Furthermore, to their contact–magic premise of human reorientation through 'direct perception,' I want to oppose two questions: (1) Does this 'counter-magic' not mean playing the game of the opinion-manipulators, albeit in the contrary direction? and (2) Does this not mean playing the game on the terrain of the Establishment brainwashers, where they are much more powerful? One may discount the first question as liberal relativism. But the second surely implies that Happening techniques can have an antidote effect only if and when television programming, newspaper and film financing and distribution, town planning, and so on, are under the control of their producers and consumers, and that, in the meantime, the alienating powers of the system are such that 'live' performances can do little to influence it.

I believe the greatest possibilities for Happening techniques do in fact lie in a diffusion through media such as film and television, which are already using some of them (e.g. in *Laugh-In* or *Blow Up*). Obviously, the exploration of such possibilities is at least a worthwhile pursuit in *avant garde* finger-exercises. At best, it might become of great influence as a laboratory experiment in new perception.

The foregoing discussion of Happenings may make clearer why they did not outlast their socio-political moment. A magico-religious stance is not able to cope with the world (or the USA) of today, and therefore cannot give birth to a major spectacle and theatre form. Such a form can, I believe, arise only in so far as it becomes steeped in and adopts the ideal of philosophical humanism. As Lukács, Merleau-Ponty and many others have noted, present-day humanism no longer takes the side of man against body, of his spirit against his language, of values against facts; people are not given, they *become* in the process by which the body becomes a gesture, the language a deed, and the facts a point of view.[16] Adopting a humanist point of view, a new theatre coming after the Happenings would have to face some basic dichotomies they left as legacy: e.g. between emotion and reason, facts and values, objects and persons, estrangement and cognition, wit and language. The new theatre would have to acknowledge openly that the nexus of the sensorium is, after all, the brain.[17] This means above all that the Happenings have not faced *the use of language as verbal poetry and not as noise.* Yet the spoken word, the conceptualised sound, is of paramount importance in establishing a continuity between past and present: 'The loss of word means a loss of memory.'[18] Loss of contact with the past leads to a perpetual point-consciousness shifting with but never widening beyond the fleeting point of the present: it is thus equivalent to the loss of contact with *future* too. An allegorical genre without memory of antecedent and without anticipation of posteriority must flounder in pure naturalism and phenomenology: the meaningful word seems to make the difference between nihilism and cognition. Its adoption would probably entail structural principles more sophisticated than simple permutation or quasi-circular repetition.

Richard Schechner believed that the delicate balance 'between revitalisation and fantasy, control and freedom, reflection and participation, complexity and simplification... can be maintained' (Schechner, 155). Unfortunately, I think we must recognise that Happenings have achieved this balance only in exceptional cases. The failure to achieve it, because of subjectivity, imprecision and dogmatic blindness to history, has prevented them from becoming more than a possibly fertile footnote in the history of theatrical spectacle. But then, as I remarked earlier, books and special issues of professional periodicals have been and are being devoted to less significant footnotes. And the dossier is not quite closed: the implication of this genre may hold some surprises yet.

Notes

1 Apart from the classic approaches of Aristotle's *Poetics*, Diderot's *De la poésie dramatique* and some other writings, Lessing's *Laokoon*, and Brecht's *Schriften zum Theater*, the following secondary literature has been most useful in these reflections (and some of my conclusions and indeed terms are obviously indebted to them, whether I agreed or disagreed with them). When quoted, they will be indicated in parentheses by author's name with the pages following, otherwise they are not as a rule acknowledged.

Baxandall, Lee, 'Beyond Brecht: the Happenings', *Studies on the Left*, (January–February 1966).
Eco, Umberto, *Opera aperta (Milano, 1967)*.
Higgins, Dick, *FOEW & OMBWHNW* (New York/Barton/Cologne, 1969).
Kaplan, Donald M., 'Character and Theatre', *TDR* no. 32 (1966).
Kaprow, Allan, *Some Recent Happenings* (New York, 1966).
Kaprow, Allan, *Untitled Essay and Other Works* (New York, 1967).

Kirby, Michael, *Happenings* (New York, 1965) (wih statements and scripts by Allan Kaprow, Claes Oldenburg, Robert Whitman and others).

Lebel, Jean-Jacques, *Le Happening* (Paris, 1967).

Manifestos, by Ay-o and others (New York, 1966).

Schechner, Richard, *Public Domain* (Indianapolis & New York, 1969).

Sontag, Susan, *Against Interpretation* (New York, 1969).

Tarrab, Gilbert. 'Le Happening', *R. d'histoire du théâtre*, special issue (1968).

TDR no. 30 (1965), issue devoted to Happenings.

Let me also make clear that, though I have seen a number of performances billed as Happenings in Europe and America, I have worked basically from scenarios and descriptions, just as if discussing the *Commedia dell'arte*, since my chief interest is in this case not that of a chronicler but of a 'socio-formalist' theoretician of spectacle.

2 See an account of it in Kirby, *TDR* no. 30, 34–6, and of its direction by Judith Malina in Pierre Biner, *Le Living Theatre* (Lausanne, 1968), pp. 52–3.

3 Cf. Schechner on Ann Halprin's dance-Happening, *Esposizione*: 'the similarity of one human being to another and the ineluctable unity which comes from a group doing roughly the same thing together' (Schechner, 149). Kaprow himself lucidly notes that his symbols 'are so general and so archetypical that actually almost everyone knows vaguely about these things,' since he tries to keep them 'universal, simple, and basic' (*Happenings,* ed. Kirby, 50).

4 Oldenburg himself mentions that in *Fotodeath* 'events repeated themselves in superimposed lines of movement,' which seems a brief painterly way of saying much the same I was trying to get at above.

5 The main works dealing with this theory are:

Shklovskii, Viktor, *Rozanov* (Petrograd, 1921).

Shklovskii, Viktor, *Khod Konja* (Berlin, 1923).

Shklovskii, Viktor, *Literatura i kinematograf* (Berlin, 1923).

Tinianov, Yury, *Arkhaisty i novatory* (Leningrad, 1929).

Tomashevskii, Boris, *Teoriia literatury: Poètika* (Moscow-Leningrad, 1925).

Most quotations can be found in the excellent study by Victor Erlich, *Russian Formalism* (The Hague, 1955); see also René Wellek and Austin Warren, *Theory of Literature* (New York, 1956), chapter 17. The translations in *Russian Formalist Criticism: Four Essays*, transl. and ed. Lee T. Lemon and Marion J. Reis

(Lincoln, 1965) have gaps and terminological difficulties. Since this essay was first written, a number of other translations have been published, e.g. *Readings in Russian Poetics*, ed. L. Matejka and K. Pomorska (Cambridge MA, 1971).

[6] Whitman was quoted to that effect in *Happenings*, ed. Kirby, 180.

[7] Michael Kirby developed the hypothesis of Happenings being defined by a performance non-matrixed by time, place or character in the Introduction to his anthology *Happenings* (see note 1); Donald M. Kaplan was referring to the restatement in Kirby's article 'The New Theatre' in the *TDR* special issue on Happenings which Kirby co-edited. I would like to stress that though I disagree with Kirby in some basic aspects, I found his notion and term of matrixing a really useful contribution to a not merely impressionistic discussion of the genre.

[8] Etienne Souriau, *Les grands Problèmes de l'esthétique théâtrale,* (Paris, 1962), p. 11. Souriau has enlarged on this score in several other works, e.g. in his presentation of the anthology *L'Univers filmique* (Paris, n.d.), and in the well-known *Les Deux cent mille situations dramatiques* (Paris, 1950).

[9] For a reading of mimesis as (re)presentation or performing preferably to copying or simple imitating, see my brief argumentation in chapter 4.

[10] An excellent formulation of that process can be found in Allan Kaprow, *Assemblages, Environments and Happenings* (New York, 1967), pp. 165–6.

[11] This section uses, beside Masque texts and the accounts of E.K. Chambers, *The Elizabethan Stage I–IV* (Oxford, 1923), insights from:

> Cunliffe, John W. 'Italian Prototype of the Masque and Dumb Show', *PMLA*, 22 (1907).
> Evans, Herbert Arthur, *English Masques* (London, 1897).
> Frye, Northrop, *Anatomy of Criticism* (New York, 1966).
> Furniss, W. Todd, 'Ben Jonson's Masques', *Three Studies in the Renaissance* (New Haven, 1958).
> Gilbert, Allan H. *The Symbolic Persons in the Masques of Ben Jonson* (Durham N.C., 1948).
> Honig, Edwin, *Dark Conceit* (New York, 1966).
> Nicolson, Marjorie Hope, *The Breaking of the Circle* (New York, 1960).
> Orgel, Stephen, *The Jonsonian Masque* (Cambridge, MA, 1965).
> Prunières, Henri, *Le Ballet de cour en France avant Benserade et Lully* (Paris, n.d.).

Reyher, Paul, *Les Masques anglais* (Paris, 1909).

Rossiter, A.P., *English Drama from Early Times to the Elizabethans* (London, 1969).

Schoenbaum, Samuel (ed.), *Essays Principally on Masques and Entertainments* (Chicago, 1968).

Talbert, Ernst W., 'The Interpretation of Jonson's Courtly Spectacles', *PMLA* 61 (1946).

Taylor, R.A., *Aspects of the Italian Renaissance* (London, 1923).

Welsford, Enid, *The Court Masque* (Cambridge, 1927).

These books are quoted by author's name and page in parenthesis. See also R.B. Parker's parallel of 'Dramaturgy in Shakespeare and Brecht,' *Univ. of Toronto Quarterly* no. 3 (1963).

[12] Haskell Block, *Mallarmé and the Symbolist Drama* (Detroit, 1963), p. 86. I have already mentioned affinities with Expressionist, Surrealist, and Futurist drama, and Kirby has gone much further in following *one* tradition behind the Happenings (the so-called Dadaist one) in the 'Introduction' to *Happenings*.

[13] This section owes much to Lee Baxandall's article (see note 1); though I am dubious about his basic stance, he had the perspicacity of first posing and problematising the crucial comparison of the two estrangements – Brecht's and the Happenings'. It also owes much to discussions with Richard Schechner, before and after his quoted book.

[14] Al Hansen, *A Primer of Happenings & Time/Space Art* (New York/Paris/Cologne, 1965), p. 34.

[15] See, on the other hand, Oldenburg's remarks on his *Gayety*, a very interesting manifestation of the tension which went into the making of that 'civic spectacle': 'In *Gayety* I want to create Chicago, in the way I see it .... I think of O Henry's or anyone elses municipal report, sociological studies etc. but that mine is poetic/satiric/symbolic. The enigmatic portions may be taken to be the situation of the spirit in the community, often these have a violent turn. – The relation of the incidents is fortuitous as is the case in real life .... Unfortunately I am limited to typicalities, but the spectator may imagine the numbers. – The piece closes with a Finale, an apotheosis, in the form of a destruction which always seems appropriate in which the forces of the community are released functionlessly in relieving chaos' (*Happenings,* ed. Kirby, 234–5).

[16] See George Lukács, *History and Class Consciousness* (London, 1971); and Maurice Merleau-Ponty, *Signes* (Paris, 1960), *passim*.

[17] I am indebted for this observation, as well as for stimulating my interest in a possible parallel between Masque and Happening, to

Professor Donald F. Theall of McGill University, and to his
unpublished manuscript of an address to McGill alumni from
Autumn 1968.

[18] Georg Lukács, 'Gedanken zu einer Aesthetik des Kinos', in
Schriften zur Literatursoziologie (Neuwied, 1968), p. 78.

APPENDIX: Happenings: An Exchange Between
Lee Baxandall and Darko Suvin

Lee Baxandall
The analysis by Darko Suvin in regard to Happenings has
much in it of interest – but much also, I fear, which
obfuscates the last few years of theatrical experiment, and
which wrongly discredits the Happenings tendency. Since
Professor Suvin paid considerable attention to an article of
mine on this topic in formulating his view, perhaps you will
permit me to respond.

Foremostly, the Suvin piece smacks of remoteness from an
adequate experience of Happenings and related theatre
pieces. To found this suspicion, one need not have picked up
on the statement that his theorising about this mode of
theatre proceeded 'basically from scenarios and descriptions'
rather than from first-hand contact. ('Just as if discussing the
commedia dell'arte,' Suvin hastens to add – but the *commedia*
and Happenings are very different animals indeed, as even a
cursory comparison will prove! And even assuming Suvin's
analogy were accurate, should we then regard our impoverished means of knowing about the *commedia* as an appropriate
and adequate means for approaching contemporary theatre
pieces?)

Suppose that his contact with Happenings had been more
frequent than he suggests. Would Suvin's conclusions then
tend to be less remote from the function of perceptual
phenomena which Happenings constitute? We can doubt it.
For Professor Suvin proceeds very consciously on the basis of
a theory of cognition. His particular idea of a real or material
theory of knowledge is unsuited, I submit, to understanding
the function of the best of the Happenings and also to
describing the cognitive process we all undergo. Yet Suvin's
premises are none the less lucidly held by him. And this

makes difference and discussion more valuable, more productive with him than if one were to differ with others who
vaguely hold a comparable prejudice (here, against a non-
conceptualising theatre) but fail to conceptualise their own
particular values. Hence, Professor Suvin does more than
assert that Happenings exhibit a 'nihilist' attitude toward
reality. Suvin makes clear that when he says that Happenings
are 'strictly magical ... religious, non-cognitive', he judges
them by a gnoseological standard. He explicitly tells us: 'The
meaningful word seems to make the difference between
nihilism and cognition'; 'the spoken word, the conceptual-
ized sound, is of paramount importance.'

Now, an obvious and, I think, irrefragable retort would
consist in asking Suvin if he believes that *no* cognitive
expression occurs among the non-literary arts, for example,
in painting. But to point up Suvin's fundamental error
merely by taking note of his bias for the literary genres and
for the more conceptualising examples of those genres is not
sufficient. We should also directly indicate a theory of
cognition more adequate to life, and art, than his highly
rationalistic, almost eighteenth-century, limited idea of
cognition.

The alternative to an overly exalted idea of the roles of
Concept and Reason is not anti-intellectualism, and not
irrationalism – as, in the theatre world, the likes of Robert
Brustein want to cause us to believe. No. The alternative to
an enthronement of Reason is a more comprehensive
material theory of cognition.

I hesitate to bring the outstanding statement of a more
comprehensive theory of cognition to the reader's attention—
for, although written in 1950–1, it unfortunately has only
been published to date (and this is truly extraordinary) in
Serbo-Croatian. The work I refer to is the masterful *Theory
of Creativity on a Marxist Basis* by the outstanding philosopher
and visual arts expert Max Raphael, whose *Demands of Art*
was published by Princeton University Press in its Bollingen
Series in 1968. Yet so prevalent and misunderstood does the
prejudice exhibited by Professor Suvin in the realm of theatre
remain, that perhaps an overview of its basis in a faulty
notion of cognition can well be justified.

In the view of Max Raphael, then: Cognition must be seen

as a dialectical process arising with the human experience of the world. The process, which occurred historically for the species, occurs anew with each infant that is born. Raphael locates the initial cognitions in *bodily activity*. The animal begins to know its way about the dark night of protozoic existence, while the infant threshes in its crib or at the breast. Then, the cognitive function is built upon by the *experience of the various senses*. Perception and its transformation and expression are learned by trial and error and with growing assurance. But in the initial stage, that of bodily activity, sensations can be affirmed or rejected at once: a tree and a crib are hard and they hurt when struck; water is soft, but one sinks in water. At the level of experience through all of the senses, perception is not that readily verified. Hence, sensuous experience must isolate a *sign* from the environment; the sign stands for a perception. It is fixed and distanced from its source; the sign enters 'within' the subject and, subsumed in the process of cognition, is transformed and synthesised with other perceptions on a basis of continued dialectical interaction with the environment.

In the third stage, cognition is comprised of thought that understands or *comprehends* the world. The baby and man-the-species begin to seek, 'in what is common to all the particular images, for the force that inheres to reality as such and that regulates the relation of all its parts to one another, i.e. for the generality that dominates the particular. Understanding is thus linked to the perceptions, in its effort to encompass all the particular determinants.'

At the last stage of development, Raphael locates *speculative reason*.

We will define reason (on the basis of our total historical data) as the mediation which is predicated on the unmastered world in its entirety, which seeks to construct that world theoretically from a single source point and to master it in the imagination, and which constitutes the unity of all contradictions, therefore, the Absolute.

Note that speculative reason is not only the final cognitive faculty to develop; *its reliability is contingent* on the reliability of the faculties that are developed earlier.

The three mediations of cognition – the body, the senses, and the understanding – are in a dialectical relationship which historically has arisen under the impress of the outer world, in such a way that these mediations, in association and with continual interaction, have developed into a higher unity from whence, with different means, they confront the same task: mastery of a theory that will dominate practically the impingent outer world.

Reason, moreover, is in the process of development. Early in the history of the species, a kind of reason developed; not a scientific reason, but not wholly untrue to the external world, either. The Absolute, or source point, from which the world is mastered in theory, has progressively grown more equal to its practical task, therefore, objectively more absolute. Raphael describes the emergence of Reason from magic through religion and metaphysics to Marxism.

I should wish to emphasise, *contra* Suvin, Raphael's notion of the interpenetration of reason – as it is developed in any individual and at a given period – and the earlier-developed cognitive faculties of *the body, senses and comprehension.* These at once aid in determining the nature of reason and are in turn shaped by reason. Accordingly, it is incorrect to find *no* cognitive aspect in art that refuses to interpret, to comprehend or to reason, for the apprehender. The art which is only made up of 'sensuous qualities' is also cognitive; it also represents a subject in dialectical relation with the world-as-object.

In the above, I have not given specific instances of the cognitive properties of non-conceptual elements in Happenings. But the reader undoubtedly has had many examples occur to him.

A final important matter raised by Suvin is the question, Where have Happenings gone? Does their displacement indicate their inadequacy or their insignificance?

I would place the downturn of the Happenings trend in 1967. Now, at least two major practitioners (Carolee Schneemann and Ken Dewey) turned up that autumn at the Siege of the Pentagon, and it should have been no great cause for surprise. I have a hunch, and I am sure that it is not mine alone but would be found widely among Happeners, that the development of political struggle and also the *dramaturgical character* of the struggle have perhaps been chiefly responsible for the eclipse of Happenings. And this development I would describe not as the rejection (a mechanistic concept) of Happenings, but rather as a stage wherein a historically necessitated and validated phenomenon was incorporated, revised, and *superseded* (a dialectical concept) by a further stage of historical activity.

Darko Suvin

Obviously, we all start out from working hypotheses (which those who disagree are free to call prejudices) and the utmost a discussion can achieve is to clarify their thrust and limits. Lee Baxandall's rejoinder to my 'Reflections on Happenings' contributes to such a discussion, and I agree with much of what he says. Now, as to some matters arising out of our disagreements:

(1) I do not want to comment extensively upon his contact–magic assumption that the understanding of an aesthetic activity is directly proportional to temporal exposure to it. Obviously, there is a necessary minimum of exposure: anything beyond that seems to equate sensual perception with dialectical understanding. Mr Baxandall proceeds to buttress this later – I think mistakenly – by paraphrasing Raphael. In that view, the greatest expert on rodents is undoubtedly Mickey Mouse. This seems to me to be a (or *the*) heresy of the American New Left, and probably the basis of our disagreement. As an anti-toxin to it, a Diderotian type of rationalism is sometimes indicated.

(2) Nothing in Raphael, if I have not forgotten something, applies specifically to theatre arts. Theatre arts are *not* painting. (That is only what some Happeners would like to think.) The history of *homo sapiens* in the last five or ten thousand years indicates that the significance and meaningfulness – the power to express human relationships – of theatre arts has been wedded to the growing sophistication of their verbal signs' level. Nobody in his right mind claims this is the only, or even the basic, type of signs employed by theatre. But it is the type which has permitted it to transcend the static ritual stage and its magico-religious approach to the world, and engage in understanding the dynamic world of changing human relations. I would therefore maintain that a return to nonverbal rituals cannot *today* fail to be nihilistic.

(3) Yet Mr Baxandall throws into relief the constrictive aspects of our (mine, his) present-day 'artisanal' criticism, with each critic sitting in his private little workshop, alone or – if he is very clever, and lucky to boot – with a few apprentices. It is a sad reflection on North American life that out of 2000 universities and colleges teaching theatre and/or dramatic arts, as far as I know none has an Institute for Theatre Theory (or Aesthetics or Poetics). If some such centres existed, presumably Lee Baxandall and I would have had an opportunity to discuss my essay before publication, as part of a learning process in such an institution. I do not doubt that some possibly one-sided emphases in my reflections (all emphases are by definition one-sided – his, too) might have been rendered more adequate. Nevertheless, I'm somewhat puzzled that he should think I was simply rejecting Happenings. I have received comments from the other side of the spectrum disagreeing with my too great concern with, and the importance accorded to, Happenings. But I was not trying to write either a pro or a con article; I was just trying to reflect on what could be learned from Happenings, negatively and positively, about further developments in theatre (or spectacle), and about its theory. I agree with Baxandall's conclusion about a possible dialectical superseding by political 'street scenes'. But, as that development also shows, a superseding is not simply incorporation and revision; it is also rejection. The reader might have noticed that the structure of my essay is not an 'either-or' one, but a 'not-only-but-also' one. Baxandall's critique has – as is perhaps proper to a rejoinder – fastened only on one aspect of that structure.

Afterword (1982) to Part 2: Looking Forward From Brecht

1. *The four chapters on Brecht in Part 2 (as well as chapter 2 in Part 1) structure its historical domain as a basic scansion: historically, the chapters could have been divided into 'before Brecht', 'Brecht' and 'after Brecht'. Brecht's opus is central to this book because he gave the central (though, of course, not final) pertinent formulations for the point of view and the concerns of any reflection on the role of culture or art – or should one simply say social discourse and verbal behaviour – within the horizons of political salvation. It is a happy chance – but perhaps not a chance? – that he did it largely (second in importance only to his poetry) by means of dramaturgy, presenting us thus with a felicitous union of message and code, with a feedback between ends and means. As a practical achievement, Brecht's system is, I believe, so far the highest vantage point for a survey of dramaturgy. Although, in theory, we can by now see where it stops short (e.g. evaluation of Stalinism, treatment of female dramatis personae), climbing up to and looking around from its peaks is still the way to see most of the land.*

At the beginning was the sheer joyous shock of reading Brecht and seeing the Berliner Ensemble. This has been perhaps best formulated by Roland Barthes' recollection of the 'Brechtian bedazzlement' [l'éblouissement brechtien] in the May 1965 special issue of Esprit: 'Cette illumination a été un incendie: il n'est plus rien resté devant mes yeux du théâtre français' [This lighting up was a conflagration: no trace remained before my eyes of French theatre]. All of us in the student theatres mentioned earlier (of which Barthes was also a part) stood largely under the sign of Brecht. Barthes also gives an excellent first explanation of why Brecht at one swoop swallowed up all of his precursors – the populists, the avant-gardists, and so forth – and rendered apparent their subsequently intolerable limitations: his was simultaneously 'un théâtre populaire éclairé par le marxisme et ... un art qui surveille rigoureusement ses signes' [a plebeian theatre enlightened by Marxism and an art that rigorously watches over its signs]. It contested, and yet recuperated the best in, all the known historical dramaturgies, and it gave forth the sensually present feeling of a different theatre and dramaturgy, equivalent to the highest cognitions of the revolutionary sciences and experiences of our times. Once again, as in every great age of theatre up to Shakespeare, dramaturgy had become a possible partner on the front-lines of cognition, with the added advantage of a sensual and collective pleasure attendant upon it. As all good revolutionaries, Brecht's theatre too proclaimed – with Sorel and Gramsci – a pessimism of the intellect conjugated with an optimism of the will. Heady stuff, all of this! It became difficult to see or read something that did not come up or at least tend to this standard – the Angry Young Men, the Left humanists, most Absurdists, impressionistic experimenters and fragmentary technicians of all kinds – without getting irritated to the breaking-off point. How could one go on producing or watching, at any rate taking seriously, Gorboduc *or* The Four PPs *after* King Lear *and* As You Like It?

The parallel is inexact: Brecht's age had more radically divergent tendencies in theatre than Shakespeare's could, or perhaps was allowed to, have; this is to my mind the main reason why he did not achieve a summa *as persuasive as Shakespeare's. But even the partial parallel may transmit the silent explosion of clarity that many of us derived from the appearance of Brecht on the world stage. What he untranslatably called* die sanfte Gewalt der Vernunft *(the mild violence of reason?) had us in its thrall. All the familiar landmarks regrouped themselves. The great tradition of plebeian narrative ('epic') theatre from the Asian dramaturgies through the European middle ages to the burlesque, the* agitprop, *and the rebels pushed out to the margins of Individualism (Ruzzante, the German Romantics, Nestroy, Büchner, Jarry, Wedekind, Mayakovsky, O'Casey, early Krleža, dozens of others from every language) reassumed its historically central position. Logically, Individualism now became a historical aberration (as argued in chapter 1), while some of the greatest names (Shakespeare, Aeschylus, Chekhov) could be seen as largely non-Individualistic and rescued for the new tradition, and others (Sophocles, Schiller, Ibsen) could be downgraded to redress the balance.*

I wish I could – I hope I shall one day – pursue at great length the parallel between Brecht and Shakespeare, indispensable to do full justice to both. I have cautiously approached it in the Coriolan *chapter, choosing the terrain most favourable to Brecht. For the present purpose I shall mention just one crucial parallel. It has again been best formulated by another member of the great team from the 1950s* Théâtre populaire *journal, Bernard Dort. In a retrospective, twenty-five years later (now in his* Théâtre en jeu *[Paris, 1979]) he pointed out that the force of Brecht's dramaturgy resides in its fusion of the critique of the world by the theatre, and of the theatre by the world. For me, that is exactly Shakespeare's strength too, however different both of his critiques may have been. In this book I have looked at how the two critiques intertwine in Brecht, an intertextual focus that differs from a search for fictional sources and influences. His critique of theatre is mentioned incidentally in* The Chalk Circle *chapter, somewhat more in the case of the* Coriolan *adaptation, most in the 'Mirror and Dynamo' chapter, and it underlies chapters 2, 8 and 9. Its absence from the* Saint Joan *chapter in the traditional philological form is due to the fact that the parallels to* The Maid of Orleans *and* Faust *seem to me – once Schiller and even Goethe have ceased to be living presences in world dramaturgy – of interest mainly to Germanists, and possibly Germans. But, even where less explicit, the critique of theatre by the world is constantly present in these chapters. It is addressed directly in the* Saint Joan *chapter too: how may the stage talk about the stock exchange and the depression in verse (and in dramaturgic situations) is perhaps one of its* leitmotifs.

The discussion of Brecht in this book is not presented as final, but as ongoing. Some points, especially some soundings in the early attempt at an overview, 'The Mirror and the Dynamo', could already be viewed with scepticism. I would hope this chapter formulates some centrally pertinent insights about the whole dramaturgical tradition culminating in Brecht: the slaughterhouse age looked at; the (model-type, i.e. exaggerated) polarisation between the 'mirror' and the 'dynamo' stances; the look backward as a pleasingly Galilean resultant of the two component forces of a plebeian look from below and an intellectual look from above, both of them vectors running aslant from the postulated utopian future to our times. But I am by now dubious about the too neatly Hegelian three-step dividing Brecht's development into a non-consenting, a consenting and a mature phase. It is probably still of some introductory value, but the main reason I have let it stand is that no acceptable alternative is yet to be seen. Even Dort repeats in his cited 1979 book this same Hegelian triad – much superior, of course, to the Esslinian bisection into immature (read political) and mature (read aesthetic) phases. But we need more reflection on the significance of Brecht's sometimes zig-zag developments. The stimulating, but one-sided, assumption of a lay religiousness in his 'consenting' phase, pioneered by West German critics, does not adequately explain the tangled dialectics of the Lehrstücke, *which are not merely (if at all) a dip toward Stalinism. I go into Brecht's variant of Leninism – clearly inflected toward the self-managing concept of workers' councils – in chapters 5–7 but these are among the first probes into a complex matter. Allotting to Brecht the political thinker an original position somewhere between Lenin, Luxemburg, Korsch, Gramsci and Bloch – which could explain also some of his rare but huge mistakes, such as his understandable (and before 1968 perhaps defensible) reluctance to abandon the hypothesis that the Warsaw Pact countries were, in however contradictory ways, still on the road to socialism or communism and not to what Marx calls Asian despotism – remains a desideratum of Brechtian criticism. I shall note here only that the 1960s, when chapter 4 was written, were for reasons both of infrequent performance and ideological limitations (including mine) an unpropitious time for understanding these 'didactic plays' or 'plays for learning': they still remain a part of our most distant horizons. The particular investigations of chapter 5–7 are, then, attempts to approach these horizons.*

Another, by now debatable, point may be whether there is not too much talk of 'aesthetics' in chapter 4. This is useful in so far as it succeeds in stressing that and how central features within *a dramaturgy are historical, a proceeding which subverts and adapts – as I argue Brecht did in his practice – classical 'mirroring', or static, or formalist aesthetics. In this view the inner-directed autonomy of a text itself (which I assume as the first indispensable step of materialist investigation) works against its being understandable in isolation from the socio-historical practice which is its inherent intertext. Possibly a better balance might be suggested by another terminology. Yet the 'contrary' use of such classical aesthetic terms and debates as that of mimesis seems to me necessary. It recognises that the theatre as an institution depending on audiences and the State has – as Brecht recognised by the 1940s – not radically broken the continuity of problems existing from the middle ages and the Renaissance (and from the recuperation of Antiquity).*

Finally, Brecht – and these investigations into him – leaves us

with some quite basic, quite fascinating and quite urgent questions.
For this book, the most encompassing of them could be called
'dramaturgy and intervention into history'. It is, of course, a
particular form of Marx's Eleventh Thesis on Feuerbach: *can the*
production of culture contribute to changing human relationships?
Before being ethical, the question is epistemological: Is this possible,
and if yes, just how? I argue in the Paris Commune chapter that for
theatre in particular this is not possible in any immediate and nation-
wide way since the rise of a mass and industrialised society. But is
what Brecht called intervening, effective or engaged thinking (in the
technical sense of meshing or being in gear [eingreifendes
Denken]*) possible in dramaturgy at all? In these post positional*
notes, I shall point out only that for Brecht such transmittable,
connected or fitting thinking consisted of 'practicable definitions ...
permitting to manipulate a defined domain', and always incorporat-
ing the behaviour of the definer as a factor of defining (GW XX:
168, and see the whole section 158–78). In particular, an image or
model – say, of a person – can be drawn up into which would be
inserted attitudes that the person observed might not have found by
her or himself: 'but these imputed ways of behaviour do not remain
the observer's illusions; they turn to realities: the image has become
productive, it can change the person modelled, it contains (realis-
able) proposals. To make such an image means to love.' (ibid.,
170). The great Brechtian (and Marxian) theme of a productive or
creative eros *culminates in such suggestions, which he wanted put*
on his gravestone ('He made proposals. We used some.'). I do not
think this solves the problem; but it does pose it anew. And Brecht's
pioneering status as a precursor of media (radio and film) criticism,
together with his precursor position for modern epistemology or
semiotics (e.g. of Prieto or Eco), indicates how dramaturgy is, in my
opinion, 'practicable' today. Or at least it indicates how we have to
bet – not so much for theoretical reasons as by induction from its
abundant abuse by capitalism – dramaturgy can be practised and
used: as a theatrical laboratory for transposition into film, television
and other mass media. In that sense, the communicational and
power-political lesson I was tracing in the Saint Joan *chapter is the*
most urgent possible application of the Eleventh Thesis on
Feuerbach, *of Brecht as 'The Philosopher in Theatre'. It is also his*
channelling of erotics – so evident in his poetry, and yet, as I discuss
in chapter 5, conspicuously absent from the dramaturgy – into
societal production. As he noted in the Introduction to his Short

Organon, *dramaturgy was for Brecht the equivalent of sexual cohabitation: a domain of erotic productivity. But as different from an insurrection, a new factory, or a sexual encounter, I would argue that dramaturgy (and, modifying Freud, culture in general) is not immediate but mediated and mediating, signifying and significant, inter personal behaviour. By definition, culture – semantically half- way between cult (worship) and cultivation (labour) – is a roundabout or indirect societal practice. Thus, if theatre can only take up a freely or productively critical stance (freedom was for Brecht always simply productivity, and socialism the Great Productivity or Creativity) on condition that 'it deliver itself up to the most turbulent currents in society'* (Short Organon, GW XVI: 671) – *this is a paradox on the order of the Christian 'Whosoever loseth his life shall gain it.' And it speaks as much to theatre (dramaturgy) as it does to society: it is the* theatre's *vitality or productivity that is at stake, more immediately than society's. But this vitality is predicated on the theatre erotically assuming society (grown turbulently attractive) into itself. That is their way of becoming the ancestors of a new future: Judge and Wise Fool interpenetrating to produce the Princely Child. As in the dynamo of* The Caucasian Chalk Circle; *or as (by frustrated contraries) in the mirror of* Saint Joan of the Slaughterhouses *and* Mother Courage and Her Children.

2. *The final two chapters, then, read the dramaturgies of Beckett and the Happenings as counter-projects following on Brecht's dramatur- gy because of the (temporary) loss of the Brechtian bet on the coming about of socialist, de-alienated relations between people. In the ongoing great salvational debate whether the socialist movement for de-alienation is a believable alternative, the dramaturgies of Beckett and the Happenings are two among the best examples of the negative or nihilist alternative. But these are ambiguously rich dramaturgies. True, both are predicated upon a* non-dit: *the non-existence of a general societal movement for de-alienation. But their other face is a rejection of and horror at the result: these are dramaturgies honestly translating pain and want. It is met by Stoicism in a particular segment of the European, and by attempts at an epistemological fix in the equivalent US intelligentsia. Of course, neither is Brecht a mindlessly triumphant alternative: at best, I think his worlds are capacious enough to accommodate both consenting and non-consenting, positivity and negativity toward*

*political de-alienation and therefore toward life in general. This is
why I have cautiously used some aspects of Brecht when evaluating
these historically (not always chronologically) later developments,
though I would acknowledge that Brecht's premises need further
differentiation and possibly some fundamental enrichment – precisely
in the light of later developments in human relations, signified in
probably distorted but certainly indispensable ways, for example, by
these two dramaturgies. Yet this juxtaposition is, I hope, methodical
rather than dogmatic: the fate of the Berliner Ensemble functions as
an awful warning against 'Brechtianism'. Centrally, Beckett and
the Happenings have to be judged by juxtaposing their own
epistemological and axiological horizons to the global picture of
relations between people in their time. The juxtaposition is
mandatory because these two dramaturgies are as intimately bound
up with political de-alienation – namely, with what they perceive as
its failure – as Brecht's is. In the terms of Part 1 they are every whit
as political as Brecht (usually more so).*

*Brecht once remarked that in his time great theatre happened in
four countries. One had had a revolution, one a demi-revolution, one
a quarter-revolution, and one an eighth of a revolution (respectively:
the USSR, Weimar Germany, Czechoslovakia, and New Deal
USA). While this was a witty note rather than meticulous
overview, the basic correctness and fairness of his quip is easily
re-established by applying its premises to some missing times and
places (e.g. France in the 1940s and 1950s, or London after 1956).
And its wit is based on the important cognition that there is a central
correlation between the world stage and the worlds on the stage.
Chapters 8 and 9 go into somewhat more (though perhaps not
enough) detail on the particular correlations between their subjects
and the stagnation of human relationships in the western Europe of
the 1930s to 1950s, or in the USA of the 1940s to 1960s. It is not
necessary for Beckett to have been a Rimbaud, first involved in and
later disenchanted by the Paris Commune and its failure – though of
course Beckett did participate in the Resistance, clearly if marginally. It is enough to note how his universe is defined by the obsessively
horrible scandal of the tendency towards zero-action and zero-value.
Value must be: and yet there is none. Instead of salvation, empty
duration engulfs the (non-)agents. The homologies to what any
socialist in the original, Paris Commune sense, or simply any
humanist, can identify as the state of the world today (at least within
the author's societal experience) seem to me as striking as the more*

overt homologies between Brecht and the ideals-cum-difficulties of socialism. They are elaborated further in the chapter on Waiting for Godot *as an anti-Mystery play.*

Similar observations applying to the Happenings are discussed in the chapter 9. They extend into epistemology of perception rather than only into axiology, and as far as genre is concerned into spectacle rather than only dramatic theatre. This is, again, necessitated by the more exasperated position of the bohème *in the USA twenty years later. This chapter is followed by an exchange with Lee Baxandall to which it gave rise. In my opinion, much of my friend Baxandall's defence of Happenings knocks on an open door. The very fact of having written that chapter – rather than, as I explicitly noted, on Albee or Tennessee Williams, on Noel Coward or the later Ionesco – is surely overriding proof that I thought this spectacular genre was important. I am, I hope, poles apart from, say, Adorno's élitist refusal of Happenings, where his* Mitteleuropean *'high art' bias overrode even his affinity to the negative (such as his canonisation of Beckett). Further, I have caused some scandal among literary critics by staunchly insisting that the pertinent framework of dramaturgy is theatre (many kinds of signs) rather than literature (verbal signs only). But of course, some of Baxandall's argument I simply disagree with. I am very suspicious of romantic immanence, the inexpressible, the breathlessly numinous. I may not go as far as to accept Voltaire's position of an irreconcilable enmity between romanticism and reason, since I deeply admire some writings historically called Romantic: Hölderlin, Shelley or Keats, say. But I find that such writings are also classical in the sense referred to in the conclusion to chapter 9: they refer to an ideal and formulatable (though perhaps not yet formulated) historical norm or purpose. The merely romantic Romantics seem to me too ephemeral. Their expression of irrational aspects of life is not a critique but a – possibly plaintive – identification. To the contrary, I believe, with Brecht, that a classical form (not a fixed style of classicism) is not only a critique of irrational human relations but also the guarantee of a durability. The classic's union of richness and stringency can arise only from tension with a supra-individual purpose; this is why the text can then turn up new facets for new historical contingencies. As I said in my rejoinder, even Diderot is a good anti-toxin to irrationalist romanticism, of which (alas) the Happenings had more than a fair share, and which led to their lack of durability. But as Baxandall rightly wrote to me, when graciously giving me permission to reprint our little debate, it raises questions of sufficient theoretical importance to warrant preserving.*

Let me conclude by noting a textual point, susceptible to long developments which I in part suggested in my Introduction. In my definition of Happenings, I spoke of 'semiotic signs and media'. This is not the methodological perspective of the book. But if 'semiotic' is not to be found in the original 1969 publication, that does not betoken my late jumping on a bandwaggon. The term was already in my manuscript, and was cut by a Drama Review *editor anxious about comprehensibility.* Sic transit gloria mundi: *or, as Shakespeare put it, thus may we see how the world wags.*

Acknowledgements

Acknowledgements are due to all copyright holders, to the periodicals of first English publication detailed at the beginning of my Introduction for chapters 3, 4, 6, 8, and 9, and to the University of North Carolina for chapter 5. I would like to thank warmly for their encouragement and critical comment on the early drafts the editors of *The (Tulane) Drama Review*, Richard Schechner and Erika Munk; of *The Massachusetts Review*, Jules Chametzky, John H. Hicks and Robert Tucker; of *Clio* (Wisconsin), Robert Canary and Henry Kozicki; of *Essays on Brecht*, Herbert Knust and Siegfried Mews; and of the *Working Papers Series* of the McGill University Graduate Program in Communications, Jane Bisel.

Chapter 1 owes a good part of its present form to the encouragement of my colleague from Zagreb University, Zdravko Malić, and to the help of my classmate and friend from Bristol University, Valery J. Owen; and chapter 2 to my friend and McGill colleague Donald F. Theall. He was also responsible for making possible the teaching experiment without which chapter 5, on Brecht's *St Joan*, could not have been written; my thanks for help with materials and indications for this essay also go to Gisela Bahr, Bernard Dort, Werner Hecht, the late Elisabeth Hauptmann, and Patty Parmalee. Debts to Michael Bristol, Richard H. Howe and the performance cast are indicated in the notes to the chapter, as are debts for chapter 6 in its notes. The *Coriolan* chapter would most probably not have been written without R. Brian Parker's invitation to read a paper at Toronto University for a performance sponsored by his Graduate Centre for the Study of Drama, and it is indebted to his paper on the *Coriolanus* plays and motifs between Shakespeare and Brecht as well as to insights by the cast and director of the

McGill performance. Indirectly, discussions over the years with Joachim Bunge, Bernard Dort, Reinhold Grimm, Hans Mayer and Käthe Rülicke–Weiler probably helped as much as anything else in crystallising my views on Brecht. The chapter on Beckett would not have been written but for an invitation from Ruby Cohn, who helped with then inaccessible materials. Finally, chapter 9 on 'Happenings', though clearly a counter-project to Richard Schechner's and Lee Baxandall's views, owes much to their stimulation and friendly introduction to the 1960s New York scene. It would have been difficult to work productively without such living oases of friendly sanity.

Further, I owe thanks to the staff of the following libraries: Nacionalna sveučilišna biblioteka, Zagreb; the McLennan Library, McGill University, in particular to Mme Hélène Bertrand of its Acquisition department and to the Interlibrary Loans department; the University of Toronto, Library of Congress, New York Public, Lincoln Center, Chicago and Yale University; the British Museum, Bodleian, and Cambridge University; the Bibliothèque Nationale and Bibliothèque de l'Arsenal, Paris, the Biblioteca Nazionale, Firenze and Roma; the Deutsches Literaturarchiv, Marbach, BRD, and the Bertolt Brecht Archiv, Berlin DDR.

I am also most grateful for the financial support of the Social Sciences and Humanities Research Council of Canada, given to me in two Leave Fellowships, 1973/4 and 1977/8. The first was partly devoted to studying the semiotics of dramatic performance, a course I held at McGill Graduate Faculty in 1974/5. The second allowed me to work on Ibsen, Brecht and theory of dramaturgy, and led in particular to the *Coriolan* chapter. A further research grant in 1979 incidentally helped with materials and insights, and a McGill Graduate Faculty Humanities Research Grant contributed toward the expenses of typing the manuscript.

Finally, the book as a whole was discussed with Marc Angenot, Fredric Jameson and George Szanto, who read much of it and helped me to find the final form for it. If the form is effective, this is due largely to them – and to the two people who participated most, and to whom the book is dedicated.

Index

Names and titles from notes and bibliographies have as a rule not been listed.

277